THE INDUSTRIAL ESPIONAGE HANDBOOK

THE INDUSTRIAL ESPIONAGE HANDBOOK

HUGO CORNWALL

EBURY PRESS LONDON

Published in 1992 by Ebury Press
an imprint of the Random Century Group
Random Century House
20 Vauxhall Bridge Road
London SW1V 2SA

Second Impression 1992

A catalogue record for this book is available from
the British Library.

Typeset by SX Composing Ltd, Rayleigh, Essex
Printed and bound in U.K. by Clays Ltd, St Ives plc

ISBN 0 09 177343 1

Contents

Introduction

Where does 'pro-active market research' or 'competitor intelligence' end and 'industrial espionage' begin? What is the difference between 'a due diligence investigation' and 'an unwarranted attack on the privacy of individuals and companies'? The answer in both cases is: you can find the border wherever your own code of ethics tells you it is.

The thesis of this book is: nearly everyone is both a customer and a victim of industrial espionage. Not potentially: actually. Technological advances – particularly those to do with computers, changing styles of corporate management, new legal requirements for information disclosure, and the growth of new professions of 'knowledge workers' have made industrial espionage a great deal easier to carry out.

This is a handbook on the collection and compilation of commercial intelligence. It tells you how to spy, how others could be spying on you, and the resources, disciplines, techniques and technologies available in the service of the industrial espionage operative. It also tells you the methods of concealment, risk reduction, prevention and counter-espionage. There are no chapters on ethics, not because I dismiss the notion of morality, but because it really is a quite separate subject. What is acceptable behaviour in business ethics varies from industry to industry, from company to company, and according to circumstance. You may find yourself approving certain courses of activity simply because you strongly suspect the same is being done to you – or because your very survival is at stake. So, what you will find in these pages are descriptions, not prescriptions.

Most of the activities described here are not illegal; however, the law is in places quite astonishingly inconsistent in what it seeks to criminalise or to grant remedies in civil law – it is only particular forms of electronic and other eavesdropping that are currently punishable, for example. Of those actions that are illegal, the chances of detection let alone conviction are often relatively slight. I will describe the way the law works, where relevant. But one of the things you soon learn is that the best results do not necessarily come from illegal or even ethically difficult methods, nor from ones that grip the imagination because of their technological ingenuity. The most effective method in industrial espionage is thorough and creative acquisition of openly obtainable information – which is then carefully analysed.

Why would you want to indulge in industrial espionage? Here, in no particular order, are some of the more common reasons:

- to help formulate your own business plans
- to gain economic, or possibly unfair, advantage over a competitor in business
- to obtain market research material at the lowest possible cost
- to establish bona fides before embarking on business deals
- to exercise "due diligence" in the investigation of companies, individuals or products in whom investment is about to be made
- to lower your own research and development costs by discovering what has already been achieved by others
- to acquire new technology at the lowest possible cost
- to expand your list of potential customers/clients by seeing who buys from your competitors
- to determine your competitors' detailed sales figures
- to discover the trade terms being offered by your competitors
- to ascertain if you are paying the lowest possible prices for your raw materials
- to calculate your competitors' detailed costs breakdown
- to discover potential employees

- to acquire the data with which to perform "competitor analysis"
- to uncover marketing plans, product launches, etc, planned by your rivals
- to win a competitive tender or auction
- to aid a merger or acquisition
- to fight off a hostile take-over
- to discover what others think of you
- (if a professional advisor or consultant) – to help secure a contract or to enhance services being provided to a client
- as a precursor to fraud or forgery
- to counter business fraud
- as a first step in the planned sabotage of a company or product
- to locate information that will aid the destruction of an individual's reputation
- to pursue a personal vendetta
- (if employed by a foreign power) – to help your country's economy prosper more rapidly and at lower cost than would otherwise be the case
- to obtain information for the purposes of journalism
- to prevent others from spying on you – or to detect if they are trying to do so

Let me tell you how this book was written. I have never offered my services directly as an industrial spy, nor do I go in for 'covert' work – there are those that do – but I have had an unusually varied career and have been in many circumstances in which the possession or acquisition of good business intelligence has been of the highest importance. I have also come to know, more by accident than deliberate act, many individuals whose own professions have required them to develop similar skills, though from different perspectives.

My first career after university was in book publishing. For all but the first few months, whatever my title, my job was to commission non-fiction books. People with ideas approached me, or I approached them, and they could be commissioned to write a book based on a synopsis of a few pages. I was a 'trade' or 'general' editor – the books could be on almost any subject that might be sold in a bookshop; in the latter half of my publishing career I worked for one of the big mass-market paperback houses. The books to which I could

commit my employers usually took more than a year to write; that might be followed by a further nine to twelve months in the publication process. (Book publishers *can* get books out extremely quickly, but not as a matter of routine.) I had to be able to forecast what people would be reading two years or more ahead. Each time I contemplated a book proposal I needed to have a great deal of information very quickly in order to make a proper decision:

- what other books on the same subject were already available? Did the new book have anything additional to offer?
- what was the market for such a book – did people who were interested in the subject-matter actually *buy* books? How many copies could I expect to sell? What production values would the customers expect – what price could they be expected to pay?
- what other books might be being written that I didn't know about but that could be published before the one I was thinking about?
- was my proposed author the authority s/he claimed? Was there someone better – and what was I going to do if there was?

But these questions were just for openers: if more than one publisher was competing for a particular book, I might have to participate in an auction. Book auctions are nearly always carried out over the phone rather than in person; you are often bidding blind – not knowing what the competing bids are, or who might be making them. Book auctions are usually spread over a period of a few days, rather than the few minutes in which a painting or item of furniture is knocked out in a formal auction room. Under these conditions, I needed to know who my competitors were and to second-guess how highly they valued the acquisition of a particular book – could they be regarding it as a loss leader, and not subjecting it to normal book-trade estimating disciplines? Or were they offering more money against a promise to acquire some other product from the same author? Or, yet again, was I being invited by a literary agent to 'bid' against some non-existent other publisher? Could I by-pass the auction by getting to the author and convincing them that I was really exceptionally good to work with? Could I convince a newspaper to serialise the book – how much could I expect them to pay? And so on.

Beyond all that, I needed to keep up with trends in the book trade. What was business confidence like in the bookshops? That might affect print runs. Were there any important long-term trends in buying habits – for example: was biography becoming more fashionable at the expense of books on politics, were celebrations of rural nostalgia still selling well, was the market for 'popular science' on the decline, were showbiz biographies invariably successful? What were the trends in pricing levels – how much dare we charge without compromising sales volumes? Which publishers were losing money – or being acquired by large conglomerates? Which editors were on the move? That might indicate which authors might be wooed away.

The methods of intelligence acquisition I used in those days were good, but disorganised. They also took place at a time when desktop computers were only to be found, if at all, in labs or in the homes of hobbyist enthusiasts. My obvious reference books were the Whitaker's *Books in Print*, Bowker, the US equivalent, and a fat twice-yearly publication called the *Export Bookseller* which contains advertisements and editorial coverage of most of the books UK publishers hope to publish during the following six months. I would also keep catalogues from rival publishers. Beyond that, for editorial research, I got very fond of the London Library. For industry trends there were magazines and newsletters but they usually printed information too late for some of my actual needs. But thereafter my skills became a great deal less obvious. I did not realise it at the time, but I used prototype versions of many of the techniques described later in this book.

It was nearly all done on the phone – friendly intermediaries who, in return for similar favours that I had done for them in the past or would do in the future, provided essential bits of information. The intermediaries might be journalists, academics, literary agents, the occasional well-informed bookseller, freelance copy editors and readers who worked for several publishing houses, over-

seas publishers – even those who, most of the time, were my immediate commercial rivals. The sales force could tell me about opinion and events in the bookshops. Visits to the United States or to the great annual book fair at Frankfurt would, in addition to their overt purposes of buying and selling the rights to publish books, bring me a great deal of information, otherwise unobtainable, about what was going on in rival, British publishing houses – and the books they were to bring out. Then there were the copies of books and synopses which I got to see, but which had not been formally offered to me. . . . The other great intelligence aid is publishers' social life: at every lunch, party and reception some time may be spent discussing ideas and literature, but most of what goes on is gossip in the aid of the exchange of business intelligence. . . .

But book publishing is a fairly slow-moving business and more aggressive techniques are necessary in other industries. As I moved from books into the publishing of electronic databases (I had wanted to make use of my growing interest in computers), I found that I needed to be able to predict complex technological and commercial trends. I had to bet – or advise others to bet – on which new information technologies would win through – videotex, online databases, closed user teletext, laser-disc, multi-media and so on. Such judgements must not only evaluate technical excellence and relevance but also identify which commercial interests are needed to provide the backing to ensure acceptance and success. If you are in such a position, how do you mould your views? Why, at trade exhibitions, conferences, seminars, via specialist newsletters – and a whole underground of informal networks of acquaintances.

Since much of my electronic publishing activity was for the City, a quite separate chunk of intelligence data had to be at my disposal – yet another network of sources and contacts among securities analysts, City PR folk, technicians in the various service industries upon which the City depends, had to be built up.

After publication of *The Hacker's Handbook* I found myself being wooed into computer security consultancy; inevitably although my speciality is what goes on in and around computers one must consider the overall security threats that face the companies that own the computers. I began to have a great deal of contact with the world of corporate security and spookery, which in turn overlaps with those individuals who are commissioned to execute the specific deeds – dirty work – that often makes the headlines of industrial spying scandals.

These experiences have provided the personal core of this book. As you might expect, I have combed the newspaper and magazine clippings libraries for anecdotal material. Inevitably the stories for which there is the greatest amount of detail and highest level of verification are for incidents of industrial espionage which were at least partially unsuccessful in that the perpetrators were caught. I have also gone to university, business school and polytechnic libraries for relevant academic work.

But I also carried out a number of interviews – no, let's call them loosely structured informal conversations – with various people whose professions require the rapid acquisition of commercial information. They included:

    investigative journalists
    technical newsletter journalists
    corporate security advisors
    City PR executives
    merchant bankers
    stockbroker's securities analysts
    former intelligence officers
    management consultants
    head-hunter/recruitment consultant
    business librarians
    'technical resources' specialists

However, this is a handbook and not an exercise in exposé journalism. These people were asked about their experiences and not invited to break confidences. I have used their material throughout, often without specific attribution. You can probably guess the reason why.

Finally, there were a number of areas of information acquisition, not necessarily particularly controversial, where I had not already had direct experience; accordingly, I set myself a series of exercises to review the practical difficulties and to see how successful I would be.

The basic arrangement of the book is this: the first two chapters are about the setting of spying

'targets' and the analysis, storage, dissemination and retrieval of raw intelligence. We then look at the various potential sources of data: the next two chapters deal with overt sources: print media and libraries and electronic media and online databases. However, here I concentrate on the principles of using these sources effectively and creatively; there are no long would-be-definitive lists of facilities and publications in specific areas – these are available elsewhere. Then: covert sources of intelligence: human beings (humint in spy-speak) and how they can be induced to give information that they should keep confidential, office materials, elint (the intelligence community's umbrella word for bugging, tapping, computer hacking and radio eavesdropping). After this, we examine specifically the principal subjects of much industrial spying: individuals, companies, and products. Towards the end of the book we turn to the other face of the coin: how to prevent your enemies spying on you – and if they do, how to react. The last chapter looks at the interplay between national intelligence agencies – NIAs – and commercial industrial espionage. Finally, there are glossaries of terms and sources, and appendices explaining some of the technical facilities, giving costs for various industrial espionage services, and listing useful addresses.

This edition of the book is optimised for the needs of readers in the United Kingdom, though I have assumed that most of these will want to be able to locate information in the rest of the EC, the USA, Canada and the Pacific Rim; however the principles are more-or-less instantly transferrable to most First World countries. Please bear in mind also that it does not claim completeness – there are whole shelves of books devoted to subjects that barely rate a chapter section here. What is on offer is an unusual starting point for exploration. . . .

One of the popular stereotypes of the industrial spy can be found in an extreme form in Stephen Barlay's 1973 book *Double Cross* (called *The Secrets Business* in the United States). Barlay's writing style borrows somewhat from the spy fiction popular at the time. He introduces us to a character whom he calls Mr Kubik – 'one of the scores of major operators in this field, which just about puts him in the millionaire class'.

Barlay spread the word that he wished to meet him and in due course received a call from an air stewardess – 'You remember the friend you were once so anxious to meet?' She tells him that, for his next visit to New York, he should check into a particular hotel – 'My friend finds it handy'. Barlay flies to New York and hangs around the hotel for three days. Eventually a note is pushed under the door to his room, telling him to await a phone call. The next day, a woman phones and arranges to meet him. The car in which they travel takes elaborate evasive action to forestall any followers. After talking in riddles for a while, the woman reveals she is an auctioneer. 'I don't care what's offered for sale, I sell anything, including my hammer, to the highest bidder.' Could Barlay, who had already travelled from London to New York, now be in Bangkok at a certain date in the following month?

Barlay, apparently unaffected by the normal budgetary limitations of self-employed journalist/authors, is in Bangkok at the appointed time and installed on a terrace overlooking a large hotel. Below him sits a man by a small table wearing only swimming trunks; he is the auctioneer's front man. The bidders, who appear out of the swimming pool one by one including a 'girl in what must have been the tiniest bikini between St Tropez and the South China Sea', are all similarly lightly clad – to make sure they are not wearing covert transceivers. Near by is a waterfall, so that audio eavesdropping is difficult. The auction goes a few rounds, all bids being made 'with utmost discretion' and then everyone departs. Barlay's New York auctioneer contact appears at his elbow and takes him to a cock fight on the outskirts of Bangkok – the settings for these events are nothing if not colourful. Eventually she explains what has been happening. On offer were details of a 'revolutionary life-insurance scheme that took years to devise' which had been acquired by Mr Kubik. At the end of the auction, the papers were sold back to their original owners.

Much later in the book, Barlay gets to meet Kubik – this time he is picked up in London and taken, after more evasive driving tactics, to Heathrow where he is given an airticket to Zurich. From Zurich airport there is yet more cross-country driving via Lausanne to a French holiday resort. Kubik turns out to be a Romanian who had graduated to industrial intelligence work from black-market deals in post-war Trieste.

The other popular stereotype is the technician; the unremarkable looking former employee of the phone company who installs bugs in boardrooms, under beds and in biscuit tins outside the country homes of company directors.

For all I know, characters like Stephen Barlay's Mr Kubik really do exist; the bugging technicians certainly do. But the activities of neither forms the heart of this book. We must begin with the one essential area of espionage activity that is hardly ever written about.

1 **Preparation**

Nearly every book on spying, whether overtly fictional or claiming to be non-fiction, concentrates on the agent aspect of the business. The meat is deception, or betrayal, or investigation of suspected traitors. In such books the objectives of spying seem quite incidental; they are loosely referred to as 'the plans', 'the secret documents', 'the microdots', and so on. Indeed one of the criticisms of the world of espionage is that it is largely self-referential, an endless loop of agent and counter-agent chasing each other at great expense to, and no obvious benefit for, their employers.

But the core of traditional spying is to obtain information that is needed and cannot otherwise be acquired. Long before the agents are sent out to masquerade as lowly consular officials or placed in deep commercial cover, decisions have had to be made about what is being sought. SIGINT, signals intelligence, is less popular among authors, but here too the purchase and commissioning of the eavesdropping ground-stations and satellites, and the huge computing power required to process the data they siphon in, is only made after extensive studies of costs and benefits; and the setting of targets is the subject of constant review.

Those contemplating industrial espionage also need to think carefully about what they hope to achieve; they ought to be able to cost-justify all of their activities. Just as in 'real spying', there are both costs to the spy's paymasters in seeking strategic advantage over rivals and costs incurred in failing to carry out certain anticipatory activities. This chapter is about the disciplines of setting objectives; the one following it is concerned with methods of intelligence analysis, long-term storage and retrieval of collected material, and dissemination.

How the big spies do it

In the world of inter-nation espionage, such decisions are made by an elaborate tier of committees. In the United Kingdom, for example, the key committee is said to be the Joint Intelligence Committee or JIC; among other things, it prepares the weekly assessments known as Red Books based on reports from the Secret Intelligence Service (SIS or MI6), the Security Service (MI5), the signals intelligence agency GCHQ, and the Defence Intelligence Staff (DIS). The JIC is the key group of officials involved in intelligence, the principal mediator and filter between expert assessors and ministers. It receives information from the Joint Intelligence Organisation which consists of assessment staff who draw up daily reports as well as long-term analyses.

But it also supports the Co-ordinator of Intelligence and Security, an official based in the Cabinet Office who provides an annual review of intelligence priorities and performance. The current co-ordinator, like his immediate predecessor, is a former head of SIS; earlier office-holders have come from GCHQ. The immediate customer for the annual review is the Permanent Secretaries Committee on the Intelligence Services (PSIS), which includes the Cabinet Secretary and the civil servant heads of the Foreign Office, Home Office, Ministry of Defence and the Chief of the Defence Staff. There are also other committees and, in addition to the formal structure, there are informal networks of connections as well.[1]

The role of the Secret Intelligence Service, which has between 2,000 and 3,000 staff, is to collect information which is deemed to be required and which cannot be obtained by more overt means. They step in only where the research departments of individual ministries, official embassy staff and defence attachés have failed. SIS concentrates mostly on human intelligence sources. GCHQ, thought to employ 7,000 civilian staff and 3,000 military personnel, collects its material by technical means – eavesdropping of radio signals, telephone, telex and data lines and, although this has never been acknowledged, almost certainly by penetration of computers.

This complex structure aims not only to define requirements and measure efficiency, but to avoid unnecessary duplication of effort and inter-agency rivalry; it has to do this while maintaining its own internal security on the usual 'need to know' basis. The conflict between these various objectives is unavoidable and it can be expected that any exercises in industrial espionage gathering will face similar problems.

Most countries appear to operate on a similar structure: the United States has many more semi-autonomous intelligence-gathering agencies – 17 or 18 at a recent count – and the National Security Council tends to have a more obviously political dimension than the purely official-dominated committees in the United Kingdom.[2]

We know a surprising amount about policy-determination behind Soviet industrial espionage efforts. In 1983 the French counter-intelligence service acquired a whole series of Russian documents from an employee in Department T of the KGB. They provided assessments of how successfully information requirements had been met by various gathering agencies; they also made claims about the value to the USSR of all these acquisitions. The French showed these documents – they are sometimes called 'Farewell' after the codename for the agent – to selected journalists and independent academics without allowing direct publication; nearly all of the accounts in the public domain of Russian high-tech espionage are based on them.

Since the Russian effort is easily the world's most extensive and professional industrial spying operation and because the documents show so clearly that inter-relationship of overt and covert, legitimate and illegitimate, methods which is at the heart of this book, it is worth spending some time on them.[3]

The five main documents refer to the years 1979 and 1980. At the head of the Soviet gathering of *spetsinformatsiya* – special information – is the Military Industrial Commission (VPK by its Russian initials), which is chaired by a deputy prime minister. The documents reveal its role in supervising the collection of foreign technical intelligence and incorporating that into military – and civil – research and development.

Represented on the VPK are the nine defence-industry ministries plus those of chemicals, petrochemicals and electrical equipment – twelve in all. The VPK member-ministries set 'collection' tasks – in plans running on two- and five-year cycles, just like the main civil Soviet economy was itself managed until 1990 – for acquisition agencies to carry out. These are the KGB, the GRU (military intelligence), the State Committee for Science and Technology (GKNT), the USSR Academy of Sciences, the Ministry for Foreign Trade, and the State Committee for External Economic Relations (GKES) which deals mainly with the Third World.

The last three agencies have open and legal functions, and only small *spetsinformatsiya* teams within them. Finance (mostly from the funds of individual VPK member-ministries) is allotted to each 'task'. Advance plans and targets for technical acquisition are set out, as in the Soviet civil economy. Once the material comes in from the West, the VPK or its technical centre advertise the processed results to users, such as ministries and factories, via internal newsletters.

The results are extensive: in 1979 317.5 million roubles were saved, 164 military R & D projects were started, and 1,262 projects accelerated or shortened as the result of 5,824 samples and 88,516 documents obtained. In 1980, the 4,502 samples and 25,453 documents obtained resulted in a saving of 407.5 million roubles, with 200 R & D projects started and 1,458 projects accelerated or shortened.

Some key qualifications must be made. For 1980, the VPK judged only 3,167 samples and 8,836 documents as useful, the rest being deemed fit only for 'comparison and information'. The rouble 'savings' – which are much smaller than the guesstimates the Reagan Administration was once making to justify Cocom, the much-criticised export control programme – are probably inflated.

Some of the same points are borne out in the detailed report (dated July 1981) of one collecting agency, KGB-T (for which Farewell worked). It managed to get hold of 15,072 types of samples and 11,396 documents over a three-year period. It should be kept in mind that the agency 'collects' not only on behalf of the PK and the GKNT (in general economic matters), but also 'freelances' on its own initiative and for its own use (such as seeking information on foreign intelligence services and their equipment).

Two of the KGB-T's three aims are unexceptional: 'Timely identification of the military/technical plans of the US, the other Nato countries, Japan and China with respect to preparing a possible nuclear attack on the Soviet Union and the countries of the socialist community'; and 'identification of any breakthroughs in the US, capitalist countries and China in the military field'. This is exactly what Western intelligence agencies do. It is the third goal that is special to the USSR: 'Acceleration of Soviet scientific and technical progress by acquiring information and samples of equipment'.

The reports describe the extensive support given by other Eastern European intelligence agencies which, until the various revolutions of late 1989, were closely linked to the KGB. Besides these, the KGB-T can draw on those of its own amateurs. There is a reference to these in the report for 1980 which states that, of all materials on aerospace and space missiles acquired and disseminated, 28 per cent came from 'co-opted Soviet citizens'. These probably include journalists, trade officials and businessmen, and exchange students, most of them not officially KGB. The co-opted citizens have at least one advantage over Soviet officials: they are far less restricted in their travel movements in sensitive parts of the United States, such as California's Silicon Valley.

In addition to the information supplied by co-operative Soviet citizens, 39 per cent of what was acquired was said to have come from 'overt methods' – this would include reading Western technical journals, accessing commercial databases, collecting product literature, attending international conferences and exhibitions and, on the edges of legitimacy, purchasing Western high-tech equipment for the purposes of reverse engineering. 6.9 per cent came from 'foreigners under development', and only 2.4 per cent 'with the aid of operational equipment'. This probably refers to bugs and computer 'hacking'. According to the report, it spent 850,000 foreign currency roubles in 1979 for 2,800 items, and 1.5 million roubles got 1,500 samples of 'measuring, recording and reproduction equipment, radio receiving, transmitting, signal protection and locking devices, and outfits for special purpose services'.

The Farewell documents pre-date *perestroika* and *glasnost* and subsequent upheavals in Eastern Europe and the Soviet Union; a view currently popular in intelligence circles is that KGB industrial espionage activity has increased since the arrival of Gorbachev, a theme which will be picked up in Chapter 14.

Planning for industrial spying activities

Every industrial intelligence operation, however small, however great its intention to behave ethically, needs its own JIC or VPK, even if it is no more than a senior executive holding talks with himself.

The first thing you have to decide is what it is you ought to know – and why. For those who haven't thought about such matters, the initial reaction to being asked to define this is usually a nervous giggle of complicit naughtiness; the next stage is to say: 'Well, it's obvious, isn't it?'

In fact, it is not obvious at all: whilst for a journalist the aim may be clear – 'I'm trying to write a story that is both interesting and true', for most people decisions about aims, requirements and methods vary extensively from company to company, from industry to industry and from time to time. One of the more important criteria in deciding what sorts of information to collect is an idea of how it is going to be used. The remainder of this chapter poses these issues.

In a commercial situation, the agenda of intelligence requirements can be surprisingly complex, even for quite small companies. There are almost as many ways of dividing the agenda up as there are writers on the subject, but here are some of the more useful:

The classic divisions of intelligence
All companies need to know about the immediate commercial environment in which they are operating – they need to have accurate information about the pricing of competing products and services (and where appropriate, competitive prices of essential raw materials) and immediately changing market conditions. This would be **operations intelligence** and much of the harvest will come from

salesmen, mutual customers and the acquisition of catalogues and price lists. For companies facing an immediate crisis – a take-over for example, or participating in a critical competitive tender – operations intelligence will also include the answers to 'What exactly will X do next?' – X being the predator or competitor.

Operations intelligence is by its nature limited to the almost-immediate – it doesn't help an organisation make even short-term plans. It is essentially reactive; the company which relies solely on operations intelligence runs the risk of being constantly surprised. **Tactical intelligence** concentrates, for example, not on the pricing of a rival's products, but on the reasons behind the pricing and seeks to anticipate what new products might appear over the next few months. The gossip of salesmen and the acquisition of price guides is of only limited value here, and much more sophisticated intelligence sources are required. Tactical intelligence tells you how to play that competitive tender or to anticipate several moves ahead in a take-over. Good tactical intelligence removes some of the surprise from daily life.

Beyond tactical intelligence in time-scale and degree of overview is **strategic intelligence**. This helps you anticipate that a take-over may be made or decide whether you should turn predator. Strategic intelligence is for the pro-active. It tells you whether to start a new line, open a new factory or new offices. Headings here might include:

- Markets and customers (up to a point, this overlaps the subject-matter of conventional market research)
- Technology developments and sources
- Corporate security threats
- Competitor capabilities, plans and intentions
- Political, economic and social forces
- Industry structure and trends

Clearly some of these headings can be subjects of study only in the larger sort of organisation. Sophisticated analytic tools are available to those who are interested, heralded in Michael Porter's pioneering 1980 book *Competitive Strategy*. He identifies five areas of threat to businesses:

- rivalry among existing firms

- bargaining power of suppliers
- bargaining power of buyers
- new entrants into the business area
- the possibility of product/service substitution

But the analysis is only of use if you can locate the data.

Tasking
This approach avoids the operational/tactical/strategic divisions and concentrates on identifying a series of desirable specific objectives – the 'we really need to know this' approach. For example:

- We really need to know more about our major competitors – what makes them tick, how healthy they are, who are the major personalities, what they could be planning – next week, next year, in five years' time?
- We really need more technical knowhow on such-and-such a technology – are there any easy, non-expensive ways of finding out?
- X has come up from nowhere, they could be a threat, we really need to know a lot more about them
- Y is offering us an interesting deal – we really need to know who they are, have they the resources they claim?
- We want Z as our client – we really need to know what we have to do to achieve our aims

The disadvantage of the tasking approach is that there is never any attempt at building up long-term background information – everything is done for a very specific purpose – desired information may cost more to obtain and may not arrive in time for when it is needed (or at all). However, the disadvantage of gathering too much strategic information is that by definition large quantities of information will be gathered which will never be used – only, like the 60 per cent to 70 per cent of advertising that is alleged to be wasted (or select your own figure), you can seldom identify the waste in advance.

Customers
This is a combination of the 'we really need to know' and operational/tactical/strategic intelli-

gence approaches. Instead of looking at the needs of a company as a whole, the requirements of individual **customers** within the organisation are examined. Thus in the typical sort of manufacturing company the following departments would be major customers:

> sales
> purchasing
> marketing
> production
> research & development
> CEO's office/financial planning/board

Outside manufacturing industry the emphasis may be slightly different, though the principles remain.

In practice, what you often find is that each of these departments carry out – informally and with varying degrees of determination and efficiency – their own 'industrial espionage'. When that happens the harvest is retained for the most part within the area that sponsored it in the first place, even though the benefits could be much more widely shared.

Value-for-money approach

This method seeks to relate the cost of intelligence acquisition directly to advantages that are expected to flow. It begins with a list of anticipated benefits – the opportunity to grow or retain market share, the acquisition at low cost of new customers, the obtaining of a new technological advance earlier and more cheaply than would otherwise have been the case, the securing of a take-over or merger at more advantageous terms than might have been expected . . . and so on. Anything you spend on industrial espionage that brings in the desired result more cheaply than by conventional means is then deemed worthwhile.

But here again you have the problem of anticipation – how do you know in advance what will be useful?

Baseline/Hybrid approach

This is a pompous way of saying that most companies that go in for organised research don't follow pure versions of any of the approaches so far talked about, but use most of the arguments reviewed above in evolving the pragmatic policy that

actually suits them.

Organising industrial intelligence

Let's suppose you have your agenda of intelligence objectives – how do you organise the process whereby they will be attained? Do you have a separate department, preferably with some non-committal title like 'Long Range Planning', 'Policy Development', 'Infrastructure Research' or 'Library'? Do you integrate it within existing departments? Do you pass some, or all, of it to outside consultants? What sort of relationship does this type of activity have to things you might be doing already – like market research, or corporate planning?

Who do you pick as your intelligence staff – former employees of the intelligence and special services or ex-policemen, or bright young people on the fast track to rapid promotion? Or do you really need librarians – or ex-investigative journalists?

There are no straightforward answers to these questions. A great deal depends on the internal culture of the company – is it strongly ruled from the top or is the management style predisposed to delegation? As we have seen, the disadvantage in intelligence terms of multiple collection agencies is that the same bits of information are being acquired over and over again. No one has much sense of what the company 'knows' already. The bigger the company, the greater the problem.

In the United States there is a Society of Competitor Intelligence Professionals. Founded in 1986 it has 1,400 members, but estimates suggest that more than 10,000 people work in competitor intelligence for hundreds of companies, many of them in marketing or financial departments. Fifty-six per cent of them earn more than $50,000 a year, and most work for companies with more than $1 billion in annual sales. Starting salaries for those with degrees and a few years of business experience are at least $30,000. A study by John E. Prescott and Craig Fleisher of the University of Pittsburgh shows that 59 per cent of the Society of Competitor Intelligence Professionals members have master's degrees, 29 per cent have bachelor's degrees, and 6 per cent have doctorates. Only a handful of US universities, including Michigan

State, Pittsburgh, Boston, Stanford and Harvard, offer courses in competitor intelligence, but none offers a degree.[4]

Again, few companies are willing to think of the subject in the candid way adopted in this book. They prefer to think that all they have is a department called 'Library' that simply has books and magazines and conducts online computer searches. Dirty work is passed on to third parties, preferably under a charter that says 'I had absolutely no idea they were going to use illegal/unethical methods.'

The biggest argument for a separate department, however, is the requirement for organised dissemination and analysis. Mere collecting information by itself is not enough. The classic intelligence cycle provides some guidance as to what ought to happen:

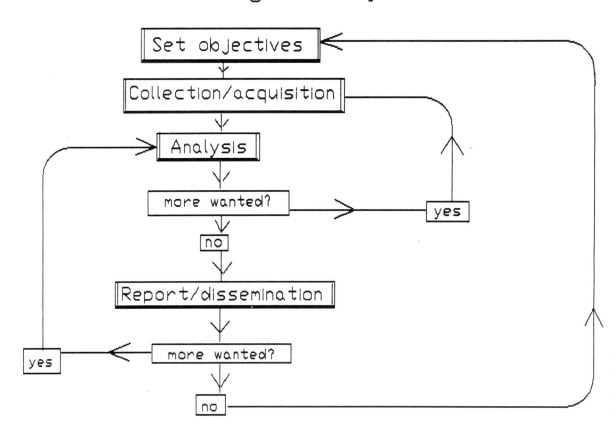

The Intelligence Cycle

What analysis consists of, and how to store and then retrieve your intelligence harvest, is the subject of the next chapter.

(1) Much of this is based on Richard Norton-Taylor's long article in the *Guardian*, 6 April 1988, a follow-up on 26 August 1989 and his book *In Defence of the Realm?* (Civil Liberties Trust, London, 1990).

(2) See *The Armies of Ignorance*, William R. Corson (Dial Press, New York, 1977); *The Puzzle Palace*, James Bamford (Houghton Mifflin, Boston, Mass, 1982); *The Ties that Bind*, Jeffrey Richelson and Desmond Ball (Allen & Unwin, Boston, Mass and London, 1985); *The Agency: the rise and decline of the CIA*, John Ranelagh (Weidenfeld & Nicolson, London, 1987); *American Espionage and the Soviet Target*, Jeffrey Richelson (William Morrow, New York, 1987); *Veil: the secret wars of the CIA, 1981-1987*, Bob Woodward (Simon & Schuster, 1987).

(3) The three main accounts I have used are: *Financial Times*, 17 May 1986; 'Soviet Industrial Espionage' by Philip Hanson in *Bulletin of the Atomic Scientists*, April 1987; *Washington Post*, 2 April 1985; *The New Wizard War*, Robyn Shotwell Metcalfe (Tempus/Microsoft Press, Redmond, WA, 1988).

(4) *Los Angeles Times*, 29 April 1990.

2 Analysis

All the businesses, organisations, individuals, situations, new products and new technologies that you are likely to be interested in have antecedents. Leading up to them is a trail of events: businesses and individuals have histories that tell what they have done before, what resources they possess, their patterns of behaviour, what their preferred method of operation is. Few significant changes within a business can take place without a great deal of preparatory work – which will have been accompanied by legal activity, hiring of executives, purchase of equipment and rental of buildings, public announcements containing hidden clues and coy or not-so-coy news coverage. New products and technologies, however revolutionary, develop from what has gone on before; any product of some sophistication goes through a period of secret research, but leaves evidence of its existence all over the place, provided you know what clues to look for.

It is proficiency and creativity in the process of careful inference, rather than ingenuity with technology or ability to corrupt, that marks out the good intelligence analyst. The process is shown in the figure opposite.

In the take-over fever of the late 1980s one particular prize was a manufacturer of foodstuffs. Part of its strength lay in its well known brand-names, but it also possessed an extensive distribution system that consisted of regional warehouses and trucks and vans of every size. Large trucks ferried foodstuffs from the manufacturing plants to the company's localised warehouses and to those owned by the large supermarket chains. Smaller vans left the regional warehouses to drop goods off at High Street retail shops in response to orders that had been placed. The questions for the predators were: how effective was the distribution system – what was it worth, could it be better managed, what would the effects be if it were integrated into their own operations? From trade magazines they found what manufacturing plant was in use at the factories. From the catalogues of the makers of the various manufacturing equipment they determined possible output levels. These they correlated with industry figures for the market share of various critical brand names and 'own label' supermarket products. From the large-scale ordnance survey map series and from local planning offices they obtained site-plans for each of the regional warehouses – and from these they were able to calculate the volume of foodstuffs that could be held. From reference books and from suppliers of comparable foodstuffs they were able to calculate shelf-life – and hence have a rate of spoilage of unsold or undistributed goods. By planting watchers outside the gates of the factories and asking them to note vehicle registration plates and clock them in and out they could plot traffic movements. The size of trucks and vans likewise gave volumes – and guesses at values – of goods moved. Teams of watchers in cars followed designated trucks and vans as they went on their rounds making 'drops' – how many did each do in a day? More enquiries, this time around the retail end of the food trade, brought information about discount levels. Back at corporate headquarters bright young people were evaluating the various items of data and reconciling them where there was a conflict of evidence. Using spreadsheet software on desk-top personal computers they assembled their best assessments into final calculations – what was it all worth?

We know that the calculations were surprisingly accurate because, in this particular case, the predator who was funding all this activity decided in the end on a friendly rather than a hostile approach and the managers of the foodstuffs company ended up being presented with a bound copy of the research findings! The foodstuffs company would undoubtedly have placed a high security tag on any internal data about its distribution system – but there was enough information available in the outside world for someone to infer nearly all of it.

The Inference Cycle

```
                              ┌─────────────────────┐
              ┌──────────────>│     Suspicion       │
              │               └─────────────────────┘
              │               ┌─────────────────────┐
              │               │     Hypothesis      │
              │               └─────────────────────┘
              │               ┌─────────────────────┐
              │               │  Identification of  │
              │               │  possible evidence  │
              │               └─────────────────────┘
              │               ┌─────────────────────┐
              │               │   Collection of     │
              │               │   evidence          │
              │               └─────────────────────┘
              │               ┌─────────────────────┐
              │               │   Verification      │
              │               └─────────────────────┘
  ┌─────────┐ │               ┌─────────────────────┐
  │ New     │ │               │  Acceptance, or     │
  │ suspicion│ │              │  possible modification│
  │ ?????   │ │               │  of Hypothesis      │
  └─────────┘ │               └─────────────────────┘
              │               ┌─────────────────────┐
              └───────────────│  Suspicion sustained,│
                              │  modified or rejected│
                              └─────────────────────┘
```

Here is another example, this time drawn from that most difficult of journalistic areas – the investigation of things which are alleged to be 'official secrets'. In the late 1960s a journalist called Peter Laurie was working for the *Sunday Times* colour magazine. Laurie was not one of those writers motivated primarily by some strong political belief. He had written on a variety of subjects and, prompted by a series of full-page government advertisements extolling its achievements, decided one day to write a feature on civil defence. This was a period when fears of nuclear war were more immediate than they are in the 1990s.

At first he received a reasonable amount of official co-operation, certainly enough for a single magazine feature, but, as his research progressed, he became aware that the government civil servants wanted him to concentrate on those areas where they thought they had been particularly clever – so many miles of special communications cable installed, local command posts (Regional Seats of Government or RSGs in the jargon then being used) with cutlery sufficient for 400 souls – rather than on what all the effort and expenditure was for. What sort and scale of disasters were being planned for, Laurie wanted to know. Who was going to be protected? What level of casualties were to be expected? Were the plans realistic?

Can't let you know that, said the civil servants, mustn't tell the Russians too much. Laurie was unconvinced – his subject was the ultimate protection of the civilian population, not the details of how the military might cope with escalating threats on the global battlefield. The officials seemed to want to talk only about the local specifics and not the big picture. He wrote his magazine piece but, surprised that his – as he thought – reasonable questions were not being answered, decided that he would try to write a book. At Cambridge he had read maths and law and these two disciplines helped him in gathering together the large number of elements required to describe the big picture without his ever seeing a classified document. His initial problem was to determine what he should try looking for – such things are much more evident in retrospect.

By the late 1960s the libraries and the specialist literature held plenty of technical detail about the effects of nuclear explosion – that gave some idea of the scale of potential disaster. From HMSO came copies of successive Defence Reviews, the annual official overt explanation and budgets of the armed services – these provided considerable detail on policies, expenditures, and specific plans – they had names like Backbone and Rotor.

What Laurie had to do was to step inside the brains of the people who had devised the broad sweeps of policy – and also of the technicians who had to give reality to the various projects. Military history books, as well as accounts of emergency planning in World War II helped here. He realised quite early on that there was very little 'policy' that was purely to do with civil defence: those who devised it were concerned about the whole range of national defence. By looking at the plans as they had been announced – a series of semi-autonomous Regional Seats of Government (RSGs) with a National Seat of Government taking what centralised decisions were possible – Laurie decided to see if he could find where all these mysterious places were – and what resources they had. How many people would each of these protect? And what did 'protect' mean? During the research for his initial article he had visited one RSG. None of these places were going to be marked on a map, but might they appear in telephone directories, perhaps under some anodyne name? The various seats of government would need to be able to communicate with each other and, given the disruptive conditions of a post-holocaust Britain, in a variety of ways – radio as well as telephone. Were there clues in the UK telephone map – and in the way in which long-distance STD codes were organized? What about the network of microwave towers – were they simply for commercial telecommunications and TV signal distribution? Once you had identified one 'bunker', could you, by looking at the alignment of the VHF radio antennae, using a knowledge of VHF radio propagation and a medium-scale contour map, pinpoint other likely sites? Once you had found these further sites you could visit them – and discover, for example, that there was a standard design of fake 'cottage' that concealed the entrances to certain classes of site. Each new antenna mast yielded fresh bearings to be deciphered.

There was also a rich streak of rumour to be quarried: the nuclear disarmament movement of the time had amassed a great deal of anecdotal material of variable quality. There were people who could hint at hidden features of the domestic telephone system, others who said that parts of the London Underground (and indeed other tunnels beneath the metropolis) had important defence implications. There were people who 'knew' where the Royal Family would go just prior to a nuclear attack. Yet others pointed at some of the BBC's secrets: assuming that a bunkered government would still wish to communicate with survivors on the outside, what role would the BBC play – and what conclusions could be drawn from that?

The subject became something of an obsession for Laurie, but when the first edition of *Beneath the City Streets*[1] came out in 1970 (it has appeared in new editions many times since) it became a cult among several different sorts of people. The nuclear disarmers welcomed it and so, for different reasons, did all those people who like the revelation of secrets for its own sake. But it also acquired a classic status among some journalists because it had shown so well what could be done by hard work and inference; speak to many of today's stars of British investigative journalism and you'll discover the inspiration *Beneath the City Streets* gave them. Unlike some who followed in his footsteps, Laurie was never the subject of a Special Branch raid or charged under the Official Secrets Acts. There is a belief among the public that 'investigative' journalism consists mostly of receiving anonymous brown envelopes stuffed with illicit photocopies – and buying drinks for leakers, turncoats, deep throats and gossips in out-of-the-way bars. For the best investigative journalists some of the best stories require almost no assistance from such means; indeed any unexpected information windfall is itself subject to careful scrutiny: is it genuine? Is it a trap? Why am I being singled out to be told all this? What is the motive of the teller?

Both of these investigations are much more complicated than most commercial research investigations, but they illustrate some valuable themes about inference:

- the importance of identifying possible alternative sources of evidence for the hypothesis you wish to test
- the importance of distinguishing between various *qualities* of information
- the importance of seeking *collateral* evidence for information and rumours of doubtful quality
- the importance of identifying the 'inner logic' or 'inner dynamic' of a situation or individual
- recognising that if there is some complex process or technology to be understood, that there are only a limited number of ways of achieving it – and that the one that strikes you as most likely is probably the one that is actually being used
- the importance of being prepared to discard theories for which the evidence is insufficient

In the subject-specific chapters that follow and in the various accounts of effective industrial espionage, these themes appear over and over again.

Disciplines of analysis

Within the area of analysis there are a number of useful disciplines.

Chronologies

One of the major ones used by all researchers is to set out chronologies and tables of their subject-matter so as to identify what is already known, what can safely be inferred, and which gaps of information are yet to be filled. The very process of writing up reports of research activity – even if they are never circulated – is part of the discipline of investigation. Specifically: researchers create chronologies of events, histories of companies, biographies of individuals and development histories of products. These tables can also reveal any inner logic or pattern of behaviour that may give a clue to future activity. Most people and companies tend to repeat their past successes – and are often doomed to repeat their failures also. We will explore this more fully in Chapters 10 and 11.

Qualitative analysis

The second is to value qualitative techniques as well as quantitative. Quantitative techniques are ones that rely on figures – the monetary value you can place on a specific company or product, the market size for a particular product, the net worth of any given individual, and so on. Figures-based research has the twin attractions that the effort that has gone into collecting it is obvious and the results can easily be manipulated by computers and presented in a variety of ways.

Quantitative research is more subjective: in traditional market research quantitative techniques invite respondents to give their views and impressions of a product or service, rather than a simple statement as to whether they would buy it, and if so how frequently. In competitor intelligence, or industrial espionage, quantitative techniques try to describe such features as management style and corporate culture. But quantitative research is not wholly impressionistic – within it there can be objective standards of measurement. The specifics are explored in Chapter 10.

Content analysis
In the early years of the Cold War, Western intelligence analysts – and journalists too, for that matter – had considerable difficulty in determining the flows and changes of Soviet policy. Neither Stalin nor those who followed him – Bulganin, Khrushchev, and Brezhnev – felt any need for publicity for the proceedings of the Supreme Soviet or the Central Committee of the CPSU, in so far as those were the places where real policy was actually formed. The publication of economic data was largely an act of propaganda.

Some intelligence analysts, and one notable journalist, Victor Zorza, decided to apply techniques which had originally been developed for literary criticism. The Soviet Union was not completely silent; indeed its leaders favoured the making of long formal speeches. In fact it was the very rigidity of the language that gave most clues. Adjectives, nouns and verbs were always given very precise meanings and any deviation from the expected showed, so these Kremlinologists argued, that significant policy shifts had taken place – or that there had been failures in the implementation of an economic or military plan.

The predictions of the content analysis buffs passed many tests – in many cases what they said was happening could later be proved in other ways. In fact similar techniques had been used earlier, during World War II, when analysis of German newspapers showed the Allies the strains

in supplies, production and morale that the Axis powers were hoping to conceal. The process continues: monitors at the BBC's foreign broadcasts listening post at Caversham in Berkshire, for example, one of the main funding sources of which is the UK Foreign Office, are under instructions to adopt formal dictionaries for translating certain official speeches – the same word or phrase must always be translated in the same way. As a result, Foreign Office and other analysts are able to read their transcriptions and have confidence in their ability to detect subtle shifts in policy.

In more peaceable times the management guru and social forecaster John Naisbitt claims that content analysis enables him to identify the main new trends developing in the USA – and his source material is newspapers. This is what he said in his best-selling *Megatrends*:

Why are we so confident that content analysis is an effective way to monitor social change? Simply stated, because the *news hole* in a newspaper is a closed system. For economic reasons, the amount of space devoted to news in a newspaper does not change significantly over time. So, when something new is introduced, something else or a combination of things must be omitted. . . . In this forced-choice situation, societies add new pre-occupations and forget old ones. In keeping track of the ones that are added and the ones that are given up, we are in a sense changing the *share of the market* that competing societal concerns command.[*]

But content analysis can also be used on a much smaller scale: companies in particular are always issuing statements – six-monthly or quarterly financials (together with CEO's statement and all manner of photographs of factories, products and people) product releases, catalogues and so on. Their leading executives address seminars. At a commercial level it is entirely possible to analyse these statements for subtle shifts of emphasis to reveal important new developments – is the company meeting its objectives and expanding – or has

* *Megatrends*, John Naisbitt (Warner Books, New York, 1982). Content analysis is also used to help predict the importance of new emerging technologies – see, for example, Jan Wylie's *Trend Monitor* newsletter.

it had some recent setback that they are for the moment unwilling to talk about? Even a change in style of presentation of a financial report or press release – even down to quality of paper used – can be revealing.

Cost effectiveness

Whatever methods are selected, it is important to anticipate the costs likely to be involved. Leaving on one side for the moment the staff and overhead costs of an intelligence operation and looking simply at the direct costs of acquiring specific items of information, we can produce a jokily idealised Management Consultant's Strategic Overview of Information Acquisition Costing Methodology (see opposite):

Like many products of the management consultancy industry, this diagram assumes that life is neater than is the case. Nevertheless, the chart is important for much that is to come in this book. Some sources of information are quite expensive – the per-minute rate for some electronic online services, for example, which are covered in the next chapter, or anything that involves any form of surveillance.

There is a great deal of trading-off between the various elements in the chart: again to anticipate the next chapter – the high cost-per-minute of online databases can be offset against savings of having staff traipse off to the nearest business library, the speed with which the desired information is obtained and the considerable possibility that the local library's resources are less complete than the big database hosts.

Again, if you are assessing the threats of someone watching your business, it is helpful to know that they too have to subject themselves to similar costing disciplines. As we will see when we come to look at some of the much-vaunted advanced electronic eavesdropping technologies, you really have to be convinced that you have exhausted most other forms of intelligence acquisition and are still missing some vital ingredient before they become worth the money. Bugging always involves high transcription costs; the use of VDU radiation detection equipment means employing skilled operatives with high-cost technical equipment in a specially designed van possibly for long

- Define information required
  - define data
  - calculate value to customers
- Select & cost methodology/methodologies
  - is information available openly?
  - what benefits are expected?
  - cost out – what is cheapest method of acquisition? Which is easiest, or runs least risk?
  - is information time-critical?
  - if information not available openly
    - are you prepared to use covert methods?
    - what are the consequences of discovery
      - in commission?
      - afterwards?
    - what value do you place on the risks?
- Estimate costs of collecting raw data
  - direct fees (e.g. online services, external staff fees)
  - support cost (e.g. telecommunications costs, transport, own staff, staff working expenses)
  - amortised costs of capital equipment (e.g. computers, specialist electronics)
- Transcribe raw data (if material is not instantly usable, e.g. tape recordings, print material needed in electronic form, computer-readable material requiring to be transferred into another format)
- Analyse data and prepare report
- If necessary, redefine information required

hours and, depending on the exact equipment they have, there may be additional transcription costs also.*

Intelligence retrieval

In US intelligence circles, they call it in the Pearl Harbor predicament; for British police it is the Yorkshire Ripper problem; in truth, there are many instances where an organisation has already

* See Chapter 12.

acquired the vital data which decision-makers turn out to need, but that information has simply not reached the right people at the right time. US signals intelligence staff had intercepted and decoded Japanese diplomatic traffic indicating the imminent outbreak of hostilities in 1941, but warnings did not reach the authorities at Pearl Harbor in time.[2] Peter Sutcliffe had convictions for sexual offences and had been interviewed eight times by police investigating a series of murders of at least thirteen women, but his details and lack of convincing alibis did not reach the relevant investigating police officers. The Yorkshire police had almost drowned in the information they had collected – over 150,000 people were interviewed, there were 27,000 house-to-house searches and 22,000 statements were taken. When he was finally identified it was almost by accident.[3]

In these days of electronic and automated means of information gathering – we will be seeing the industrial version of this in Chapter 3 – the main problem is information overload: raw reports must be properly evaluated, assessed, and distributed correctly in the first instance; and in the future must be locatable by anyone who may come to need them.

Fortunately the task of maintaining a library of information is made much easier by the existence of the desk-top computer as a cataloguing device. It is even possible, given the low cost of large hard disks, to store useful amounts of raw data, but it is important to understand where the substantive costs actually fall. The elements are:

- capital cost of computer hardware
- purchase price of database package
- costs of categorising raw intelligence material
- costs of inputting selected materials
- ease and speed of retrieving desired materials when required
- maintenance and back-up costs
- the costs of any system of internal security you may need to impose (what you have gathered by way of intelligence may be of considerable direct value to your opposition as well as telling them what you know, and by implication, what you might be thinking)

In reverse order of expense: the price of the database software, the price of suitable hardware to run it on, the human beings who must make it all work.

Types of database software
The big divide in terms of software and size of computer required is between a bibliographic and a full text approach. If you use bibliographic methods, you are essentially asking the computer to act as a catalogue of material which you have in your library. The advantage over traditional card-based methods is that each item of information can be searched for in a larger number of different ways – by author, title, subject, date, keyword and so on. Various database packages offer varying degrees of sophistication – total amount of data that can be held, variety of ways in which information can be sorted and searched, extent to which on-screen designs can be adapted to precise requirements. You only have to enter such data once. However, the drawback is that raw material can only be located if the person entering the data on the electronic file card forecasts adequately to reflect the ways in which some future enquirer may wish to locate it.

Under a full-text approach you more-or-less throw away the original print material. You get it into electronically readable form and the database software is able to search *every* word in every document (common words like 'the', 'and', 'of', 'but' and so on are excluded). The advantages are that, once introduced, nothing in the library ever goes missing and the searcher is never limited by the lack of imagination or forethought of a predecessor or librarian who has failed to provide adequate keywords in a bibliography. The disadvantages are: you need a bigger computer, in particular a much larger hard disk to hold all the files; if a great deal of your raw material is in print form, you need to find a way to make it electronically readable; in any search you may get quite a high level of 'false hits' – information you don't actually want.

The costings are not completely straightforward – the bibliographic approach has 'hidden' costs in terms of the skill of the librarians or whoever enters the information into the computer and the physical storage of the print material. Over a quite short period of time these can easily exceed the greater capital costs of the full-text retrieval approach where less skilled operators are needed, where the physical space required is much less and where there may be important convenience and speed factors. However, against this, if a considerable quantity of the raw material is difficult to convert into computer-readable form, the benefits might be much less.

Appendices III and IV give more detail on all of this.

There is one additional hazard of storing intelligence information on a computer: if you are not careful, the computer can confer spurious authority on data which it produces. Proven facts and idle rumour can be made to appear to have the same status, or even be confused with each other. No matter which of the various bibliographic or full text database solutions you select, you should make sure that the *source* of the original material is clearly identified and cannot easily be detached. The computer, remember, is not analysing the information for you; it is storing it and bringing to your notice material for which *you* must decide the ultimate relevance and value.

Security

The computer 'solutions' posed here have all been in terms of a single desk-top PC. There is no reason why, at greater expense, such solutions cannot be implemented on larger computers such as minis or, more sensibly, on a PC network, with one PC acting as librarian and cataloguer but with the results being displayed on all (or selected) PCs also on the network.

But the security problems multiply. You may not want everyone to see everything you have collected – or even to know that you have collected it. Although there are technical solutions to running databases with different rights of access, the substantive problem is that someone has to **manage and administer** the access rights – who is allowed to see what, and in which circumstances? As with so much to do with computer security, the problems have less to do with technology than with human management – the eternal security conundrum of restricting need to know whilst ensuring that all who need to know have unfettered access to anything that might help. No computer program has

automatic answers to that.[*]

If you hold information about people you also have to consider your obligations under the Data Protection legislation – the data subject (the person about whom you have information) is very likely to have rights to see the information. It is an offence to deny that you hold information when in fact you do. However the data subject has to be fairly precise in what they ask you – and you don't have to be help them in framing their requests. Personal information not held on computer is outside the coverage of the Act.[4]

Final output

The final stage of any intelligence exercise is dissemination of the findings. The shape that any report takes will depend partly on the agenda of the original commissioning exercise. For example if it was one of the 'we really need to know about . . .' exercises, then clearly what is needed is a report that specifically addresses that requirement.

But, as we have seen, much useful intelligence gathering is carried out for background: the gatherer/analyst has secured agreement on the range of activities and must now present some results. There are several items on the agenda, some of them less obvious than others. First, you are delivering information to people who have asked for it. Second, you are telling them that you have done

[*] The problem is this: for a data retrieval service to be used by several people simultaneously and have an internal security system, each item of information has to be coded with a security classification as it is input. This classification may be quite complex – it will be more than just 'Confidential', 'Secret' and 'Top Secret' or whatever. Usually you will want to have a departmental or job-specification-oriented classification as well. The original inputter has to think through the security implications of his data quite carefully: remember there can be as much danger from denying information to those who might need it as revealing it unnecessarily. There is a further difficulty if at a later stage you want to give information to someone who would not ordinarily be entitled – your devised classification system may not be precise enough for you to give them just the information they require and they will see more than you want them to. Again, it is quite difficult to withdraw information privileges on a computer once they have been awarded. The solution is often not to rely exclusively on the computer facilities but to have a mix of human and computer controls.

so, that your presence is therefore justified and that you could do more. Third, you are asking for feedback, so that your targeting can be more refined in future. Lastly (though these elements are in no particular order), the act of writing a report is itself part of the discipline of intelligence. It forces the analyst to rethink what the purposes of the exercise are and to re-assess the quality of material. Intelligence analysis is more than collecting 'information' – it is about evaluation and what seems clear when you merely think about something can reveal itself to be quite muddled and incomplete when set down on paper.

Written intelligence reports create security problems: first, you have to think about the distribution list – who gets to see any individual report and how you can see that the distribution list is not exceeded by the making of illicit copies. As we have noted elsewhere in this chapter – both the raw materials and the evaluations of your intelligence effort are among the most prized targets for your opposition.

There is a final warning that all intelligence analysts ignore at their peril: do not let your findings be influenced by what you think your customers may prefer to be told. There will already be a bias in your activities in that those who pay for your activities will tend to want to impose an agenda on you that may be more restricted than desirable. In national intelligence agencies, for example, the problem has often been that a significant amount of the funding has come from the armed forces which has thrown an emphasis on the military capabilities of the enemy – at the expense of the identification of long-term economic, political, social and religious trends. Recent lack of preparation to cope with the various Iranian, Iraqi and Eastern

European crises shows the consequences of that. The industrial equivalents can be an obsession with obtaining opposition sales figures or advance details of advertising campaigns at the expense of looking at long-term changes in the nature of the market for the product or new technologies to aid the manufacture and delivery of the product.

But the predicament for the analyst can be greater than that – you may find yourself being asked principally to confirm the prejudices of your paymaster; or, if you are your own paymaster, you may tailor your efforts too tightly to validating your own existing beliefs. The problem is at its height when a management perceives itself to be under threat; it can persuade itself that the opposition has some unfair advantage – they are using spies, they have corrupted suppliers and customers, they are spreading malicious stories to the press and in the financial markets, and so on. It finds it difficult to accept that the opposition may have reached its ascendancy by nothing more than honest management skills and good business fortune. Over and over again, private detectives operating in this area have told me that one of their biggest nightmares is clients who cannot accept that their opposition is simply better at what they do than they are themselves.[*]

(1) Allen Lane, the Penguin Press, 1970; Penguin Books, 1972; Granada/Panther, 1979.
(2) See *The Man Who Broke Purple*, Ronald Clark (Weidenfeld & Nicolson, London, 1977).
(3) See Gordon Burn, *Somebody's Husband, Somebody's Son* (Heinemann, London, 1984).
(4) Data Protection Act, 1984.

[*] Of course dirty tricks are played, but see, for example, the National Car Parks case, p. 39ff.

3 Overt Information Sources: Databases

If any one single technological advance has transformed the business of industrial spying it has to be the availability of vast amounts of information, quite legally, via telephone lines onto the screens of personal computers. It is the electronic extension of conventional publishing enterprises. However, as with so much that is offered by the computer industry, the services are not fault-free and the true benefits can only be obtained if the customer is prepared to make quite extensive efforts in self-education.

The vision offered by the publishers of electronic databases of commercial information is that all you have to do is type a few words on to a computer keyboard and masses of essential, apposite information comes rushing down the telephone line to be printed out on a machine right by your elbow. Huge amounts of data are indeed available, but most people's first hands-on experience of the 'online' world is off-putting. The per-minute costs can appear to be extraordinarily high, the instructions you must send to the remote computer seem obscure, and the information you decide you want cannot be obtained from just one service; you have to use several – and each one operates quite differently from its rivals.

Online databases – as they are often referred to – do indeed provide research resources of astonishing power, but the reason for their imperfections must be appreciated before their true value is understood; it is to be found in the way in which they developed.[*]

The online industry

In the middle 1960s research workers were becoming aware of the enormous difficulty of locating academic papers relevant to their interests; they had to wade through index after index of journals for material – and to rely on gossip and recollection as to whether a paper on a particular topic existed. So a few people started to gather into computers the indices of important academic journals, together with a series of keywords indicating the broad themes of the subject-matter of each article. Later researchers could then locate articles simply by typing in –'searching against' – one or more of these keywords.

The database programs that were used to hold this information were by today's standards crude and because computing resources in the mid-1960s were expensive, everything about these early databases was abbreviated. The information provided was not particularly detailed – it was bibliographic, pointing the inquirer to the *existence* of a paper or article rather than immediately providing the paper itself – and the commands that had to be used at the keyboard to locate the information were curt and obscure: it was not envisaged that a researcher would carry out his or her own enquiry, but that a separate computer operator or 'information professional' would be used.

These facilities were not started as commercial ventures but that is what the more successful of them became. Instead of limiting the material to what their internal researchers needed, the managers of these systems started informally to sell access to external scientists as well and, after a while, to carry information that was only of use to these outsiders. One of the more successful of these systems was owned by the aircraft and armaments manufacturer Lockheed. They had started a service called Dialog. It had been conceived as early as 1963, was first demonstrated in 1965 and in 1968 won a contract from NASA to provide a 'citation' service for 500,000 documents. The commercial service started in 1972. By the beginning of the 1980s it was carrying around 100 different databases, nearly all with an academic/scientific slant. Ten years later it was no longer owned by Dialog but had been acquired by Knight-Ridder, a large

* The full-text database facilities running on large personal computers described in the previous chapter have borrowed many ideas from the online industry.

multi-media group; the original scientific databases were, for the most part, still there, but of the total of over 350 separate information services, a majority of them were now business, news or consumer-interest oriented. At the beginning of 1990, Dialog held over 200 million 'records'.

Several things had happened. First, a number of publishers of existing print publications had moved over to computer origination and thus had their raw data readily available in electronic form. Reference book publishers, particularly of trade directories, had found annual updating much easier if it was computer-aided. Newspapers went over to 'direct input' electronic newsrooms – instead of having separate print workers who would compose journalists' stories on 'hot metal' machines. Today you can scan several years – eight or more in the case of the US material – of the full text of the back copies of, among others, the *Washington Post, Los Angeles Times, Wall Street Journal*, many other leading local US newspapers and, in the UK, among others *The Times* and *Sunday Times*, the *Financial Times, Guardian, Daily* and *Sunday Telegraph*, the *Independent*, and *Today*. You can also, for a similar period, access newsagency tapes from United Press International, Associated Press, and (in some countries only) Reuters. Trade and special interest magazines and specialist newsletters are also available electronically. These electronic by-products of the print publishing process can, at very little additional cost, be uploaded on to the existing online hosts and thus earn additional revenue for the publishers. Already some traditional print publications earn more in their electronic form than they do in the paper versions. Publications previously updated annually (and typically several months out-of-date by the time they were distributed to customers) are now updated monthly or even weekly – and are instantly available.

Second, many of the world's financial markets started trading electronically (or had electronic forms of price reporting) – and this data became available for later historic analysis.

Third, of course, was the arrival of the desk-top computer and the democraticisation of computer power. There are many more customers than any of the online pioneers had ever imagined.

Fourthly, computer costs have dropped for the online services as they have for the customers, so that it is possible to store much more information – including the full text of newspapers for several years – and also to develop easier ways for information to be extracted, menus instead of obscure commands – a friendlier user-interface.

The trouble is that online industry is a product of its history; no one sat down and planned it. Information, although it is often there to be had, is not available in any unified coherent fashion. The electronic publishing industry operates in a highly imperfect market and is full of inconsistencies.

Structure of the online industry
The originators of the information on the electronic databases are known as **publishers** or **database producers**. Database producers normally do not supply direct to the public.[*] The intermediary is usually called the **host**. The host owns a very large computer with considerable storage capacity, some special software for processing the raw files from the producer so that they can be searched, some further software to enable large numbers of customers (users) to access large quantities of information simultaneously (and be billed appropriately), and an extensive facility for users to dial in from all over the world.

As a customer, your immediate commercial relationship is with one or more hosts – like Dialog, BRS, Profile, Pergamon Financial Data Services or Nexis/Lexis, to name some of the bigger operators. Typically you will pay a sign-up fee (and in many cases be compelled to pay for a training course whether you need it or not) and then you pay for each minute you are connected to the system. The host works out which of the database producers should receive revenue (which is usually a percentage of what you have paid to the host). Within this general scheme there are variants: different databases on the same host may carry different connect-time charges; some databases charge on the basis of *records* displayed (essentially you pay heavily only to see worthwhile in-

---

[*] Some database producers, however, will only make their data available through their own hosts – this applies especially to some of the credit information services – like CCN and Infolink in the UK and TRW in the USA.

formation, not for time when the computer is sending you messages saying it is searching for the information); charges can vary according to time of day (Dialog makes some 80 of its more popular databases available outside business hours under the brand-name 'Knowledge Index' at bargain rates to reach a domestic – or freelance writer – type of audience); some databases are only available for large annual fixed fees, though access is then unlimited; some hosts demand largish minimum monthly invoices; although it is now increasingly rare, some hosts insist that you lease specialised terminals from them in order to receive the service; some hosts will accept direct debit arrangements via a credit card (useful because it avoids the costs of generating foreign-exchange cheques), others refuse. Some databases are completely free, except for telephone call charges. In the UK the Yellow Pages directories are available in a 'consumer' form at no cost. A professional version, aimed at people who need to generate mailing lists, is published on a paid basis. There is little consistency, either, between charge rates for individual databases and charges seem to have little to do with value. (Except, of course, if one database uniquely has the information you actually want, you'll probably be prepared to pay for it.) One thing you quickly learn – in contrast to print libraries, electronic data libraries are not places for leisurely browsing.

One host can hold several hundred databases and little attempt may be made to link the separate databases so as to make the host service appear as a coherent whole.* Many databases are available on more than one host; when this happens, although the underlying information is the same, it may appear different because of variations in 'search' software (see below) from one host to another. What is more, charge rates for the same information may vary quite widely from one host to another. At the time of writing it is significantly cheaper for a UK-based researcher to search the full text of the London *Financial Times* by using Dialog, whose computers are based in Palo Alto, California, than to access Profile, the host owned by the Financial Times itself, whose computers are located just to the west of Greater London.

* But see p. 22 – link to multiple database searching.

As a further wrinkle, some electronic mail services also offer links, or *gateways* into a variety of hosts, usually making a small surcharge as they do. The advantage is that rarely-wanted services may be obtained without the necessity of making a separate contract in order to do so – you pay on the same invoice as for your electronic mail. The UK-owned Dialcom (Telecom Gold and its many cousins) service and the US-owned CompuServe, offer these facilities.

In other words, the online world is imperfect and inconsistent: information is only there if some database producer has decided it is commercially worthwhile; information has to be gleaned from a variety of different databases and different hosts, and at widely varying prices. The online world is a new business, and as a result volatile in its commercial strategies.

The 1990 edition of the reference book *Computer-Readable Databases* lists 199 online hosts (services offering more than one database) and 5,043 publicly available files and sub-files. Thirty-three per cent of the files are for business and nineteen per cent are scientific. Twenty-eight per cent of them are full-text (see below).

Types of database
Several different types of database are now available:

- **bibliographic** these databases contain references to articles, with keywords to give an indication of what is in them. But all you get is a list of articles etc. relevant to your search; you must then go elsewhere to get a physical copy of each article in which you are interested. Sometimes you can order a photocopy of the desired article via the host, but it may be quicker and cheaper to find it for yourself in a business library. As we have seen, this is the oldest form of online database.

- **abstract** this is one stage better than a bibliographic entry – you get an abstract of the desired material. Abstracts are sometimes produced to save the customer reading time and to conserve computer space, but also to avoid copyright. Reuters Textline is mostly an abstract service.

- **reference** these tend to be databases based on traditional reference books: ask the right questions, and the software finds the 'entry' for you. However, it is the whole of the entry which is searched; most reference books consist of one main index with perhaps a further subsidiary (or cross-) index at the end. In an electronic version you can search by any field – company by director name or registered office address, for example, or company by both of those and product lines and turnover size. The marketing databases published by Kompass are an example of this.

- **structured** here, once you have defined what you want, the database finds all the elements that satisfy your criteria, and displays in any of a number of formats which you can chose – many company databases fall into this category. You could for example use the results as a basis of a highly selective mailing, or for direct importing into a specialised computer application of your own.

- **full-text** here the entire original article (typically from a newspaper but Lexis, for example, provides law reports) is available: the computer searches every word (except for short ones like 'the', 'and', 'of').

- **videotex** strictly speaking, videotex is a form of display rather than a database format. Popular in Europe rather than in the USA, it derives from a mid-1970s attempt to provide simple data services to a mass audience. The most successful is the French Teletel/Minitel service; in the UK Prestel set the fashion, though there are private videotex (viewdata is an alternative, older name) services as well. Videotex presents an electronic file card or 'screen' to the user, mostly in colour; online services are text-based and 'scroll' – that is to say, when one screen is full, a new line appears at the bottom.[*] In the UK some company and

some credit information is available in videotex format but most worthwhile services are also distributed in text-based formats as well.[†]

Online Information Categories

Individuals
Verify addresses
Verify individuals sharing home
Credit worthiness
Company directorships held
News coverage in a wide variety of newspapers, specialist magazines and newsletters and reference books – going back 5–8 years

Companies
Statutory returns for UK, US and many European countries
Cross-ownership, holding companies, subsidiary companies
Major shareholdings
Brokers' analytic comment
Key accounting ratios etc.
Market research reports
Credit ratings
News coverage in a wide variety of newspapers, specialist magazines and newsletters and reference books – going back 5–8 years – UK, US, European, some Far East

Industry-specific
Trade directories
Market research reports
Magazines, bibliographic, abstract and full-text
Newsletters
Advertising data
Facilities for mailing list creation

Patents
UK, US and some European patent and registered design data

Search languages

You specify the information you want by means of a **search language**, a series of English-like commands. Typically, you link together lists of words and ask the software to find you all the 'records' (individual blocks of information) the database

---

[*] Videotex is really suitable only for material that can be conveniently displayed on the simple 40 characters by 24 line display that has become the convention.

[†] See below, p. 114 for technical requirements for receiving videotex services.

has which contain all those words. You can also *exclude* words in your list: HACK *not* COMPUTER should limit your search to references to journalists, lawyers and horses whilst excluding computers. You can define alternate words (synonyms). Sometimes you can say that one listed word must occur within so many words of another listed word. You can also use wildcards, so that HACK* brings up HACKER, HACKERS, HACKING and so on. Some search languages let you search by date, or other critical element.

The trouble is that whilst the principle of all search languages is the same, the exact syntax varies from host to host, and even from database to database, making the searcher's task rather difficult. It is as though you are being asked simultaneously to memorise – and distinguish between – ten different word processors; they all do more-or-less the same things but require radically different keystrokes from the operator in order to achieve their effect. One host may use a search language in the form GET to chose a particular database, then SELECT to provide a selection of search words. Another host may use SELECT to identify the specific database and FIND to chose the words. Some databases use * as the wildcard indicator, others adopt the ? And so on.

Some hosts offer a menuing system – that is, instead of typing in direct commands, the host asks you to reply to a series of questions which are designed to refine your search; it then comes back with the results. Menuing systems are a good idea for new users, but because they take longer to find results and because the charging clock is ticking away all the time, they are more expensive to use. For real experts, most hosts let you use abbreviations for commands.

Most databases offer a variety of **output formats**, (what they actually put up on the screen for you). You can usually choose the level of detail you want – headlines, summaries, full 'record', and so on. In any search you are bound to get **false hits** – unexpected results which conform to the list of words you have defined, but which are not actually relevant to the line of research in hand. (You may find several people with similar names – when searching a full-text newspaper database for a named individual, for example, you almost

invariably find that someone with an identical name has played in some sports match or passed an accountancy exam and if you are not careful you may spend many valuable minutes capturing quite useless bits of information. Again, references to HACK* may bring up Hackensack, New Jersey as well as computer hacking). You should look at a headline to an 'entry' in order to make sure you really want to read the whole piece. Sometimes you can also look at your selected search words 'in context', i.e. surrounded by a few of the lines in which they occur in the full record. The various hosts all have their own syntax for selecting output formats. Different formats may attract different levels of pricing.

The secret of using online services economically can be set out in a few simple rules:

- identify carefully your requirements in any one enquiry before you go online in the first place;
- work out the commands you will need to locate the information in the hosts and databases of your choice;
- capture all that the database services are chucking at your computer on to a disk as you go so that you can examine it afterwards at your leisure without the revenue clock still ticking away;
- be prepared to log on to and off from a service several times during a session while you decide what to do next.

Technical requirements, costs

All this takes us to the type of equipment that is required to receive the services. Most of it can be found in most offices.

You need a simple low-cost personal computer, preferably though not essentially with a hard disk, a modem (the device for linking a computer to the public telephone line), which these days typically comes as a card which fits inside a personal computer, and some communications software. Once set up, using a computer for online searches is no more difficult than using any other software package; in fact there is far less to learn than for, say, a word-processor or spreadsheet. However the setting up sometimes gives difficulties and Appendix

II is designed to take you through most of them.

There is, of course, no such thing as a typical online search, but representative costs could work out at £1.40–1.80/minute connect time for a service with no separate record charge, or £1/minute connect time but with record charges of £4–9 each, say for detailed company information. Useful information about a company or an individual would thus gross out at £18–30, though detailed searches may be much more expensive. In this you must include telephone costs, the amortised costs of computer equipment and, frequently forgotten, the time of the searcher who, in turn, must have had some form of training. Costs, of course, have to be compared with alternate means of getting the same information, for example by visits to Companies House or libraries – travel time has to be included also, of course; clearly expenditure must be justified by results.

Advanced services

The online business is still trying to improve itself. In addition to the menuing system with easier commands already mentioned, some of the larger hosts are providing a database of databases – which helps you select which databases may be most promising for a specific search. Another promising feature for the novice or occasional user are **grouped** searches. Here the host has arranged for a number of separate databases on overlapping themes to be grouped together and searched with just one set of commands (otherwise you would have to call each database separately and key in the same set of search instructions over and over again). The Dialog Finbus category, for example, searches 16 separate financial industry databases simultaneously; another 16 are included in Biotech which covers biotechnology. On Profile, *uknews* includes the full text of several leading British daily and Sunday newspapers, but you can still search each one separately, or just two or three together. On PFDS, a host owned by Robert Maxwell's Pergamon Group, you can search all files simultaneously via the XFILE command.

Another feature is **automated alert**. Suppose you want immediate warning of new developments involving a particular company, individual, product or technology. You already have your background information – but how do you discover fast-breaking but highly specialised news? A number of hosts let you define a search request, if necessary over many databases and of considerable complexity, and will then run it for you automatically either every time the database is updated, or at intervals of your choosing. The resulting searches are then gathered together into one place, which is then translated into electronic mail, a fax or ordinary mail. You are charged for the facility, the regular searches (which may of course not yield results every time they are run) and for the mailing. Some hosts roll all the charges into a single flat fee. The alternative is to log on to each database at just the right interval and conduct manual searches. The determining factor in the existence and variety of these services is usually the ability of the host to negotiate contracts of cooperation between various database producers.

CD–ROM

As an alternative to using hosts and telecommunications networks, some database producers also sell their databases via CD–ROM. This uses the same disk medium as is used for audio compact disks; it is possible to store several hundred Mbytes of data on a single disk. You need a CD–ROM player attached to your personal computer. The low cost of the disk media (and the players are not expensive either) means that an *entire* database of several hundred thousand records can be distributed at very low cost.

However, the database producers still need to earn money from the exercise and the pricing strategies they adopt tend to favour those who are likely to be heavy users of just one particular database, or perhaps a small number. Company information databases are an obvious candidate for stockbrokers and financial institutions, *Books in Print* can make sense for libraries and booksellers. Increasingly, back issues of newspapers are being offered this way, in addition to the older microfilm methods. CD–ROMS are often sold on twelve-monthly subscriptions – you get a completely new and updated disk each month. More static publications, for example encyclopaedias and dictionaries, are being targeted at a domestic market, though this has yet to open up.

The obvious advantage of the CD–ROM is that,

once the hardware and the disk have been acquired, there are no further running costs. Searchers really can browse at their leisure. As with so much to do with electronic databases, you have to carry out careful costings before committing yourself.

Professional researchers (intermediaries)

An alternative to doing your own search, or maintaining someone on your staff, is to use a **professional intermediary** or **information broker**. It is a fairly young job and most of the people who do it tend to have had experience as librarians, indexers or working for one of the hosts or database producers. In 1988 in the UK, for example, there were 129 independent information brokers, some of them one-person businesses; some of those specialised in particular subject areas and were unwilling to work on anything else. The biggest UK information broker is the Financial Times Business Research Centre which is covered in more detail in the next chapter – see p. 30 – as it deals with much more than electronic sources of information. There were also 38 fee services attached to large institutions and organisations. Business schools and libraries will often carry out online searches for a fee. Local reference libraries are usually the best place to start to locate an information broker.

However, if your subjects of interest are unusually sensitive, you may feel it is a security risk to involve too many third parties.

Online searches can be enormously cost-effective, if carefully planned and carried out by someone with a knowledge of where to locate information quickly and cheaply. But they can also be extremely expensive if searchers spend long hours online thinking what to do next, or if they request too much irrelevant information.

Online Services

Main advantages
- almost instant, generally up-to-date information saving on visiting libraries and people
- an 'invisible' form of enquiry, unlikely to alert subjects unnecessarily
- gives enquirer an edge before conducting face-to-face interviews or making visits
- very cost-effective if used properly

Main disadvantages
- information patchy – and unexpectedly so
- information not always accurate
- complex nature of online business means money can be wasted looking unsuccessfully for information
- many search languages required slows up search process
- can be extremely expensive if search requests are ill-defined and undisciplined

4 Overt Information Sources: Print

Had this book had been written only a few years ago there is no doubt that a chapter on print information sources would have preceded one on electronically held data. Of course it is true that there will always be substantial amounts of desirable information available in print and via no other medium. What decided the ordering was less a fanatical love of computers or a desire for gimmickry than my experience during the rather eclectic and wide-ranging research for this book. Although there is plenty of print material that most commercial researchers may be happy to buy or can obtain for free – often from the subjects of their activities – until very recently most people have assumed that the obvious starting point was the library system. Unfortunately, in the 1990s, this is no longer what it was.

Libraries

I live in London. Within 30 or so minutes of my front door is a huge range of libraries: the copyright deposit library of the British Museum, the university libraries of the London School of Economics and King's College, London, and the City University Business School, polytechnic libraries such as the one at the North London Poly, specialist libraries like the City Business Library funded by the Corporation of the City of London and the one attached to the Royal United Services Institution, local authority public reference libraries and those supporting private institutions like the London Business School. As I sought my material I found I had to visit all of these to track down the articles and material I wanted. It was not only that it was impossible to predict which library would excel at which topic, but that all of them suffered from incomplete and broken runs of journals that their catalogues said they kept. The bibliographies I have generated from various Dialog databases list a large number of articles I would like to read but which I have been unable to locate anywhere in

Britain's capital city.

With the exception of the privately funded libraries, the effects of lower political priorities for public spending can be seen everywhere: library opening times are shorter and less convenient for those who must be in offices and places of work during ordinary business hours, libraries are reducing the purchase of books and are cancelling subscriptions to magazines and journals, and there are fewer librarians with the result that there is less help for readers, and catalogues tend to be more out-of-date.

All this makes using libraries much more expensive than first appears to be the case: it takes time and costs money to travel to these places; it takes time to use their catalogues and wander around their stacks. And although reading the books and journals may be free, each sheet passed through their photocopying machines costs – and you may have to wait in line before you can use them. And many of your trips may be unsuccessful.

Libraries, therefore, have become simply another source of information, sometimes immensely useful and cost-effective, sometimes very frustrating.

Reference libraries
The most obvious first port-of-call for most enquiries is the local authority-run **reference library**. All big cities and (in England) large boroughs and county boroughs have one main reference library and will also have basic source materials at all but the smallest branches. At the very least you can expect a range of all the standard reference books, local phonebooks and local trade directories and so on. These are the very stuff of initial research into any company, individual, and specific industry. The librarians at these local libraries usually have directories of other sources of reference – lists of relevant trade directories, yearbooks and

journals in particular areas.* Unless you are very lucky, though, the quality of information may peg out quite quickly – local authority-run libraries are those that have been hit hardest. They'll tell you that these further publications exist but won't have copies for you to look at. They may know of other neighbouring libraries that are supposed to keep copies but, if my experience is anything to go by, the subscriptions may have been cancelled since the directory of further sources was last compiled.

But local libraries excel in one area: local information. In addition to the phonebooks and trade directories, they'll have detailed local maps, back numbers of local newspapers, copies of the minutes of local council meetings. If there is one industry or company that dominates the area, expect to find a great deal of detailed information, possibly kept in a separate special section. Even these days, most libraries try to keep a local history collection. Local librarians may know of local societies that contain historic information which may be of use.

Some large cities have separate **commercial libraries** associated with their biggest reference library. Some of these are beginning to charge for some of their services, which sometimes means that they have a broader range of materials than would otherwise be the case. You may find some of them willing to carry out online searches of the sort described in the previous chapter.

Legal deposit libraries

Top of the heap in the public sector are the **legal deposit libraries**. In the UK, under the Copyright Acts, all British publications must be deposited in the British Library, the Bodleian Library, Oxford, the University Library, Cambridge, the Trinity College Library, Dublin, the National Library of Wales and the National Library of Scotland. Most countries have similar arrangements – the premier US equivalent is the Library of Congress in Washington. For the seeker after business information, however, the benefits of the legal deposit libraries are less than may first appear. Admittance to the UK libraries is not instant: you have to

* The two main guides to reference materials in the UK relevant to this book are: Aslib's *Directory of Information Sources in the United Kingdom* and Croner's *A-Z of Business Information Sources*.

show you have exhausted other means before they will give you a reader's ticket. Service, the time it takes for a book to be delivered to you, is often quite slow. If you are writing a thesis and can order your books in advance, this is almost no problem, but it is bad news for the business-oriented researcher who tends to want information almost immediately. The catalogues may not be up-to-date, which in a business research context can be fatal. Lastly, what the legal deposit library holds is *one* copy of each publication issued within its jurisdiction – that means that, for a UK deposit library, any US or European material has to be bought and paid for, just as in any other library. It also means that if the library needs to have more than one copy, or its one copy is lost – then that too has to be bought and paid for.

For the UK-based searcher of commercial information, the section of the British Library of most use is the Science Reference and Information Service (SRIS) in Southampton Buildings off Chancery Lane, London WC2. This holds materials in science, technology, business and commerce, patents, trademarks and designs, and international standards. It keeps extensive records of British companies and product information and has the single most comprehensive collection of published market research reports. SRIS allows admittance without a special reader's ticket. Although it is the best the UK can offer, it is certainly not a one-stop location for business information – here, as elsewhere, subscriptions have been cancelled, runs of journals and magazines are incomplete, coverage of US, European and Antipodean trade magazines is relatively disappointing, important market research reports which have been stolen or otherwise mislaid are not always replaced.

British newspapers and a fair number of Commonwealth and foreign newspapers are kept at the British Newspaper Library at Colindale in northwest London; however, for most purposes, searching newspapers is best done via online interrogation (see previous chapter).

University and polytechnic libraries

Although they may not advertise the fact, most **academic libraries** are quite happy to admit researchers from the outside world – provided such researchers have shown that they have already tried the public library system and found it wanting. You may be told that you must give precedence to students and members of staff, and some academic institution librarians may warm more to you if they think you are academically rather than commercially inclined. You'll probably be asked to sign a visitor's book – it's up to you what you actually write.

Oddly enough, the most useful form of academic library for the commercial researcher is not those at the great universities, but the ones at the more humble local polytechnics. In the first place, courses there tend to be much more vocational than at universities, which means that the books and journals held in their libraries rather favour trade and industrial material. Secondly, many polytechnics regard it as part of their remit to keep good contact with local industry. Local industry may have rewarded them by donating relevant reference materials to the library.

Business Schools attached to polytechnics and universities often have their own separate libraries and these can be extremely useful. They should have reasonably up-to-date company information for major and local companies – annual reports and Extel cards and their equivalents. You should also find company histories and industry-specific analyses. If you treat the librarians nicely they may also do part of your research for you – identifying other libraries that might have information that they do not have.

In some academic libraries it may even be possible to negotiate the *loan* of some materials, so that you can read and photocopy at your leisure.[*] In any event, although it may not be the prime consideration, photocopying in academic libraries is easier and cheaper than in public libraries.

Other Libraries

There are also some **private business libraries**, usually attached to private business schools, like the London Business School in Regents Park. Here, for anything other than the most basic enquiry, you will be expected to pay an annual fee (it may be called something else, but that is what it is). You may be able to commission the librarians to carry out research for you, perhaps over the phone and with the results faxed to you. For this you'll pay an hourly rate plus any direct costs. These can be good value. Many specialist libraries of various sorts also exist, either attached to specialist academic institutions, pressure groups or trade and professional associations, chambers of commerce,[†] or funded by some benefaction. The City Business Library in Fenchurch Street is run by the Corporation of the City of London and has a wide collection of domestic and foreign materials and a complete set of Extel company cards. Although some of these are open to the public almost without question, admission will usually be by arrangement with the individual librarians in each case: if they let you in at all they will want to be strongly convinced that they represent your last resort and that the objectives of your research are suitably worthy. It is sometimes possible to gain admission to libraries owned by private companies and even to government ministry libraries,[‡] but your reasons for wanting to do so have to be extremely good. Your local reference library is usually the best place from which to identify and locate these specialist libraries.

Security

There is one hazard of using specialist libraries and making friends with librarians of which you should be aware: you and the things you were researching may be remembered. If you wish to conceal your

---

[*] This seems a good point at which to remind the reader that photocopying may be an infringement of the rights of the copyright holder – the original author and/or journal publisher. Some publishers, particularly those of market research reports which may never have sold many copies in the first place, absolutely forbid libraries to sanction any form of photocopying. However, for most purposes, there is a recognised exception for 'fair dealing' in photocopying: you can copy reasonable amounts for the purpose of research, particularly from books and journals no longer in print.

[†] In many European countries, chambers of commerce have public law status, and are the places where local companies have to deposit their annual returns (whereas in the UK it is to Companies House in Cardiff).

[‡] Useful UK examples for business information are: the Statistics and Market Intelligence of the British Overseas Trade Board at the DTI, the Library of the Office of Fair Trading and the Library of the Monopolies and Mergers Commission. But even the Ministry of Defence will allow you into its library if you have sufficient reason.

activities from those who are the subjects of your research you will have to use a false name and invent a plausible alternative reason for your enquiries. You may even have to request the librarian for a whole range of materials in which you have no conceivable interest in order to disguise your real intents. As we will see, this is what you have to do whenever your subject-matter is sensitive and where you have to rely partly on the efforts and co-operation of those whom you do not know well.

We must now look at the principle categories of print materials that are available – in libraries, from official sources, for direct purchase, or for free:

Statutory and other official information

Large quantities of information exist in the public domain because of laws requiring companies and individuals to provide data about themselves. The information is often free or low cost if obtained from official sources, though there are may also be commercial services that provide the same data in a more usable or convenient form. Many of these sources are considered in more detail in later chapters.

Company information

Statutory information about UK companies can be obtained either from Companies House in Cardiff or at the search room in City Road, London. You can get outline information for nothing by using the computer terminals in the search room.[*] Full information is delivered at the cost of £2.50 per company on microfiche which you can inspect using the equipment on the premises or by using your own fiche-reader.

For every company that is publicly quoted in the UK there is an **Extel card** which is updated regularly for every significant change. Extel cards are usually sold on subscription to stockbrokers and to lawyers and accountants specialising in corporate work, though you can buy them individually. Some large reference and business libraries

* This same service is due to be made available via online hosts sometime during 1991.

have a complete run.

The US equivalents are various SEC (Securities and Exchange Commission) compulsory filings – the annual **10–K** for all companies and the quarterly **10–Q** for publicly quoted companies. In a number of European countries company filings are made to a local body, sometimes the local chamber of commerce, rather than to a central authority, as in the UK and USA.

Company information is dealt with in much more detail in Chapter 10 but the basic material you can obtain includes:

> Balance sheet
> Profit & loss account
> Source and application of funds
> Directors' report
> Registered office
> Register of members
> Directors, company secretary
> Directors' interests in shares
> Mortgages & charges
> Register of debenture holders

In many countries, though not the United Kingdom, it is also a requirement that commercial mortgages and other finance agreements are available on a public register, often held at local authority rather than central government level. The US version is known as the Uniform Commercial Codes and by using these records you can uncover such items as new plant and equipment that has been purchased – and how much they cost.

Patents, registered designs

In order to secure patent protection for a product details must be published – in the UK the process is overseen by the Patents Office. Further details appear in chapter 13.

HMSO, GPO

The governments of most countries publish a huge selection of official and semi-official statistical and other data about a wide variety of industries and professions. This is in addition to the official reports which provide information about government policy. Often this material is published at bargain prices. In the UK the official government publisher is Her Majesty's Stationery Office

(HMSO) and the US equivalent is the Government Printing Office (GPO). The complete index of publications of both of these is available online and both offer good mail order facilities.

Births, deaths, marriages, wills, probate
When seeking information about people, the official registers of births, deaths and marriages are the definitive place to check. If someone claims to have obtained wealth by inheritance, for example, you can verify this by asking to see the will of the alleged donor.

Electoral roll
The electoral roll, often to be found in local libraries, confirms addresses that people claim to live at, and who else lives at that address. Historic electoral rolls show how long people have lived at the same address. Rolls of electors, of course, do not include details of children below voting age. The raw data from electoral rolls is used as one key source in credit databases – and these, even if you have no particular desire to secure credit information, are often a good fast way of tracking down people's addresses and those of possible relatives. Information from the electoral roll is sometimes duplicated for local government purposes – in the UK, one example is the registers of individuals liable to pay the community charge or poll tax.[*]

Telephone books
Another obvious, frequently forgotten, source of name and address information is telephone books. In those countries where a significant section of the population are without a phone this source is slightly less useful and in most countries individuals can choose to go 'ex-directory'.[†] A company that you can't trace via the telephone directory either doesn't exist, or is in a very peculiar line of business. Overseas telephone directories are available in some UK libraries – the City Business Library has quite a good collection. Increasingly telephone number information is available electronically; the first country with a complete electronic phone directory service for consumers was France with its Teletel service. The UK, among a number of countries, has made the Yellow Pages (classified business information) available for some time and in 1990 launched its complete directory in online form under the title Phonebase. British Telecom also sells its directories in microfiche and CD–ROM formats.

Law Courts
Court records are the definitive places to obtain confirmation of any legal action, including writs and petitions issued, pending cases, actual judgements, bankruptcy and divorces. However less reliable information in this area, though more easily located, is to be found in newspapers, especially local ones and in trade magazines. The big credit databases contain details of judgement debts.

Information about yourself which you can obtain as of right
There are a number of items of legislation which permit individuals to obtain information *about themselves* and, with a bit of masquerading, they can sometimes be abused by others in order to get the same information about third parties. In the UK there are four categories of such legislation: the Data Protection Act, 1984, which allows individuals to demand from database holders the contents of any file that is held about them – this is a European Community-wide law. It applies only to information held on computer, not to paper-based records. The Consumer Credit Act, 1974, governs the special case of credit databases and is intended as a protection for individuals who feel that they may have been declined credit on the basis of wrong information. In addition individuals have the right to see some medical records and some local authority and social work files.[‡]

Land register
Details of the ownership of land are, in most countries, held on publicly available registers,

‡ But the UK also has a very large number of laws making it an offence to disclose information. In his *Freedom of Information Handbook* (Bloomsbury, London, 1990), David Northmore reminds us of the 1980 Home Office reply to a Parliamentary question that there were at the time some 89 such laws. Northmore estimates that there must be well over a hundred by now, not including Official Secrets legislation.

* Indeed, one of the many reasons for its unpopularity was the expense of collecting it, which included replicating part of the effort already expended on the electoral roll.
† See also Chapter 8.

though this has been the case in the UK only since the end of 1990. The ease with which the information can be extracted varies considerably from country to country. In the UK not all land is yet formally registered and you must first obtain a registration number and then ask for the substantive details in a subsequent stage. In the USA, by contrast, where information is held at local rather than federal level, there are specialist publishers who have most or all of the information instantly on file – their main customers are property developers.

You may have to look in a separate register for details of mortgages and charges on the land.

This subject is examined more fully in Chapter 10.

Planning applications
Also on the subject of land, local authorities in most countries tend to require that details of any planning application are publicly available. This can be one of the most useful sources for uncovering particulars of a company's future expansion plans, as detailed ground-plans are required.

Ordnance survey maps
A further source of information about land is official maps – the UK system is known as the Ordnance Survey and they are available to a very large scale – more than sufficient to see individual buildings and to calculate their precise sizes.

Motor vehicle registration
It is often useful to be able to identify the owner of a motor vehicle – you may be concerned about one which appears to be carrying out surveillance on you, or you may simply want to know whether it is wholly paid for or the subject of a finance agreement. In most Western countries this data is on public record, but in the UK, such information is only available from the DVLC – Driver and Vehicle Licensing Centre in Cardiff – if you can show 'reasonable cause', a typical reason being that you are the victim of a hit and run accident.

Freedom of Information legislation

The US Freedom of Information Act was enacted in 1966 primarily to assist the media and the public in learning about the operations of the US federal government. Whilst it has undoubtedly achieved many of its objectives, the heaviest users of the legislation seem to be companies seeking information about their competitors. One of the federal entities that has received a particularly heavy set of 'competitor intelligence' requests has been the Food and Drug Administration. Of the 40,000 requests for disclosure it received in 1988, more than 85 per cent came from the industries it regulates. Only four per cent came from reporters or consumer groups. The volume of requests handled by the agency has grown 15-fold since the Freedom of Information Act went into effect in 1974. In 1988, servicing requests cost $5.6 million. Some of the requests are simply to see how the government is likely to handle the release of a new pharmaceutical or cosmetic, but others are designed to see what the FDA knows about a competitor's activities which have not so far been published elsewhere.[1] Another US government arm that has received some attention from industrial spies is the Environmental Protection Agency. The agency's Environmental Photographic Interpretation Center (EPIC) has a staff of 50 pilots, photographers and map readers. Officials borrow U–2 spy planes from the National Aeronautics & Space Administration to map areas of potential toxic hazard. The EPA also uses an 'Enviro-Pod', which takes high-resolution pictures from small aircraft. These aerial photographs provide a cheap source of mapping intelligence for corporate spies.[2]

You do not need to be a US citizen or to prove a direct interest in the subject matter in order to make a request under the Freedom of Information Act.

Newspaper & magazine morgues, local newspapers

In addition to national newspapers, which obviously carry information of national significance, their local cousins may be as helpful; in any event they can be extremely useful for a whole variety of items of research. In the UK there are over 2,000 of them, including those special to the London suburbs and various 'county'-based monthlies. They are bound to cover the activities of local companies and personalities in more detail and with angles that no one else would be interested in.

They will also provide extensive coverage of the activities of the local government bodies, local politics and local societies.

If you are carrying out a 'lifestyle' check on an individual (see Chapter 11), it is the local paper that is most likely to carry information about appearances in the magistrates' courts. Estate agents' advertisements will enable you to price properties, not only now, but at various times in the past.

Although many national newspapers can be searched electronically, local papers have to be investigated by good old-fashioned page-turning. However, for the most part they are weekly, which means only 50 or so editions to be scanned for each year.

The newspapers and magazines themselves usually maintain their own libraries. They are sometimes referred to as 'morgues'. Whilst these were originally intended for the sole use of their staff (and the occasional freelance writer who could call in a few favours), some of them provide public services. The two most obvious UK examples are the Financial Times Business Research Centre, which is a fully fledged commercial corporate intelligence consultancy employing 20 people and which charges an annual subscription and hourly rates,* and the BBC Data Enquiry Service which also has a commercial tariff.

Many trade magazines are also willing to let people look at their back issues held in their offices, but while you do you may be surrounded by journalists, some at least of whom may be curious about what you are looking for, and why. The same can apply with local newspapers if the libraries prove inadequate. However, you can sometimes turn this situation to your advantage, as we will see in the next chapter.

Trade papers and magazines

According to *Willings Press Guide*, in the UK in 1990 there were some 7,085 magazines, newspapers and journals published to service the needs of various industries and professions and other special interests. Typically they contain: news for the whole industry, news about companies and individuals, important contracts signed, significant

relocations, and news about new products and new technologies. Key industry figures will be interviewed and will often talk more freely to a trade paper than to any other outsider. The best trade papers are regarded with considerable affection and/or in high regard by their readers.

Most of them contain appointments pages saying who has moved where and often giving photographs. There will also be lots of advertisements, which may give the first indication of new products and services to be offered – and there will also be recruitment advertisements, which are often an early sign that a company might be changing direction.

Just as with local newspapers, one of the many advantages for the researcher is that these are weekly or monthly, as opposed to daily, publications. That means that for each year that is being scrutinised, only 50, perhaps only 12 issues have to be scoured.

Newspaper cuttings services

As a substitute for, or support to, online searches, you can use the traditional method of paying someone to monitor the press for you – the press cuttings services. The UK services – the biggest are Romeike and Curice, International, Durrant's, Newsclip, CXT, and Standard Press Cuttings – date from the 1880s and have an annual turnover of £10m. Typically, you pay a basic fee of just under £40/month and then around £1 for each clipping. For a premium, high-speed service, where staff at the clippings agency work in shifts and where delivery to the client may be via fax or courier, fees are much higher.[3]

Trade directories, yearbooks

By contrast, the UK's 1,500 or so different professional and trade directories and yearbooks are far less useful. As we saw in the last chapter, because of publication schedules, many of these are out-of-date by the time they are published. The problem is likely to be greater for industries that are undergoing a fair degree of change and instability, and where management turnover rates are high.

But although there are many exceptions, large numbers of these directories may not give the sort

* See Chapter 3.

of information you can actually use. Looking at the two industries with which I personally have been most concerned during my working life: I have used the *Computer Users' Year Book* before visiting potential clients in order to find out about their computer systems; all too frequently the information has been very out-of-date, often because the DP managers were not terribly interested in replying to questions from the *CUYB*'s publishers. The *Writers' and Artists' Yearbook* is used, among other things, by potential writers seeking publishers to whom to offer their books. Though it has many useful features, such writers are usually very disappointed: the lists of subjects each publisher is said to specialise in is often little changed from year to year and the entries give no clue as to how well regarded each publisher is for each category in which they publish. The budding writer needs to know to which editor a book should be submitted, however the lists of names under each publisher entry are usually of board members – often these include people who have a watching brief from the conglomerate that owns the publisher but who otherwise have no immediate interest in publishing. Commissioning editors are often not on the main boards of the companies who employ them, and neither are art editors.

Whilst trade papers have a bright future, directories and yearbooks in print form have not, as computer-supplied versions of these become more and more common.

Market research

Although some market research is for the eyes of one specific client alone, there are about 15 UK-based companies that specialise in the regular publishing of multi-client studies of specific industry sectors. There are many others who publish more occasionally. In the USA, in addition to those organisations who will publish data on almost any industry, there are several who concentrate on just one industry, for example pharmaceuticals or high technology. A few are even more specialised – one company is only interested in trends affecting personal computers.

The world's largest research company is Dun & Bradstreet, which has offices in 40 countries and an annual research turnover of $1.26bn. Not all of their work is available to all comers, however.

Local reference libraries usually have directories of market research, though they are unlikely to hold copies themselves. Reports can cost from £20 each to several tens of thousands. Some business libraries, both public and private, hold actual copies of reports – the most comprehensive British collection is at SRIS off Chancery Lane. You won't be allowed to photocopy. Information about the existence of market research can also be obtained from various online services. The *Financial Times*'s Profile host contains a Marketing Surveys Index and also the full text of some reports, though these attract extremely high charges.

Free information

But considerable amounts of information remain available for free, or for the price of a letter or telephone call. Only very small amounts of dishonesty are necessary.

Trade magazines
In a number of industries the leading newspapers and magazines are published on what is called 'controlled circulation'. That is, although they may carry a nominal subscription, overwhelmingly most copies are distributed free to 'qualifying' readers. The practice is strongest in those industries and professions which a large number of advertisers wish to reach – medicine, computing, accountancy are obvious examples. In these situations it is more important to the publisher to be able to maximise advertising revenue by offering advertisers evidence of a large relevant readership than to charge. You can become a subscriber by filling in a reader application form – what you say is up to you.

The fact that these magazines are free does not mean that the journalism is bad or corrupted. In my own field, journalists on free newspapers have often broken stories of national interest.

Many trade magazines carry bingo cards so that readers can request further information from advertisers. Often the request fulfilment is carried out by specialist houses and not by the advertiser direct. If you wish to request trade catalogues, specification sheets and the like you may prefer to arrange to have them delivered to a 'cover' address.

PR handouts

In addition to buying advertising space, many companies employ PR agencies to win them editorial space in magazines. The main tool of the PR agency, particularly the poorer quality ones, is the press release. You can get yourself on the distribution list by masquerading as a freelance journalist. Many trade papers have only a very small core editorial staff and rely heavily on freelancers. PR agencies are so keen to tell their clients how extensive their mailing list effort has been that they are only too happy to include anyone who asks.

Trade catalogues, specification sheets

Trade catalogues and specification sheets are among the most important primary sources of intelligence you can obtain. In addition to the subterfuge of having them delivered to a 'cover' address, you can often obtain them at trade exhibitions, or you can ask a friendly trade journalist to collect copies for you. An alternative is to collect them from a mutual customer.

Company reports

The company report too is a vital tool of the corporate spying game. If all else fails you can become a shareholder and company reports and other communications from the company become yours as of right. However, most company secretaries will meet requests without any great thought – the annual report is a public document.

Stockbroker reports

If it is analysis of a company either by itself or in relation to its industrial peers that you require, one of the best free sources of analysis come from stockbrokers' analysts. Until the arrival of Big Bang, stockbrokers were not allowed to compete for customers on the basis of dealing commissions, but had to vie by offering better standards of service. The main weapon was the investment analyst and although fixed dealing commissions have gone, the investment analyst is still very much with us. The star analysts are frequently seen on television commenting on City matters. There is almost certainly an over-supply of analytic teams in the City. The London-based Society of Investment Analysts had between 2,700 and 2,800 members at the beginning of 1991, 80 per cent of them in London itself. Between them they cover every company listed on the London stock exchange, many important overseas companies and some unquoted companies that are significant either because they may at some time come to market or are key players in industries where the bulk of participants are quoted. The main audience for stockbrokers' reports are actual and potential institutional clients. Although it is possible to obtain many of these reports by paying for them – you can get some online via Profile – you can also get them for free. You can try a masquerade though it can be difficult for a private individual or an executive in an industrial company to pretend to be a financial institution; a better route is to make friends with the relevant investment analysts. Don't forget, they need information of all kinds in order to be able to carry out their work and whilst they will have access to the published figures of the companies and industries in which they are interested, they also need background about products, personalities, industry trends – much the same as the corporate intelligence executive. You can trade – your informal chat for their reports.

This trading of information is one of the most important elements in the managing of industrial espionage agents – a theme taken up in the next chapter.

(1) *Washington Post*, 5 June 1989. See also *Corporate Intelligence and Espionage*, Richard Eells and Peter Nehemkis (Macmillan, New York, 1984).
(2) *Business Week*, 28 October 1985.
(3) *Independent on Sunday*, 2 September 1990.

5 Covert Sources: Humint

Here is a quote from what seems to be one of the more authentic espionage novels of the late 1980s, David Ignatius's *Agents of Influence*, set in the Beirut of the 1960s, 70s and early 80s:

> Rogers thought back about his own career. For all his training in deceit, his successes as a case officer had most often come from being open and straightforward. The true marvel of the intelligence business, in his experience, wasn't the gadgetry or the shadowy operations. It was the simple fact that people like to talk. The old politician wants to tell war stories. The young revolutionary wants to explain how he plans to change the world. They shouldn't tell you these things, but they always do.[1]

There is no obvious border post, no Checkpoint Charlie, to mark the crossing point between overt and covert sources of intelligence, and in the use of human sources of information – **humint** in the jargon – the territorial limits are less clearly defined than most. Employees of opposing companies can be holding an open, legitimate conversation with one another, and both could simultaneously be trying to use the other to glean information that neither would readily give if asked outright. Every business person, to some extent or other, uses covert methods. We'll be looking at them in their various forms over the next five chapters.

Now is perhaps as good a time as any to make some general remarks about covertly acquired material: there is a very common temptation to over-value it. Somehow knowledge that you have run a risk to collect, or which has cost a great deal to obtain, or which you know you shouldn't really have, becomes more attractive, plausible and valuable than intelligence which has been obtained openly. Alas, some businessmen as well as some politicians believe that the willingness to use covert methods shows a degree of praiseworthy

toughness and realism on their part. Some rather enjoy the glamour of working with industrial espionage professionals who claim exotic backgrounds. And some professionals are only too happy to play up to the image their customers seem to expect.

There is of course no correlation between the expense, difficulty and risk you have gone to to obtain information and its value to your business. As it happens there are lots of disadvantages in clandestinely sourced material. Because you need to conceal your motives and methods you have less opportunity for testing its accuracy. After a while you may have spent so much money on your *sub rosa* source or taken so much risk, that you can't afford to acknowledge that it might be less than wonderful. Covert material has as much chance of being incomplete or erroneous as information more openly obtained. Covert sources may solve some problems but also give you difficulties you never had before. You may, for example, acquire worthwhile information but then be constrained from using it, either to protect a source or because it will become obvious that you have used 'unethical' means. Indeed, you have to think through what would happen if, as a result of bad luck, clumsiness or reliance on the wrong sort of person, you are found out – and if you are prepared to take the risk. Obviously the greater the element of 'unethical' or actual illegal activity, the greater the damage if you are caught. If your covert sources are human – the subject of this chapter – there is the additional dimension that they may be lying, if only to increase their importance to you – this can extend all the way from slight exaggeration to downright fabrication. Finally, the human sources may in the end betray you, intentionally or otherwise.

To use covert sources effectively you need to know what is available openly: first to prime and target the covert effort properly, and secondly to be able to verify the accuracy of the information acquired. You certainly can't abandon analysis as a discipline.

Humint vs Sigint in national intelligence agencies

There can be no doubt that nearly all intelligence operations rely in some measure on people as sources. Just how much has been a keen topic of debate for four decades or more in the various national intelligence agencies. Throughout the 1950s, 60s, 70s and 80s, the growth of the signals intelligence agencies was relentless. It was the period in intelligence circles of the movement from chaps to chips. In 1988 the budget of the NSA was, at $3bn, double that of the CIA.[2] Comparable figures for the respective budgets of GCHQ and SIS are more difficult to guess but are thought to be £600m and £160m, respectively.[3] The growth in NSA and GCHQ was not only in budget and extent of manpower but also in reputation. What they offered – and continue to offer – is high-quality intelligence-gathering at a distance. You don't need to guess about troop movements, new buildings, land development, the success of crops and mineral exploration – you can watch and plot them. In the case of economic analysis, you can correlate what your satellite imagery tells you with publicly accessible databases giving ship movements, commodities prices and other financial data and thus develop a pretty good idea of the economic health of many Second and Third World countries.

In a 1988 'Dispatches' TV documentary, an ex-CIA officer called Donald F. Jameson gave the pro-sigint arguments:

> Human spies are a mess, they are complicated, sometimes they get caught, sometimes they betray you, sometimes they have inaccurate information, whatever. All of these things make it a lot more difficult than having some nice little machine up in the air or buried under the ground or somewhere else and there is an assumption, which I don't think is necessarily accurate, that what you get through technical resources is cleaner, more reliable information than what you get from a spy.[4]

The reliance on sigint has always had its critics,[*] but until almost to the end of the 1980s it was frequently possible to dismiss the claims of the champions of humint by suggesting that they were either too old or too stupid to make the transition to a computerised world. But by then there were too many examples of failure attributable to lack of good humint. US agencies had failed to predict the fall of the Shah of Iran and the possibility of the rise of a Muslim fundamentalist state under Ayatollah Khomeini; they continued until 1989 to promote the USSR as the major threat to peace in Europe and elsewhere and produced almost no warning of the collapse of the Russian empire and the resurgence of nationalism in Eastern Europe; and they consistently underestimated Saddam Hussein of Iraq, first ignoring him, then supplying him with arms because they saw him as an ally against Iran and then, in 1990, miscalculating his invasion of Kuwait.[†]

On both sides of the Atlantic the supporters of humint within the intelligence community argued their case fiercely, sometimes to journalists so that the results appeared in print.[5] The argument for humint is this: sigint provides vast amounts of information about what is happening now or has happened in the recent past. Conclusions always have to be inferred from the collected data and the very quantity of information is itself a problem. Humint, at its best, can provide information about **intentions** and **motives**. In fact, so some members of the intelligence community have been arguing,

---

* One of the ways the US intelligence community divides its activities is between humint and sigint which in turn sub-divides down into comint and elint. Humint is intelligence from human sources, sigint is signals intelligence. Comint is derived from the interception of communications, whether via land line (telephone and cable) or through radio waves, whilst elint means electronically gathered intelligence and covers computer penetration, satellite reconnaissance and traffic analysis – drawing conclusions from the mere fact of electronic communication between two parties, without actually knowing its content.

† This list of intelligence failures is now used to advance almost any argument for change within the intelligence community; as we have already seen, it can also be used to accuse the armed services with being too narrowly interested in information about the military capability of old enemies.

the increased reliance on sigint has made high-quality humint even more important.

In corporate intelligence gathering there is, of course, no direct equivalent of the type of sigint practised by the NSA and GCHQ and hence no corresponding debate about the value of humint as opposed to, say, use of bugs and taps or research of overt sources. In industrial intelligence, the human agent, like his counterpart in international spying, can provide the human dimension on the motivations of people inside the target company which can never be obtained from a reading of overt sources.

The motivating of 'agents'

In most classic 'spy' books, agents are recruited by appealing to their ideological beliefs, by offering money or by blackmail. Agents that offer themselves to be recruited must, apparently, be 'controlled'; that is to say, the intelligence officer must take charge of the relationship and not permit the agent any great degree of self-determination.

During one of the off-the-record discussions that forms part of the research for this book, a distinguished former SIS officer said that often the most desirable attribute of the agent-runner was a capacity for friendship. Throughout his career he had met interesting people during his various postings and it was his job to extract, in the least painful and least obvious way possible, information of use to London. Which is not to say that the classic spy books are wholly wrong and that SIS officers never use some of the tougher means of obtaining information from their agents, just that SIS has a broad if hidden welcome for the unaware agent.

However much the idea of the controlled agent applies to the activities of NIAs – national intelligence agencies – in industrial intelligence operations, many 'agents' may not even be aware of their role. You can place all agents somewhere along the following 'awareness' chart:

Unaware >>
Covertly corrupted >>
Overtly corrupted >>
Volunteers >>
Professionals

Unaware agents
The unaware agent is someone who gives you information without realising, at least at the time, the benefit that you are gaining. They can include: your immediate competitors whom you meet on neutral ground, their staff, mutual suppliers, mutual customers, mutual professionals such as lawyers and accountants, management consultants, executive headhunters, journalists. In fact any or all of these people can also be the subject of covert or overt corruption; the distinction is based on attitude and motivation rather than who they are.

Later in this chapter we will examine the recruitment of unaware agents more fully.

Covertly corrupted agents
A covertly corrupted agent is one who provides information for monetary or other reward but who does so under circumstances in which s/he can believe that they are not 'really' doing anything wrong. A typical example is the payment of a 'consultancy' fee to someone who, by virtue of their job, acquires specialised information in confidential circumstances. The consultancy is designed so that the consultant is apparently being asked to provide generalised background information on, say, a particular industry or technology. In reality it is the specific confidential information that is wanted, even if it is handed over on a nod-and-a-wink basis. In covert corruption it is recognition of the sensibilities of the agent which may be as important as anything; but there are benefits for the agent-runner, too. He can deny any desire to acquire 'genuinely confidential' material. One of the more objective tests for covert corruption is the size of reward paid in relation to what the overt contract says are the services being delivered. The skilled agent-runner has to employ many of the techniques of the seducer.

A typical target for covert corruption is the technical or trade journalist. These people are frequently extremely knowledgeable and their job often pays them significantly less than those about whom they write. At the lowest level, of course, trade journalists can be used as unaware agents – treated nicely, gossiped with, given stories which they can use (punchy 'quotes', industry rumours and so on). One route to corruption is to select a suitable journalist and then commission a consultancy paper, say on 'industry trends'. You shouldn't offer to pay too much for this. In the consultancy paper, you suggest, he can write about what he really knows, freed from the restrictions of the house style of the magazine or newsletter for which he works. You can flatter the results (unless they are really bad, in which case you chose the wrong potential agent), and then suggest that the journalist might like to become more closely involved in, say, 'product development', for which a larger fee becomes possible. Trade journalists do of course occasionally move into the industries which they had previously been covering – it happens quite frequently in both the computer and financial services industries. But what we are talking about here is commissioning the journalist to visit your commercial rivals with all the privileges of being an independent observer and for the purposes of writing a story for publication but with the hidden agenda of passing the results direct to you. The corruption goes no further than this; at no stage does anyone acknowledge that anything 'unethical' is happening.

Another prime target for covert corruption is the management consultant. In Europe there are perhaps 28,000 people who call themselves management consultants and who belong to an appropriate trade association or professional body and perhaps as many again who carry out some of their functions without using that particular term.[6] In the USA there are over 10,000 consultancy firms. According to industry mythology, the first management consultant was a former student at MIT, down on his luck and temporarily diversified into brick-laying. He worked out a more efficient method of building walls and sold his tips to his fellow brickies. The split in the industry's activities is something like the table opposite:[7]

Companies use management consultants either when they wish to make a change in their way of doing business and prefer not to take on permanent staff to further their particular goals or when they have lost their sense of direction. Any management consultant rapidly gets to know the innermost workings and secrets of their client.

	% EU	UK	US
Information systems	35	15	11
General management, strategy		7	18
Manufacturing		12	17
Admin/info management	17		5
Marketing	10		13
Human resources	>10		14
Finance consulting		15	
Government admin		15	
Specialised Services			10
Executive search			3
R & D			
Procurement			

(blanks indicate significant activity but below 2%)

The classic method of corruption is to identify a consultant who is working for your competition. You approach him, say how much you have admired his understanding of the industry you are in and commission something suitably generalised such as a Strategic Forecast of Industry Trends. You stress that you understand that he may be working for your competitors but say it is the overview and not the specifics that you require. Once the Strategic Forecast has been delivered, you press for the greater detail. . . . There are variants on this ploy. If you are dealing with a large management consultancy you can commission the ethical Strategic Forecast and then identify an ambitious member of the management consultant's team as being suitable for covert corruption. The unspoken pay-off might be praise to the staffer's superiors, or perhaps a direct job with you. Again, the essence is that the corruption is never acknowledged, especially by the agent.

Junior but ambitious staff at merchant banks, stockbrokers, accountants and solicitors are also candidates for covert corruption. In the United States there is one lawyer for every nine businesses.[8] Staff belonging to trade, industry and professional associations often acquire confidential or useful information about their members. Some trade associations exist principally as a convenient talking shop but others may lobby heavily for favourable attention from government and official bodies. Trade association staff are often unaware agents and may also be covertly, or even overtly, corrupted.

Overtly corrupted agents

Covert corruption can tip over into overt corruption, but it needn't. In overt corruption both agent and agent-runner know what the score is – the agent wants money, favours or a job. Whilst the corruption remains covert the likely harvest will probably be indirect, once everything between agent and agent-runner is in the open, the results are likely to be much more immediate – photocopies and disks of confidential information, direct assessments of the weaknesses of individuals, and so on. However, the fact that both agent and agent-runner know that corruption is taking place doesn't remove the need for the agent-runner to respect the agent's needs and feelings. Most agents in this category like to feel that they are only prepared to go 'so far'. What 'so far' is may change over a period of time; most forms of corruption display a slippery slope effect – getting on the slope may require courage (or stupidity), but once on it, the speed down to the bottom accelerates.

To follow two examples used earlier: the trade journalist becomes overtly corrupted the moment he visits your competitor and has no thought of writing a journalistic piece on the outcome and when the main customer is you. The management consultant becomes 'turned' as soon as he provides you with unique competitor analysis based on information obtained in confidence from one of his other clients.

The skill the agent-runner needs is to determine how to 'play' the agent – to identify the agent's needs and motivation (which may be measured in self-esteem as well as money and job prospects).

Sometimes there are agents who want to become corrupted – and end up being shafted. The best example of this is the actual or spurious job offer. These most often come to the surface when the company that has lost employees (and with them, it is suspected, commercially sensitive information) sues the competitor who has attracted the employees away. This is what happened when, in 1988, a California company called Plant Equipment tried to hire five engineers and a salesman formerly employed by a Canadian rival called Positron. Both companies specialised in emergency telephone facilities. The alleged secrets involved the design features in specialised emergency telephone line equipment that allow a caller to be traced even if she or he cannot speak. At first Positron were able to get an injunction to prevent the hiring, but after a while the Californian courts permitted it to go ahead.[9] In another case, in 1978, Mobil Oil charged Superior Oil with personnel raiding and trade secret loss over a two-year period. Mobil feared that former employees would disclose its lease-evaluation and exploration-bidding techniques.[10]

But there are also cases where overt straightforward bribery – documents for cash – occurs.

Volunteer agents

The volunteer agent is the rarest category in practice but, because this is the agent most likely to get caught, it is also the one about whom there are the largest number of detailed and attested cases. This is the individual who approaches likely customers and tries to sell confidential information – usually for cash, sometimes in the hope of getting a job. The danger for the volunteer is that they get turned in by their potential customer.

This is what happened to a 33-year-old junior researcher called John Wilson working at the Californian pharmaceutical company Amgen in 1988. Amgen had been developing an anti-anaemia product called erythropoietin – EPO. Based on gene-splicing, EPO is supposed to alleviate chronic anaemia in patients suffering from kidney disease by triggering production of red blood cells. In tests, the kidney patients regained much of their lost energy and didn't need the usual frequent blood transfusions. Amgen scientists and biotechnology analysts believed that EPO could also help patients undergoing chemotherapy or those suffering from rheumatoid arthritis. It was thought the drug and its derivatives might be worth up to $400 million a year. Wilson offered a briefcase full of blueprints, 500 pages, to Amgen's main rival – Genetics Institute of Cambridge, Massachusetts. He used the covername Pimpernel and his asking price was $200,000 in cash. He hoped to complete the deal at a restaurant in Ventura, to the northwest of Los Angeles. Unfortunately Genetics Institute had tipped off Amgen and the FBI. FBI agents took a seven-week course in gene-splitting tech-speak and it was they who appeared for the restaurant rendezvous. Wilson was eventually sent to prison for 15 months.[11]

In a similar case, two scientists formed a consultancy company called Biopharm Research. One of them worked for Merck, the other for Schering-Plough, both leading pharmaceutical companies. They allegedly put together two packages – samples and documentation – on ivermectin, an anti-parasitic drug, and interferon, used in the treatment of Kaposi's sarcoma, a frequent side-effect of AIDS. The hoped-for price tags: $1 million in cash plus $500,000 in bonds for the ivermectin and $6-8 million for the interferon, which Schering were making under license from another pharmaceutical company, Biogen. An FBI agent posing as an 'international broker' made the arrest in Atlanta.[11]

In another case, an employee of a company called Arbitron, which provides instant TV ratings data to TV networks and advertisers, attempted to offer equipment and documents of a new device called ScanAmerica. This gave out data overnight rather than within a few days and would have provided Arbitron with technology that thus far was only used by its main rival, AC Nielsen. The employee offered the information, valued by prosecutors at $240,000, anonymously and apparently in the hope that he would be employed as an 'independent consultant' by Nielsen. Again a trap was set by the FBI.[13]

Professionals

Finally we come to the professionals, those with specific skills for hire or who go into business on their own account. They include private detectives employed to follow individuals around, watch the factories and offices of the targets, infiltrate staff into the target's premises, scavenge waste paper, and so on. They also include the technical specialists – buggists, tappers and the like. The agent-runner's skills here are to identify who the appropriate professionals are and to find a way so that their involvement can be denied.

Most of the professionals hired to do the dirty work are private detectives. It has become something of a cliché to say that most private detectives do not conform to the two clichés about them: that they resemble Philip Marlowe and all his literary descendants, and that they only do divorce work. Some of them don't even call themselves private detectives, preferring the title 'security consultant' or sometimes simply 'management consultant'. In the UK anyone can call themselves by any of these titles and set up in business without any need for a license, qualification or membership of a professional organisation. Some 500 private detectives companies list themselves in the Yellow Pages; perhaps there 5000-6000 individuals; but not all of them advertise or take a listing. If you are going to employ one of them, you need to be able to work out what you hope they can do for you and whether the particular firm or individual can deliver what they promise.

Most private detectives/security consultants come from one of a limited number of backgrounds – the police, customs investigation, the special forces of the armed services, and the intelligence community. The first thing the potential client must do is to see if they can establish whether a particular individual really does come from the background claimed; the second is to decide what relevance that background has to the activity you hope will be carried out on your behalf. Whilst some people are undoubtedly repelled at the thought of dealing with private detectives, many more tend to overestimate the value of a glamorous or mysterious background – the Special Air Service trains its officers and men to cope with a huge variety of unusual situations, but these do not normally include making commercial enquiries or investigating fraud. Being ex-SAS or ex-MI5 or MI6, therefore, is by itself not enough.*

In practice, many companies specialise in a small range of jobs and don't touch anything else. Liberalisation of the divorce laws has meant less of the classic work of arranging correspondents in hotel bedrooms; though increasingly some detectives are being employed by women to check on boyfriends and potential husbands.[14] A number of security companies concentrate on process serving – delivering writs to reluctant defendants and repossession of assets. Some concentrate on the vetting of personnel being considered for sensitive jobs, others on the investigation of insurance claims, especially those involving personal injury. The larger and more skilled companies carry out fraud investigations and international exercises in the tracing of assets that have been the object of

---

* See the NCP case below.

disputed contracts or alleged frauds. A few have had great success in tracking down counterfeiters – manufacturers, among other things, of fake perfume, watches, pharmaceuticals and vehicle parts.[15] Another specialisation of the larger international companies is 'due diligence' research. Due diligence is a legal term, indicating a duty on the part of someone – a company director, a professional advisor – to take adequate steps to verify the truth of statements they are making. Due diligence is of particular importance in company prospectuses, where the public is being invited to invest on the basis of various assertions about a business. Whatever they call themselves, due diligence investigators are in fact high-class private detectives for the corporate market. The best-known of the due diligence operators of the late 1980s/early 1990s is Kroll Associates which has eight offices worldwide, employs 250 staff direct with another 500 part-time 'operatives' and claims annual revenues of $50million.[16] Kroll has managed the growth of his business and in particular the publicity for it, with considerable skill and to the annoyance of many of his rivals who suggest that he vastly overcharges for the services he provides. Yet another specialisation of the high-end firms is 'crisis management' – helping a company through a kidnap and ransom ('K and R' in the jargon) of a senior executive, the malicious tampering of a food or pharmaceutical product or a computer-related disaster or threat.

On the whole, the higher the public profile of the private detective company, the less likely they are instantly to agree to carry out dirty work – they have to be seen to be behaving ethically if they are to work openly for blue-chip clients. Kroll went to extraordinary lengths to protect its reputation when, in 1989, one of its San Francisco staff was accused of masquerading as a congressional investigator.[17]

Most of the private security industry tends to rely on sub-contracting: few firms can afford to keep a permanent staff with the range of skills and experience necessary to carry out all the activities that may be required in a typical investigation. Electronic sweeps and visits to public record offices are two services very frequently sub-contracted.

As a customer you may want to know about these sub-contractors – on the other hand, you may not. You may want deniability – so the investigators are hired by some professional intermediary like your lawyers with a broadly phrased remit which says very little about the precise methods to be employed, and your investigators employ sub-contractors to carry out the really dirty work, like pretext calls and bugging. That way, should anything go wrong, you can be as 'shocked' as everybody else. However, you may actually prefer to know who the sub-contractors are and the remit to which they are working.

The allegations in the National Car Parks case of 1990, if true, show professionals operating with less skill than the customers might have hoped.[18] Perhaps that is why so much of their activities came to light. The story was substantially uncovered by reporters on the London *Sunday Times* who in turn received information from a former accountant to a private security company. As this book is being completed, various forms of litigation are in contemplation and the descriptions given here are as a result less full than one might like. NCP, with a turnover of £151 million and profits of £37.5 million, controls more than 650 car parks throughout Britain, 70 per cent of the private sector. It is the largest car parking operation in Europe. Its joint chairman is Sir Donald Gosling, one of Britain's richest men with an estimated personal fortune of £145m.

Despite its market dominance, in 1985 NCP suddenly felt threatened when a rival company, started by a 28-year-old former clerk from Manchester City Council, began to woo its best customers. Stephen Tucker's Europarks company won the parking rights at the South Bank in London, the largest arts complex in Europe, with the National Theatre, Festival Hall and Hayward Gallery. In 1986, Tucker managed to break NCP's virtual monopoly on airport parking and won a contract at Heathrow. NCP's chief executive, Gordon Layton, could not believe that Tucker's successes were honestly won. He apparently became convinced that Tucker was using underhand methods.

He turned to KAS, a company formed in 1986 by the founder of the Special Air Service, the late Sir David Stirling, and Ian Crooke, a former SAS officer who had played a leading role in at least two of the SAS's big success stories of the early 1980s.

Layton seems to have told KAS that NCP was hunting for a spy within the company who, it believed, was feeding Tucker confidential information which allowed Europarks to undercut NCP. This apparently proved untrue.

KAS, according to the *Sunday Times*, produced a report suggesting a variety of 'methods of penetration' of Europarks. These featured many of the methods described in this book. They included the bugging and surveillance of designated Europarks offices in London and Manchester and 'long-term infiltration'. The report stated: 'The long-term aim of this operation would be to place out operators in the Europarks hierarchy as a mole in either the London or Manchester office.'

The report suggested that the operation should begin with surveillance against Tucker and other key Europarks directors. For more than two years KAS allegedly followed and photographed Tucker and at least one other Europarks director, Oren Barrie. KAS employed a man to get a job as a car park attendant. The man described himself to Europarks as a former navy diver and newspaper salesman. The man's reports contain entries about business and social engagements and even trips by Barrie's wife to Harrods. KAS also built up a dossier containing letters, credit card accounts and mortgage payments rifled from Tucker's and Barrie's bins. Later the man was caught by Europarks but managed to persuade them of his innocence. At about this time too, attempts – by someone claiming to come from Europarks – were made to get copies of Tucker's bills for his cellular phone. These, being itemised, would have shown with whom he had been speaking.[*] There were also attempts at tapping ordinary telephones.

KAS then recruited a 30-year-old former army captain called Jane Turpin. She got herself a job as a personal assistant to Tucker. She allegedly stole copies of management accounts and gave weekly briefings to NCP on the company's progress as well as providing a wealth of informal and anecdotal information about her 'boss'. She also allegedly provided NCP with details of which contracts Europarks was bidding for, and how it was able to undercut rivals and in particular on the lucrative operations at Heathrow airport. The overall fee allegedly paid by NCP to KAS was in the region of £30,000. Jane Turpin was able to leave Europarks in October 1989 without having been detected. Her own fee was about £3,000.

The story was broken by the *Sunday Times* in June 1990 and among other things, the paper was able to get an alleged confession from Turpin. KAS subsequently went into liquidation. When the operation became public, Tucker filed a complaint with Scotland Yard and a police inquiry began. Tucker also issued a writ against NCP claiming damages for industrial espionage. In an out-of-court settlement, details of which have not been released, Tucker later agreed to drop the case. In exchange, NCP paid Tucker an estimated £30m to buy his controlling stake in Europarks and gave him a place as a consultant on the NCP board.

The NCP story has almost everything a newspaper can hope for: rich secretive men, one of whom was friendly with a junior member of the Royal Family, a secretive company which nevertheless most car-owners have had to patronise, ex-SAS men, all the traditional technical apparatus of industrial spying, even, at one point, a hint of Masonic influence. The senior police officer initially asked to make enquiries about possible criminal offences ruled himself out – he was the secretary of the Masonic Manor of St James's Lodge, which consists largely of retired and service police officers, whilst NCP's security chief was Lodge Grand Master.

The NCP case represents one extreme of what the professionals can get up to and, though fun to read about (provided you are not an immediate participant), it is also misleading. Because it includes so many of the features of the traditional industrial espionage newspaper story it is tempting to think that it is typical.

Another sort of professional is the individual of the sort described by Stephen Barlay's Mr Kubik,[†] who operates on his own account. Hard evidence of the existence of this type of industrial spy is difficult to come by, but one candidate that keeps coming up is Robert S. Aries, a former professor. His victims included Rohm & Haas, the chemicals manufacturer, from whom, according to *Business Week*, he stole the formula for an oil addi-

---

[*] See also Chapters 7 and 9.

[†] See Introduction.

tive, Merck & Co, the pharmaceutical company and Spargue Electrical. He also pirated various trademarks belonging to British and French companies. In 1979 a Paris criminal court sentenced him to two years in prison for the attempted blackmail of a West German drug manufacturer.[19]

Agent opportunities

We must return to the sorts of agent recruitment which go on all the time but which, because they are so difficult to pin down and because they are mostly completely legal, never make the newspapers. The typology of agents we have used so far has concentrated on their degree of awareness of what they are doing. Whilst most of your intelligence gathering from humans will be of the informal variety, it is possible to think about the problem in a more ordered fashion – in terms of what category of person you seek to recruit. We have already looked at such intermediaries as journalists and management consultants. However, the most obvious recruits are employees of your competitors – and it is not difficult to get to them.

It is surprisingly easy to get to meet people who might be of use to you. In his entertaining book *Innumeracy* which is a light-hearted examination of probability, John Allen Paulos suggests we assume that, on average each adult knows and is recognised by 1,500 people. Looking at the USA with its 200 million population he says that, as a result, there is a 1-in-100 chance that any two adults anywhere in the USA will have one acquaintance in common and that there are 99 chances in 100 that they will be linked by a chain of only two intermediaries. A variant of this game is to work out how many intermediaries there are between you and some well-known public figure. In my case, without any great ambition to meet either, I can report that there is only one intermediary between Prince Charles and myself and only one between me and Conservative leader John Major. (In fact it is better than that – I know the person who knows the heir to the throne very well, though that person's relationship to him is based on a few committee meetings and I know, relatively slightly, two people who know John Major rather well. Once I allow weak connections on both sides – people whom I know slightly who know the Prince

and the Conservative leader slightly – I rapidly lose count). Well, I have had some small public attention and have been interviewed extensively by various national journalists who inevitably meet lots of people but *most* individuals find that they have surprisingly few links – two or three – to one or more celebrities. The Hollywood hopeful who knows the lady who cuts the hair of the man who cleans the pool of the nephew of the well-known film tycoon is actually very badly connected indeed.

Within a particular industry where the total number involved may be in the hundred thousands (of which you are certainly one) and where the real decision-makers may be fewer than 30, the mathematics are much more favourable. You will undoubtedly be able to get to all of the 30, that is if you don't know them already, through just one intermediary.

The general difficulty about the recruitment of agents is that there often has to be a trade-off between guaranteeing the accuracy and authenticity of the material acquired and the requirement to conceal your intentions and activities. For this reason, the individuals in your target company who have the greatest knowledge are not always the best candidates for agent recruitment.

Top employees
There are really only two techniques you can use to turn a business's top personnel into agents against their company – flattery and bribery. Perhaps there's a third if you really feel you can handle all the angles associated with a complex, long-term blackmail, but then you need to find some hidden fact which your target would prefer to leave unexposed.

Of the two realistic techniques, flattery is the simpler to execute and, from the point of view of the agent-runner, incurs the lesser risk of being uncovered – top employees are nearly always unaware agents. The best method consists of arranging to meet the target in relaxed and informal circumstances and to encourage him to show off. Meetings of this sort are always the better for appearing to be accidental. By having a previously researched detailed knowledge of his business and industry you can praise his achievements to the skies and invite him to guess with you what his next move might be. In fact, here as elsewhere in this book I have been using the lazy writer's presumption that everyone who does anything significant in business is male. The techniques of flattery are different though no less effective if used between male and female. In any event, using this method, the harvest you'll get will be in the form of insight rather than hard fact.

One of the best 'relaxed and informal circumstances' is the conference/exhibition/trade show. Eventline, which provides a service for the conference industry, says that in the UK in 1990 they knew of 2,378 properly organised commercial conferences and that there were probably another 1,000 of which they had not heard. There may be as many again non-commercial conferences, that is, ones run by trade associations and professional bodies but without the assistance of the professional conference organisers. At any conference I have attended the formal elements are but an insignificant part of the reason for attending. People are there for gossip, to make deals, to recruit employees, to be recruited as employees – and to gather intelligence. If the mathematics of proximity don't work in your favour, you can always invite your chosen target to discuss the conference papers – or some third party.* The big conferences are not necessarily the best for agent recruitment – the ones you want are the slightly less grand ones and where the timetable allows for plenty of socialising. The conference provides one of the few situations in which the intelligence analyst has a chance directly to speak to the competition's top people.

Researchers/engineers

Similar techniques can be employed against lower-level employees, particularly those who are concerned with developing new products and services. The most effective route to flattering such folk is by using their peers, other researchers and engineers doing a similar job, but who are in your employ. What happens here is that information is exchanged on the basis of sharing technical knowledge, a sort of mutual support. Of course the

danger, indeed the likelihood, is that your employee is giving as much as he is acquiring.

Researchers and engineers can also be covertly or overtly corrupted – usually by the job bribery method and, as we have seen, volunteer agents often come from their ranks too.

Technical writers, a much under-appreciated form of life in the computing and engineering industries, can be approached in the same way.

Sales force

In most industries that need to employ them, the easiest agents to recruit are salespeople. The people who do the recruiting are your own sales force and their agents are the sales staff of all your competitors. The travelling salesperson's job is relatively solitary – they are out all day and may spend frequent nights in hotels. So while their loyalty is to the sales manager at head office, their regular acquaintances are their customers and their rivals doing a similar job for a similar firm.

What turns a salesperson into an agent-runner on your behalf is what you ask them to report on – and the degree of formality you put into your request. Every salesperson is expected to report back on customer visits, but not every one is given specific information-gathering targets. We are not talking about mere anecdotal material and gossip here, but requests to put firm estimates on local area turnover of their rivals, or the collection of competitor sales literature, or a report on commission and discount deals offered to customers. As an agent-runner the salesperson can decide whether to turn his customers – and the salespeople from the competition – from being unaware agents into ones who are covertly or even overtly corrupted.

Other lower-level staff

But others employees are worth attention also. Indeed one of the skills of the industrial spy is to develop a sufficient understanding of how a company operates to be able to identify where the opportunities might occur. Unless you corrupt the secretary or personal assistant of a top director – and that might be by any of the usual distasteful methods – bribery, blackmail, sex – what you will pick up are scraps which you hope you will be able to integrate into your other research.

---

* Don't ignore the conference papers themselves – they may contain statements of intention or provide technical details which might help some other part of your intelligence-gathering exercise.

You don't even need to engage some of your targets in conversation. In the immediate vicinity of most companies are the pubs, sandwich bars, health clubs and what have you that its employees attend. You merely have to sit there and listen to the conversation – it will be at its best immediately after some important but lengthy internal meeting and when some of the participants have rushed to get away from the meeting room to discuss the implications with their closest allies. An alternative is to follow key employees as they go home on public transport (this obviously works better for companies operating in city centres). Often colleagues will talk about work matters as they strap-hang. Further up the social scale for this sort of activity is the country club, the golf club and, *sans pareil*, the gentleman's club.

Professionals on the staff

So far in this chapter we have assumed a reluctance directly to employ 'spies' and 'industrial espionage professionals', that such people will remain off the staff of any respectable company. But there are situations when individuals of this type are specifically recruited to staff jobs.

At the less spectacular end of this particular spectrum are 'food detectives', people employed by the likes of the large international burger and fried chicken chains to check on the quality of food and service in their own and their rivals' outlets.[20] Similar practices are common on both sides of the Atlantic in the food, hotel, travel and retail industries. And then there is the curious case of Takashi Morimoto who, in the summer of 1989, became the lodger of the French family – father, mother, two daughters – of Costa Mesa, California. The Frenches had originally wanted a Japanese student but were quite happy to take in Takashi who said he worked for the Nissan Motor Company. Everyone got on very well and at the end of the summer they parted as friends. Then in October the Frenches read in their local newspaper what their lodger's job was: to provide Nissan with information about the way of life of a typical Californian family, presumably so that more appropriate cars could be offered to the US public. They were upset and outraged and, aided by an aggressive attorney, looked around for

people to sue and reasons to sue them. Nissan defended themselves by saying that Takashi had never concealed the identity of his employers. In the end the Frenches decided not pursue their case.[21]

At the other end of the spectrum are the activities of Melvyn R. Paisley, Richard Lee Fowler, the Boeing Company and many other US defence contractors.[22] Members of the defence industry have always had to operate under formidable difficulties. They must invest, often for years, in technology which is leading-edge, highly specialised and usually shrouded in government-imposed secrecy agreements. When they compete for a particular contract, the result is usually all-or-nothing: the speculative research and product development frequently has little value outside the specific contract for which they have been bidding. Added to that is the problem that the prime customer, the government, frequently makes decisions not on sound rational grounds – a clearly defined brief and may the best bid win – but on a complex and ever-changing agenda of political priorities. The agenda can include: changing perceptions of who the enemy is, what the enemy's capabilities will be at the time the weapons system or aircraft comes into service, regional requirements to promote industrial growth and/or employment, rivalry between various parts of the armed forces establishment, the need to make deals with other governments. And so on. The secondary customers are often Third World governments,* where the only way to trade is by finding the right officials to corrupt. Small wonder, then, that some of the most lurid anecdotes of industrial espionage activities come from the defence industry, beating by a long way those that come from the pharmaceutical and computer industries.

Melvyn R. Paisley, an ex-fighter pilot and by all accounts a larger than life 'man's man', joined Boeing in 1954. He rose to hold the position of head of international marketing. A former Boeing employee, who eventually gave a long interview to the *Los Angeles Times*, had shared a secretary with Paisley for six years during the 1970s and became

* A secondary customer is one who buys a product once it has been developed and on the strength that a major power has already committed itself to seeing the weapon system/aircraft in service.

so alarmed at his colleague's behaviour that he sought to have him fired. Later, when Paisley went to Washington, the ex-employee tried to have Paisley debarred from holding public office. 'Usually every major company has one guy who does the dirty business,' said the former Boeing executive. 'He was the guy.' Paisley is alleged to have boasted about bugging a competitor in 1970, bugging PanAm, bribing US military officers overseas and concealing pay-offs to third parties and payments to prostitutes in his expense accounts. He also boasted about the bribes he had *received*, including, of all things, a Singer sewing machine. In 1978, two Boeing executives went to their top management to complain. The meeting was not a success.

In 1981, Paisley left Boeing to join the transitional team for Ronald Reagan, who had been elected the next President of the USA. He went to work for Navy Secretary John F. Lehman, who had also been at Boeing. Former colleagues of Paisley were astonished when he survived the confirmation procedure for his job which had included a background check by the FBI and a review by the Senate Armed Services Committee. He became Assistant Navy Secretary, in effect the head of research and procurement. While at the Navy Department, Lehman and Paisley introduced a new competitive bidding system and became embroiled in arguments between two other defence contractors, Pratt & Whitney and General Electric (not related to the UK's General Electric Company, GEC) over bids for F404 jet engines for the F–18 Navy Advanced Tactical Aircraft which Pratt & Whitney won. At one point investigators during a raid found secret GE bidding documents in an office belonging to a Pratt & Whitney executive.

Paisley and Lehman left the Navy Department in April 1987 and Paisley set up a consulting business – just before rules designed to stop such 'revolving door' practices came into effect. According to 'government sources' quoted by *Business Week* in 1988, the consulting business was Paisley's base for illegally obtaining sensitive information for such clients as McDonnell Douglas, United Technologies, and Martin Marietta, which were all searched by federal authorities. The magazine went on to claim that investigators also thought

Paisley may have had questionable links with defence contractors while he was still in the Navy. The investigators were alleged to be studying whether he gave proprietary data to companies bidding on the contract to build the prototype of the Advanced Tactical Aircraft (ATA). The magazine quoted government sources as saying Paisley had fed McDonnell Douglas Corp. details of the ATA bid submitted by a Grumman-Northrop team. McDonnell Douglas and its partner General Dynamics won the competition with a bid that was $1 billion below the Grumman team's $5.2-billion proposal. The contract, it was claimed, eventually could be worth $40 billion. Investigators apparently theorised that in return for the low bid, Paisley helped McDonnell Douglas market its F–18 fighter jets overseas. Paisley also may have given McDonnell inside information on General Dynamics's proposal to sell its F–16 fighter jets to the Swiss government. Investigators also began to speculate that Paisley set up his consulting business while still in office. A source at General Dynamics alleged that Paisley, shortly before he left his Navy post, sent a note soliciting business for a consulting firm he said belonged to his wife.

In a case that came up in March 1990, it was alleged that a year before Paisley resigned as Assistant Navy Secretary, he agreed to help an Israeli company get a contract to sell ground equipment to operate remote-controlled aircraft. Israel is a major manufacturer of the pilotless intelligence planes that carry cameras and other equipment to monitor enemy troop movements. The president of Mazlat Ltd, the Israeli company, deposited $50,000 in a Swiss bank account set up by one of Paisley's consultancy colleagues, William M. Galvin, six days after Paisley signed a 1986 directive ordering the Navy to buy the ground-control equipment from Mazlat instead of another company. Galvin, Paisley, Mazlat president Zvi Schiller and Israeli defence consultant Uri Simhoni allegedly agreed to share equally the $2 million that Mazlat was to place in the Swiss account. The figure represented two per cent of the value of the contract.

Galvin pleaded guilty in an investigation which federal officials had called 'Ill Wind' and was imprisoned for 32 months in September 1990. Paisley himself remained uncharged by March 1991.

In another twist to the story, Charles F. Gardner, a former executive at Unisys, the computer manufacturer, was sentenced in 1989 on an unrelated matter of bribery for arranging the purchase of Paisley's resort condominium in Idaho for an inflated price.

Paisley is not the only former Boeing employee to have been involved in corporate espionage. In November 1989 the company pleaded guilty to charges of illegally obtaining Pentagon planning documents in 1984. This followed the indictment of Richard Lee Fowler on 39 counts of theft, conspiracy and fraud arising from alleged trafficking in classified documents. Fowler was alleged to have obtained hundreds of highly classified Pentagon documents while working for Boeing in Washington as a senior marketing analyst between 1978 and 1986. These included the Pentagon's five-year budget plan and three National Security Council decision directives signed by President Reagan. In an interview with attorneys Fowler was asked if he had been pressured into getting the documents. He answered: 'No. That's what I was hired to do.'

(1) *Agents of Influence*, David Ignatius (W. W. Norton, New York, 1987), Chapter 11.
(2) *The US Intelligence Community*, Richelson (Ballinger, Boston, Mass, 1989), pp. 13 and 26.
(3) *Guardian*, 19 June 1990; however the budget of GCHQ is in one sense artificially low as most of the hardware it uses is substantially part-funded by the NSA.
(4) 'Spytech' (Channel 4 Dispatches, 20/20 TV, 1988).
(5) For example, *Guardian*, 22 August 1990; *Independent*, 20 August 1990.
(6) 'How to Choose and Use a Management Consultant', Economist Intelligence Unit No. 1183, 1989.
(7) European Management Consultants' Federation, 1989.
(8) Quoted by Alvin Tofler in *Powershift*, p. 41.
(9) *Los Angeles Times*, 21 June 1988.
(10) Quoted in *Industrial Espionage: intelligence techniques and countermeasures*, Bottom and Gallati (Butterworths, Boston, Mass, 1984), p.19.
(11) *Los Angeles Times*, 23 August 1988, 11 April 1989.
(12) *Los Angeles Times*, 22 August 1990.
(13) *Washington Post*, 27 November 1990.
(14) *Sunday Telegraph*, 8 August 1990; *Sunday Times*, 7 January 1990; BBC1 Breakfast Time, 7 February 1990.
(15) For example, Network Security Management, Carratu International, Argen, Fairfax. See *Washington Post*, 16 May 1988; *Financial Times*, 14 March 1991, 13 April 1991, *The Times*, 23 October 1990, 15 April 1991; *Sunday Times*, 31 March 1991; *Lloyds List*, 26 March 1991; *Sunday Telegraph*, 14 February 1988, 14 October 1990; *Daily Telegraph*, 20 September 1990, 24 October 1990; *Independent on Sunday*, 21 September 1990, 6 January 1991; *Sunday Times* Magazine, 18 November 1990, *Guardian*, 26 June 1990, 22 October 1990.
(16) The press love writing about Jules Kroll: these are only some of the longer and better pieces about him: *The Times*, 1 December 1990; *Independent on Sunday*, 6 January 1991, 31 March 1991; *Observer*, 31 March 1991; *Los Angeles Times*, 9 October 1988; *Washington Post*, 16 May 1988; *Wall Street Journal*, 2 December 1986; *Financial Times*, 5 August 1989; *Guardian*, 29 July 1989. In July 1991, Kroll Associates acquired one of its largest rivals, Business Risk International, to form a company with a world-wide staff of 500, 34 offices and a $75m annual revenue. (*Financial Times*, 19 July 1991.)
(17) *Washington Post*, 4 and 17 March 1989
(18) *Sunday Times*, 17 and 24 June 1990, 5 August 1990, 7 April, 5 May 1991; *The Times*, 18 June 1990, 1 and 6 May 1991; *Today*, 26 June 1990, 8 April 1991; *Financial Times*, 1 May 1991; *Daily Telegraph*, 1 May 1991; *Guardian*, 26 June 1991, personal information.
(19) *Business Week*, 5 May 1986.
(20) *Los Angeles Times*, 6 February 1987.
(21) *Los Angeles Times*, 8, 9 and 10 September 1989, 15 August 1990.
(22) This account draws on: *Los Angeles Times*, 26 June 1988, 18 August 1989, 7 November 1989; *Boston Globe*, 23 July 1988; *Washington Post*, 14 November 1989; *Business Week*, 4 July 1988.

6 Covert Sources: Office Work

'More than half of modern culture depends on what one shouldn't read.'

Oscar Wilde, *The Importance of Being Earnest*

For the person with diminished moral scruples, the office, the workplace and their immediate surroundings offer considerable opportunities for intelligence gathering. Most of the instances never come to public attention; even when an individual is caught the legal remedy may be unreliable; victims often feel that whatever damage they have sustained the courts are unable to compensate them; often all that a victim might have is a suspicion.

Here is one case from 1986, not all that typical, which did get reported: a secretary had worked for twenty years for a London company selling film set insurance and felt strong loyalty to her boss. The boss was the victim of a board room coup, during which the boss had steamed open letters addressed to other directors whom he believed were conspiring against him. The secretary went through the briefcases of recently appointed directors and scavenged their wastepaper bins looking for evidence that they had mounted their coup illegally. Eventually she was found out and dismissed. She then sued for unfair dismissal which is how a relatively commonplace event came to public notice. In the circumstances, the newspaper coverage: 'Secretary acted like MI6 Spy' seems rather unfair.[1]

In contrast to the chapters that follow, most of the techniques described here require very little in the way of skill, rather an element of opportunism and a degree of nerve. Even for those techniques where some skill is required, what counts is mostly determination and willingness to spend time rather than the development of any difficult expertise. The fact that some of these methods may appear to be banal and 'obvious' in no way diminishes their value.

Targets

These days the obvious confidential materials – memoranda, letters, board minutes, accounts records, personnel files, sales figures, marketing reports, R&D results[*] – are likely to be kept under a reasonable level of security. Getting hold of them is likely to involve some danger – either you must hope to find someone with legitimate access who is willing to be corrupted[†] (or who approaches you – the volunteer agent[‡]) or you must smuggle yourself or a professional into a building and work with great speed.

In fact, so many practitioners have told me, what you concentrate on are collateral and discards. Collateral material, in this context, is docu-

---

[*] Computer-based material – on floppy disks and within computers – is dealt with in Chapter 8.

[†] Apart from those on the staff of a company or its professional advisors, one of the favourite targets for attempted corruption are the printers who specialise in producing prospectuses for equity and bond share issues and other financial documentation. For reasons I have never understood, the last several stages of any significant financial 'offering' tend to be negotiated over printer's proofs of the final document. There are also persistent rumours that the motorbike despatch riders who handle this material can be induced to make a detour in delivery to enable interested parties to make photocopies.

[‡] See p. 37. An interesting variant on the usual story of the corrupt employee or ex-employee approaching his company's competitors is the blackmail ploy. In December 1988 the chemical giant du Pont received an ultimatum: pay $10 million, or competitors will learn the company's secrets for making Spandex, du Pont's trade name for Lycra, the fibre used in underwear, bathing suits, and other clothing. After supplying copies of documents for verification by du Pont staff in Italy, four ex-employees, all Argentinians, hoped to receive a pay-off at a Geneva rendezvous but were met instead by FBI agents and the Swiss police and extradited to the United States. A 1989 study carried out for the American Society for Industrial Security found that 48 per cent of 150 companies queried had been similarly victimised (*Business Week*, 13 March 1989; *Los Angeles Times*, 28 February 1989, 29 September 1989).

ments and other items which contain confidential information which a company has underclassified and which a hostile intelligence analyst can use to build up a picture of whatever it is the target thought they had managed to keep secret. Classic examples of collateral material are departmental reports which refer to sales results, marketing campaigns, R&D results, and so on, without being the definitive internal documents to carry that information. In companies that go in for lots of internal presentations, the agenda and overhead projection foils also provide valuable collateral evidence of activities.

Discards are drafts and obsolete versions of documents – and many other things besides. We'll examine the possibilities of garbology shortly.

Searching methods

Perhaps one should begin with some observations about searching in general. First of all, its legality. If you can be regarded as 'invited' into an office, then your being there for reasons other than those which the owner might expect does not of itself make your presence illegal. If you have wandered into an office without being 'invited' then, in the first instance, the most you have committed is an act of trespass – which is a civil wrong as opposed to a crime. The 'victim' can sue you for damages, but has to prove that damage – and that means physical damage – has taken place. It is only if you break into an office – by forcing a door or window or using keys to which you are clearly not entitled that you commit a criminal offence. Of course the trespasser who steals something (takes away permanently, not just borrows) is guilty of theft. However, in English law at any rate, you can't steal 'information', though you can steal the paper or diskette upon which it is held.[2] Usually you can't be charged with stealing something that has been thrown away – but the contents of a wastepaper basket in an office may not necessarily be regarded as 'thrown away' until they have left the premises. In some parts of the United States there are local ordinances which state that garbage on the sidewalk may only be handled by authorised garbage collection agencies.[3]

But being caught can often have penalties that have nothing directly to do with the law. At the very least you and your intentions have been exposed. Even if you aren't caught, you will have needlessly alerted your target and made subsequent activities much more difficult. You need to pick your time carefully and you should try to have a cover story in case you are caught. Much of this will depend on who you are. If you are spying on a fellow office worker you will use your knowledge of meal breaks and the habits of your target. If you are being sent in from outside you may have to adopt the guise of an office cleaner or service technician. If you do, it is usually considered wise to spend a bit of time making yourself vaguely 'known' about the building, at least to the point when people no longer remark on your movements. More risky, but requiring less time, is to be a visitor 'lost' and looking for someone's office or the loo. There are many variants to this ploy: 'Put on a white coat; you are a doctor/scientist/researcher' is one. A friend who is a technical engineer for a television company reckons he can get into almost any important public event by putting on his expensive ski-jacket and carrying a large thick coil of cable over his shoulder. A chattering handie-talkie radio is used where an extra air of importance and business is deemed desirable.

Many professional searchers of offices and homes now take a Polaroid camera with them. People have an extraordinarily acute eye for detail about places and items around which they regularly live and work. The Polaroid camera is able to record the 'before' so that the 'after' can be as near perfectly restored as possible. The Polaroids are used not only for the general appearance of the room but for such fine detail as the contents of drawers and briefcases.

Photocopies

What is still sometimes called the xerographic process was invented by an American called Carlson in the 1930s. No longer just made by the Xerox Corporation and its licensees, significant new features appear on photocopying machines every three years or so and all but the smallest offices have devices which can print huge quantities in a very short space of time, with the automated stacking and collating of several hundred sheets at once.

Although the copied computer disk is by far the most efficient way of squirreling data away from an office, because there is still a vast population that is happier when handling print, photocopying is still the favourite method. You still have the benefit of being able to steal the contents of a document while leaving the original behind.

The owners of photocopiers have been fighting back for some time. Look to see if there is a register logging photocopies taken – and if it records the machine's counter number. You may need to make a plausible covering entry. Check if the company is one of the five per cent of the population that has a careful stationery policy. Not only is stealing stationery a criminal offence where photocopying itself may not be, but you could be starting an alert. For the price of a quire of photocopier from the local office supplies store you could be avoiding the risk of detection.

Some companies try to reduce the risks of stolen photocopies by using special paper upon which to type or print their confidential material. This reveals a 'watermark' when photocopied. If you don't mind who sees the photocopies, then the watermark may confirm the authenticity of the original. However, if there is a risk that the photocopy is shown to its real owner or to third parties to whom business ethics is important, you may have to take precautions. There may be a number of procedures in place in which the way and time at which a copy was made can be identified. The obvious method is if each authentic copy has been marked, e.g. Copy 3 of 8 and a detailed distribution list kept by the document's originator. By looking at who had access to Copy 3 the identity of the thief may be determined. A more clandestine method of 'authentic copy marking' is to vary slightly details of punctuation or wordage between the various copies. It was hidden marking – plus forensic work which identified the drums of the machine she had used – that in 1983 identified Sarah Tisdall as the Foreign Office clerk who had sent copies of a minute by the then Defence Secretary about the imminent siting of cruise missiles in the UK to the *Guardian* newspaper. The *Guardian*'s editor had kept the copies and had been compelled to give them to the police under the Contempt of Court Act, 1981.[4]

You can of course carry your own photocopier with you – portable models have been available since the mid-1980s – you have to stroke it along the surface of the paper to be copied and it can only handle a strip 5 or 6cm wide at a time. Most models use a heat-sensitive rather than plain paper which does not last indefinitely and quite a few have had reliability problems.

Cameras

An alternative to the photocopier is the miniature or sub-miniature camera. The Minox in its various forms has been a 'James Bond' gadget since the 1960s. For its time it was well thought-out – the chain connected to one end is useful not only for securing the camera against loss but also acts as a measuring device for focusing purposes. The main problem is that the film used is very small, perhaps a tenth of the size of 35mm film and once enlarged it becomes quite grainy, which makes the reading of fine detail difficult. High-definition film and the associated special developing processes mean a considerable loss of convenience to the spy. Of greater practical use is the 110 size camera which has a film 25 per cent of the size of the 35mm and which thus gives much better definition than the Minox. The other advantage is that people who find it accidentally are less likely to associate it with spying. Since the late 1980s, however, there have been considerable advances in the design of point-and-shoot miniature 35mm cameras. These often have sophisticated auto-focusing mechanisms and in-built flash lamps. At the same time they are of a size which makes concealment quite easy.

Paper shredders

A common line of defence by those with confidential waste is the paper shredder. It is only of limited value. Ever since Iranian revolutionary guards entered the abandoned US embassy in Teheran in 1979 and reconstructed shredded CIA documents people have realised that, with diligence, the work of paper shredders can be overcome. Tens of thousands of documents were captured by the guards and between 1980 and 1985, they and the Iranian government published more than fifty volumes of the documents, under the title *Documents from the US Espionage Den*.[5] In fact rebuilding sliced paper is much easier than the Teheran reports may have suggested. In all but the more expensive shredding machines the paper strips tend to fall together into a soft heap; often the cutting wheels leave slight serrations along the edge of the strips and these cause them to adhere together like velcro. If you need to play jigsaw puzzles with shredded paper, try and disturb the pile as little as possible. It is even easier if some of the correspondence or memoranda is printed on distinctive paper.

Garbology

Garbology as a respected discipline within the social sciences grew out of the work archaeologists carry out when they seek to build a picture of the fabric of life of some long-lost culture from the scraps and fragments they find in a 'dig'. The dean of academic garbology is William Rathje who for nearly twenty years has lead a multi-disciplinary team called the Garbage Project at the University of Arizona at Tucson.[6] One of his followers, Luanne Hudson, who has taught a garbology class, Modern Material Culture Studies, told the *Los Angeles Times*:[7] 'What you throw away can reveal your age, whether you have children, your economic level, possibly your educational background but at least your intellectual level, your level of health, whether or not you're a stable member of the community and many other things.' She claimed that research obtained by studying garbage was often more accurate than that collected from personal interviews. 'You can reconstruct behavior from actual items. Psychologists, sociologists and anthropologists will go out and ask people, 'How many bottles of beer do you consume a week?' A person will usually tell you what they think you want to hear. At the front door, they tell you one thing; at the back door, their garbage tells you another.'

Another of Rathje's former colleagues, an archaeologist called Fred Gorman who is a former director of Harvard University's field school said: 'We can learn a great deal about people's domestic consumption habits that span not only the range of foods consumed, but also medicines, potentially addictive substances, alcohol, tobacco and other types of narcotics. It's possible to gain information

even of a financial nature.'

Academic garbologists are slightly defensive about their subject as a result of the activities of private detectives and journalists. They have a code of ethics which tells them to discard material relating to finance and other personal matters and to draw conclusions based on a whole group of people within a neighbourhood rather than on selected individuals. The best-known journalistic garbological activity concerned the singer Bob Dylan, but in 1990 the London *Sunday Times* magazine ran a feature entitled 'Some Very Famous Dustbins' in which two journalists, Bruno Mouran and Pascal Rostain, set out to obtain and photograph 'the flashiest trash in Los Angeles'.[8] Victims included Liz Taylor, Ronald and Nancy Reagan, Princess Stephanie of Monaco, Jack Nicholson and Madonna.

The subject has even been at the centre of spy novels. In an off-beat thriller called *Dunn's Conundrum*, Stan Lee's pre-occupation is an intelligence super-agency called the Library whose staff have access to everything, including the product of all the other intelligence agencies. One of their number was called the Garbageman, who was a genius at trash analysis. He had been recruited, initially by the CIA, on the basis of a doctoral thesis. He becomes disturbed when a 'trash cover' delivered to him does not make sense.

It isn't only that this garbage is fake; it's self-conscious garbage. . . . Sanitized garbage. Discreet garbage. It's almost as though someone were trying to make a good impression with their garbage. Look at the magazines. *Harper's, Newsweek, Foreign Policy*. Where are the *Playboy*s and the *Hustler*s and the *Cosmopolitan*s? Improbable. No liquor, no wine, no beer. None. Improbable. The junk mail is totally innocuous. . . . No hot causes, no left wing, no right wing. There are four brands of breakfast cereal. Impossible? No. Three brands of cigarettes, but only a pack of each kind in – what? – two weeks? . . . A pair of children's socks. . . . They're worn but there are no holes. That means the kid outgrew them. But . . . there ought to be a lot of stuff to go with a kid.

Later it turns out that the premises from which the

trash had been collected had been set up by various people interested in compromising the activities of the Library. The 'trash' had been designed to be picked up and to confuse any would-be analyst.

Industrial spies and private investigators in their various guises have none of the moral concerns of the academics. 'It [garbage] is the single most useful tool to obtain information regarding the private lives of individuals,' Armand Grant, president of Teltec Investigations, a Malibu-based detective agency employing 13 private investigators told the *Los Angeles Times* in 1988.[9] 'People do not think of destroying envelopes from the bank. They do not think of destroying telephone numbers they have dialled that are on their phone bills. You would be surprised what one would find in trash.' An investigator for 22 years, Grant claimed he had 'broken open some monolithic cases by opening up trash. . . . It provides leads you follow on where certain other items might be found. . . . The thing you do is find out when trash is picked up and pick it up before the trash people get there. It's done very quickly.'

In March 1991 Mary Kay Corp won a court agreement from its largest rival in the cosmetics business, Avon Corp, preventing it from taking any more material out of its trash dumpster. Avon were also required to reveal material that they had previously scavenged. Avon was preparing a defence against what it feared might have become a hostile take-over bid from Mary Kay.[10]

Prime aims in any exploration of trash are discarded drafts and print-outs and obsolete documents. Before the advent of the personal computer, word processor and laser printer, carbon paper and typewriter ribbon (particularly the high quality one-strike variety) were also keenly sought. These days investigators have to hope to be able to cover latent images from scrap paper. If a notepad is used for an important handwritten note, the sheets of paper immediately below the sensitive note will carry the impress of the handwriting. Sometimes the original can be reconstructed quite easily using the 'soft pencil' technique; otherwise the ESDA (electrostatic deposition analysis) methods used in recent cases of alleged police fabrication of confessions has to be employed.[11] Another item worth salvaging – or stealing – are dictation tapes.

The Garbology Harvest

Office
  Obvious
    discarded memos, reports, etc.
    discarded computer print-out
    obsolete internal telephone directories,
      organisation charts
    obsolete computer manuals
    discarded overhead foils, slides, etc.
    used credit-card counterfoils
  Less obvious
    typewriter carbons
    discarded floppies
  Indirect
    cartons and containers
    discarded invoices, delivery notes, etc.
      for raw materials, cartons, etc.

Factory
  throw-aways from manufacturing – swarf,
    off-cuts, etc.
  cartons, containers and other wrapping
  warehouse chits
  effluent (for later analysis)

Home
  bank statements
  other invoices, etc.
  correspondence
  junk mail
  food remnants
  drink bottles, cans, etc.
  medicine containers
  clothes, wrappings thereof

Often trash from the homes of key executives are as productive as that collected from their offices. Domestic trash is less well guarded than that at workplaces. There is the possibility of a wealth of personal detail such as credit card counterfoils (also useful for the fraudster, but that's another story) and correspondence, but given that many top executives are also workaholics, scraps of work-related material may make it to the domestic dustbin where it would have been carefully destroyed in the office.[*]

Back at the factory, an examination of the changing quality of industrial waste, by-product and effluent can tell the scientist a great deal about

* See also Chapter 11.

the processes that are going on within a factory. The technique is used widely by environmental campaigners but it doesn't have to be limited to situations where pollution is suspected. An assessment of industrial scrap may yield information about metals, alloys and plastics being used. The shape of the scrap can be used as the basis of a deduction of the dimensions of what is being fabricated within. Boxes, polystyrene moulds and other wrapping materials from suppliers can provide clues about 'ingredients' and quantities.

Most covert office work requires very little technical skill. In the next three chapters we look at the technical aids available to industrial spies.

(1) 5 August 1986.

(2) The case of *Oxford* v. *Moss* [1978] 68 Cr. App. R.

(3) *Los Angeles Times*, 20 May 1988.

(4) *Official Secrets*, David Hooper (Secker & Warburg, London, 1978), p. 157ff.

(5) *Independent on Sunday*, 30 September 1990.

(6) *Journal of Consumer Research*, September 1985; *People,* 22 November 1976; *Omni*, May 1982; *Independent on Sunday*, 22 November 1990.

(7) *Los Angeles Times*, 20 May 1988.

(8) *Sunday Times* Magazine, 7 October 1990.

(9) *Los Angeles Times*, 20 May 1988.

(10) *Los Angeles Times*, 19 March 1991.

(11) *Guardian*, 30 August, 29 December 1990, 15 and 28 March 1991. An alternative interpretation of the ESDA acronym is Electrostatic Document Analysis.

7 Covert Sources: Elint

Right at the centre of popular perceptions about industrial espionage is the use of bugs and taps. A number of recent cases have caught the public imagination: the Comet 'biscuit tin' case was the first successful British prosecution for industrial espionage activities under the Interception of Communications Act, 1985. That had involved telephone tapping. Shortly before those events, officials at the Davenport Brewery in Birmingham, then facing a £38m take-over bid by the Wolverhampton and Dudley Brewery, had found a well used bug; the perpetrators and their employers were never caught.[1] Davenports was later sold to another brewery group, Greenall Whitley, and they in turn eventually closed it down. Allegations of bugging arose during the Argyll/Distillers/Guinness affair.[2] When the *Independent* newspaper was planning the launch of its Sunday edition a bug was discovered in the office wiring,[3] and during a £441m hostile take-over bid for Laing Properties by P&O and Chelsfield a bug was found at Laing's headquarters in Watford.[4]

Such indeed has been the level of press interest that the *Sunday Times* found itself the victim of a hoax involving bugs and taps.* A man calling himself Barry Gray claimed he had been retained by Alan Bond, the English-born Australian entre-preneur. His alleged targets included Robert Holmes à Court and a director of Tiny Rowland's Lonrho Group. 'Barry Gray' turned out to be a man well-known for helping newspapers make fools of themselves by identifying stories that they might be hungry for and for which he could assemble just enough evidence and 'atmosphere' to be believed. Previously he had pretended to be an IRA gunrunner who had sold a passport to ace terrorist Carlos the Jackal, had simultaneously deceived the KGB and the CIA when he claimed to know the whereabouts of a kidnapped defector, and had sold the *New York Post* a second-hand pair of shoes for $56,000 on the basis that they had belonged to ex Teamster boss, Jimmy Hoffa.[5]

There seems little doubt that large numbers of bugs are sold.[6] In the UK they are advertised regularly in newspapers of total respectability by at least five companies. There are at least three specialist retail outlets in London and any number of High Street electronics stores that carry a small basic line of bugs and taps. A crude idea of the quantities involved can be derived by examining the Companies House returns for one of the more prominent – Lorraine Electronics, which operates from a shop in a north-east London suburb but is also one of the biggest advertisers. In 1989, under its registered name of Ruby Electronics Ltd, it reported turnover of just under £620,000; since the average price of its bugs and taps at that time (according to its colourful catalogue) was just over £100, they could be selling 5,500 to 6,000 devices a year. Of course a significant proportion of the turnover could be from higher-priced items, bug detectors or from sweeping services; at any event, for the record, the four employees produced a profit of 16.36 per cent. Allowing for their competitors, both those that advertise and those that are more discreet, an annual UK sale of 20-25,000 bugs and taps seems a not unreasonable estimate. Some of these will be for overseas use

---

* The *Sunday Times* is not the only British newspaper to get into difficulties over a bugging story; in November 1988, two reporters from the *Independent* tried to find out how easy it was to hire someone illicitly to bug a business lunch. Although many of the best-known London-based corporate security companies turned them down flat, at least until the name of the 'client' could be checked, the reporters managed to find some operatives willing to be hired. Unfortunately, their activities had attracted so much attention that, at the end, several teams of private detectives as well as the police were following them around. The reporters were apparently unaware of this up to the point at which their story appeared (*Independent*, 27 November 1988; *Observer*, 31 November 1988).

and no one knows how many are bought but not used.

The time has now come to show how relatively useless these types of 'elint' – electronically gathered information – are by themselves and to show the limits of the various technologies.[*]

Perhaps one ought to start with the most obvious but also the most-overlooked aspect of all: the most a bug or tap can do is capture conversations within its range of operation. The bug can't differentiate between an important strategy conference and the noise of office equipment, vacuum cleaners and coffee cups. It won't interpret when speakers mumble or talk cryptically in the shorthand and jargon that is endemic to all businesses. By themselves, tapes of eavesdropped chat don't tell you whether you are hearing all that you think you may need to know. In other words, even where technically successful, what elint produces is hours of noise-on-tape which has to be transcribed and interpreted. The cost of this nearly always far exceeds the cost of the hardware.

And it is risky – if you are caught, because of the particular odour in which bugging/tapping is held, you will nearly always face heavy public condemnation, even if you haven't broken the law.

Wired bugging

One of things that often surprises people is that not all forms of elint are illegal. Use a radio transmitter or a radio receiver tuned to an unauthorised frequency, or tap into a telephone line and you break the law (in the UK, respectively, the Wireless Telegraphy Act, 1949 and amendments and the Interception of Communications Act, 1985).[†] But the oldest technique of eavesdropping is using your ears to listen when others believe they are not being overheard – and it is as effective today as it always was. The second oldest technique is lipreading, and these days a TV camera, a zoom lens and video recorder mean that you can have several attempts at verifying lip movements. If you leave a tape recorder running in a room, if you leave a hidden microphone in your target room and run a concealed wire to a pair of headphones or a tape recorder elsewhere, or if you use a long-distance microphone (for 'recording birdsong'), you commit no criminal offence. (You may of course trespass in the course of installing or retrieving some of this equipment, but that is a matter for the civil courts and the penalty is limited to any physical damage to the target's property).

Much of the equipment usable for wired bugging is sold in the High Street without any specific 'security' label. All but the cheapest easy-to-hide microcassette recorders feature half-speed playing, to give 90 minutes without having to turn the tape over; many of them have built-in vox (voice-operated relay) facilities, so that when there is no sound the tape stops running. Miniature 'tie-clip' microphones can be fixed to other items of clothing, concealed up sleeves, for example. The same mikes, without the clip, can have their connecting cables extended (though not indefinitely) for use in rooms where a tape recorder can't be taken. Long-range mikes are sold as accessories for video cameras.

Specialist security outlets sometimes offer the same products, rebadged and at a higher price, but are also likely to stock more esoteric microphones, ones which are built into belts or briefcases, or which can be buried in a wall (the 'spike mike' is designed for placing through a wall from the far side of the target until it is just a wallpaper's thickness away) or contact mikes which are designed to be fitted against a window and which will then pick up interior noises via vibration.

One of the many advantages of wired bugging is that, compared with methods using radio or the telephone system, it is much more difficult to detect. It is in fact possible to locate electronic components even if they are not obviously

---

[*] Not for the last time in this book, the reader is urged to return to the idealised Management Consultant's Strategic Overview of Information Acquisition Costing Methodology, p. 13 (Chapter 2). Bugging and tapping do not score well; the more sophisticated and the more expensive the technologies employed, the more important it is to ensure that the hoped-for information really can't be obtained elsewhere and that its eventual value is commensurate with the cost and risk.

[†] It is not illegal, of course, to tape telephone conversations in which you yourself are a participant; in the USA, however, you must inform the other party of what you are doing (Wiretap Act, 1968) and the convention is that telephone recorders send out a marking signal to indicate that recording is taking place.

radiating energy at the time.[*] The practical difficulty is that in most places where concealed microphones and tape-recorders are likely to be deployed there are also other 'legitimate' electronic items – calculators, watches, computers, radio receivers, and so on, which will mislead the detection equipment.

Bugging

Bugging means the use of radio transmitters. A microphone collects the noise in its immediate vicinity; this in turn is delivered via a low-powered radio transmitter and then received on a radio receiver, usually a modified or specialised one. It was in 1965, over 25 years ago, that a US Senate Sub-Committee first got excited about 'cocktail olive bugs'[7] but the capacity for the popular press to reinvigorate an old story seems undiminished so let's spend a short time explaining the basics of the physics involved.

It is true that radio-transmitting circuits of incredible miniaturisation can be manufactured easily, even at the level of the home constructor with a small-headed soldering iron. Transmitter kits requiring minimum assembly are available by mail order in the UK for incorporation into concealment housings of your own choice for under £10. The limitations come not from the size of the circuitry, but from the requirements for a power source and an efficient antenna, and the fact that most bugs are very easy to detect once you decide to go looking for them.

A radio transmitter needs to be powered. If you can't connect it to the mains (and if you do, you'll need a voltage transformer/rectifier which will bulk things up somewhat – two favourite configurations are to build everything into a power adapter or a light bulb) – or if you can't use the telephone line power, you have to feed it with a

battery.[†] The battery too will bulk things up – the longer you want the bug to last, the larger the battery; the further you want the signal to reach, the larger the battery. Replacing a battery is as hazardous as installing the bug in the first place.

The radio signal needs to get out: not any length of wire will do – transmitters are at their most efficient when the antenna length is at certain fractions of the wavelength of the frequency being used, usually one-quarter. (For bugs designed to be received on modified broadcast FM receivers, the optimum length is 75cm). For preference the wire should be in a straight line and not curled up. Any variation from this and the power from the battery is being converted into heat or otherwise lost; in other words the battery is draining away and you are not hearing anything. That is the problem with many of the 'ashtray', 'pen' and 'calculator' housings. The radio signal won't pass through metal – that's filing cabinets or walls insulated inside with foil or the metal from which the bodies of most road vehicles are still constructed. If there is a reasonable amount of metal between the transmitter's antenna and the receiver, very little will be heard. A large building or a block of landscape may have similar effects.

All of which can be overcome if you have time to do the installation properly: bulk doesn't matter if it is well concealed; a rooftop antenna will radiate more freely than any other. Given time, you need have no more than a small mike in the target room and use a length of very thin cable to a transmitter hidden and radiating elsewhere. If you do that, you'll also defeat some bug-detecting equipment, the sweeps of which will usually be concentrated in the areas of greatest sensitivity. But of course time is what you may not have.

Your next problem is that the same technology that enables you to hear what the transmitter is putting out can be used to detect the bug's existence. Anyone using bugs has to make careful decisions about power-output and hence range. The greater the range of the transmitter, the quicker any battery power gets used up, and the wider the area in which those who suspect your operations have a chance of discovering your equipment. Or

---

[*] The main piece of equipment to do this is called a high-frequency non-linear junction detector; it works by radiating a low-power extremely pure radio signal (one with no harmonic content) and simultaneously listening out for harmonics, typically the third harmonic, which have been generated by the interaction of the radio signal with the structure of an electronic device.

[†] Solar power, the other possible alternative, isn't really feasible as the size of solar cell required for even the lowest-powered bug could not go unnoticed.

the greater the chance your bug is overheard by accident. On the other hand, a bug that is too low powered may not transmit far enough – which means that your receiver may have to be located more closely to the target than is convenient.

If you have sought to keep your bugging costs down you will have bought one which you can receive on an unmodified FM broadcast radio (i.e. in the range 88–108MHz). Clearly your target, if he suspects, has only to tune across the band to see if he can hear himself. (These days many portable radios feature electronic tuning and have a scan facility – you press one button to hear, in turn, all the stations in your locality.) Most of the bugs widely advertised and easily obtained in the UK, Europe and the USA are designed to operate in the frequency band 108–136 MHz. This is used by civil aircraft and many 'electronic security' shops sell modified FM broadcast radios retuned to this band. It is also the second part of the radio spectrum (after the FM broadcast band) that any investigator will check out.

You could try going for a bug operating on a more obscure band; whatever you do, you'll have to check out if there are any legitimate users of your selected frequency – you don't want them complaining of interference. At this stage, you'll no longer be paying High Street prices, of course, either for the bug or the equipment you'll need to receive it.[*] In addition, depending on the frequency you choose, you could have either an antenna-size problem or a lack-of-effective radiation problem – radio waves vary in their ability to get through brick walls depending on their wavelength. You could have both problems, of course. In any event, either a £250 scanner-receiver (of which more in Chapter 9) or specialised bug-detecting equipment will soon smoke your bug out.

There are some partial answers: first, give your bug a vox (voice-operated relay) so that it is only transmitting when its microphone hears a noise. That will mean it can it only be detected easily

when sounds are present within its area of operation. As a by-product, this also will conserve power if the bug is being run on a battery. Second, and more expensively, you could have a radio-activated remote control switch attached to your bug so that the bug is not only a transmitter but has associated with it a receiver which responds to a specific sequence of notes on a given frequency – the surveillance operative has a miniature transmitter which sends out the signal to turn the bug on or off. Third, and still more expensively, use **sub-carrier audio**. Anyone who uses an 'ordinary' receiver will only hear a blank carrier (perhaps someone testing out a new transmitter?) and the signal you want to hear has been sub-modulated on to the 'silence' in much the same way as stereo 'difference' information is transmitted in the broadcast radio band. Again, part of your cost is the receiver that can hear the sophisticated bug. Most higher-end bug-detecting equipment can locate sub-carrier audio. The smart move here is to locate your main carrier frequency next to that of an existing legitimate transmitter (for example, a broadcast station, or a commercial two-way 'pmr' radio base which is on most of the time, such as those used by taxi and courier services, or adjacent to a paging service transmitter). The bug-detecting equipment may have difficulty in separating the legitimate from the illegitimate. Yet another route is to use infra-red transmitters and receivers. But at this level you need professionals, who will charge for their services and whom you have to decide to trust.

Another approach blurs the distinction between wired and wireless bugging: you modulate a radio-type signal on to the mains power line. This technology is used in the so-called wireless intercoms you buy at office equipment stores and also in some baby alarms. Both 'transmitter' and 'receiver' have to be connected to the electricity mains, and be within the same phase area of the local sub-power station. A similar approach is to adapt the technology used for the 'base' side in some cordless telephones: your bug operates on an MF radio frequency (above or below the AM broadcast band), is plugged into the mains and uses the power cable to radiate out a signal over a range of 100 meters or so. In this case, the receiver does not have to be plugged into the mains, but

* More expensive bugs are crystal-controlled; low-cost bugs can suffer from frequency-drift – they can go 'off' as the battery becomes exhausted – the crystal makes the circuit more stable and thus easier to receive. They are more efficient in other ways too so that battery power is more completely transferred into radiated power.

hears the result as an ordinary radio station. Both of these technologies can be detected relatively easily once you start looking for them – you can use a broadband 'communications receiver' like those designed for shortwave radio enthusiasts or specialist debugging kit.

That's about the limit as far as DIY bugging is concerned; that is, where you can buy the bug relatively easily (in the UK there is no law prohibiting the manufacture, sale or possession of such devices – you only break the law when you transmit), install it yourself and, armed with a suitable receiver, carry out your own monitoring. There are more sophisticated techniques, such as using modulated infra-red transmitters, RF flooding[*] and the oft-written-about laser beam which detects speech from the vibrations of the window of the room in which the conversation of interest is taking place,[†] but for these you need professionals – and you have to locate them, and then decide that you trust them.

Finally, what you end up with (and in this respect it shares the same problems as telephone taps) is a tape which will need transcribing. The difficulty and cost of this will depend on how clearly the bug's mike was able to pick up the noise in the room – echoing rooms are bad news – the quality of enunciation of the speakers, whether they had anything of interest to say and how good the radio reception was.

Detecting bugs

As we have seen, at the lowest possible level, an ordinary FM radio receiver can be used as a bug detector and a £250 scanner from a High Street electronics chain will cover most of the frequencies used by bugs. However, the scan rate of these (the rate at which they sample all radio channels between defined upper and lower limits) is relatively slow and of course the scanner will pause often at radio transmissions which have every right to be there. For certain other bugging techniques, a communications receiver covering 10KHz to 30MHz is also useful.

There is more specialised equipment. The low-cost 'bug detectors' sold in the same outlets that sell cheap bugs are more-or-less useless. They pick up *any* radio transmitter. They'll react to bugs, but also to a strong broadcast station if you have one in the vicinity; they'll go off in reaction to the taxi outside your office, the dispatch rider in your reception, your security guard's walkie-talkie and the cellular phone belonging to you and any visitors you have. If you turn the sensitivity down (deluxe models only), you mightn't find the bug stuck under your boardroom table.

Higher-end specialised equipment tends to need trained personnel. There are two main categories of equipment. One is sold as an item of electronic test gear – the spectrum analyser. It is used to test the purity of radio transmissions but can also give a VDU display of radio activity in a given part of the radio spectrum. If you know what you are looking for and there is a bug in the vicinity, you'll see it on the VDU. Many spectrum analysers will also let you demodulate any signal of interest – in other words, listen to it. Spectrum analysers in the hands of trained people are excellent for locating sub-carrier audio and masked transmissions.

The more popular high-end bug detection kit, though, is essentially a high-speed scanner the sensitivity of which can be carefully controlled. It needs less skill to handle than a spectrum analyser but is often less effective. The operator may concentrate on specific frequency bands which past experience has shown are more likely to be used. In some cases an audio marker tone is sounded in the suspect area – the scanner then stops only on transmissions on which the marker tone can be heard. That finds the bugs quickly – most of the time – but it also alerts those who planted them that they have been rumbled. You may not want that to happen: it might be much more productive to use the bug to feed back misleading information.

Which brings us to another point: finding a bug, even if you disable it, doesn't automatically tell you who planted it. If you want to know that you have to understand enough about the bug you have found – its operating frequency, its range, the likely place it was bought – to form a view of from where it is being listened to. You then have a chance of catching someone who may tell you who

---

[*] A technique described by Peter Wright in *Spycatcher* (Heinemann, Australia, 1986).
[†] The practical difficulties are: you have to find a site from which your laser beam can be directed without your targets becoming aware, and windows vibrate in sympathy with noises outside as well as inside.

they are and who has employed them.

After a while, everything can degenerate into Tom-and-Jerry cartoon activities as teams of buggists and counter-buggists evade and stalk each other at ever-increasing expense to their employers.[*] If you wish to avoid being eavesdropped, your best and cheapest route is to stop having important conversations in predictable locations.

TV bugs

A bug doesn't have to limit itself to voice – you can transmit pictures as well. Fibre optics means that the lens does not have to be co-located with the rest of the camera. Camera and transmitter can be condensed down to a size of 3cm by 2cm by 8cm – and that's for equipment available, more or less, over the counter. You still have all the other problems – the TV transmitter needs power and a good aerial. And of course, the signal has to be transmitted, and thus can be detected. TV signals occupy much more bandwidth than voice signals, so if someone suspects any form of bugging, the covert TV transmitter will be discovered quite quickly. Covert TV *cameras* can make sense – but only in situations where you can run cable away to a video recorder, access to which is without difficulty.

Tapping

Tapping means trying to gather information from telephone lines. The simplest way is to pick up an extension receiver on a line while a potentially interesting conversation is taking place. The legitimate participants in the dialogue will almost certainly be able to hear your activities. On many phones it is possible to use a low-cost (under £2 in the UK's High Streets) inductive microphone which is typically held in place with a rubber sucker. The placement of an induction mike is quite critical – it needs to be near fairly strong currents within the telephone.

Thereafter we're mostly talking about devices

with croc-clips that can be attached to the phone line. Many of these can be detected easily with a low-cost volt-meter – the 50-volt power from the telephone exchange that provides the juice for the telephone system undergoes typical changes as the subscriber takes the phone off the hook. If there's a cheap tap attached, the voltages will be different enough to show. (Cheap 'phonetap detection' equipment sold by electronics security retailers simply measures these voltage changes and causes various lights to go on if anything unexpected happens on the line). More expensive taps are more difficult to find with this simple voltage-detection technique.

Once you have your tap attached you, the eavesdropper, have to find a way of listening in. You can be there in person if you are intrepid, or you can use a tape-recorder, but you'll have to conceal it – near the tap itself – and you'll have to find a way of picking up the tapes. You can connect a bug – a radio transmitter – to the tap and you can then listen at a distance.[†] Providing the telephone you are interested in isn't too slim-line, has a plastic body, and is located near a window, you can put the combined tap and bug inside the phone – the 50 volts from the telephone exchange will supply the power. While you are about it, you can also add a microphone to the package as well – then you'll hear conversations in the room even when the telephone is not in use. The only trouble is, there are now two ways in which the device can be found – by the line voltage detection method and by all the methods for finding radio bugs.

In fact there are three, because anyone who suspects their line is being tapped will immediately open up their telephone instrument to look for signs of alien infestation. They'll also inspect telephone wall sockets – there are plenty of electronics security manufacturers who sell official phone sockets modified with tap/bugs in them. The suspicious telephone-owner needn't even open up a sus-

---

[*] Just as, during the big City take-overs of the late 1980s, the same merchant banks, accountants, solicitors and PR companies tended to feature over and over again, so the same sets of buggers and counter-buggers tended to surface. See, for example, *Sunday Telegraph*, 26 May 1991

[†] While I was revising this chapter a friend uncovered two phone bugs of this description attached to a junction box outside of a flat lately used by the African National Congress in Muswell Hill, North London. He brought them over for technical evaluation: we decided they were operating on well chosen UHF frequencies, would have a range of around 100 metres, and would retail in the UK at about £350, though cost much less than that to manufacture (*New Statesman*, 12 October 1990).

pect phone socket in the first instance – signs of recently cracked paintwork around the socket, or a surprising absence of dust, may be enough confirmation. A more promising place to tap is within an office's frame-room – the place where the lines come in from the telephone service, or within a PABX. But of course, you need to know what you are doing and, if your chosen method of recovering the conversations is radio-based – the frame-room or PABX may not be ideally located.

Another approach is to use another telephone line with which to transport away the contents of the line you are interested in. That is not as difficult as it may sound. Turning first to residential lines, it is not unusual for the telephone company to provide an additional 'pair', or even two, when they lay in a domestic telephone line. The additional costs are almost negligible and it means that if a further line is required at that address, installation is almost immediate. The spare pair can be used to provide a longish-distance tap – the far end may be under a cover in the road, at a junction box or up a pole. It helps if you have been a telephone engineer. You can use that approach with a small business, but a great deal will depend on the sort of PABX they have, your access to it, and your level of knowledge. With larger businesses, particularly those that use leased lines, you can approach the phone company and order (and pay for) a leased line to be installed between your location and that of the target office. Your victim isn't being asked to pay for anything and, unless the communications manager is well organised, no one may realise. You will then need to masquerade as a telephone company engineer in order to make the necessary connections.

A different sort of approach is the well known 'harmonica bug' or infinity transmitter, which is now quite widely available. Although there are a number of variants, the main use of these is to convey *room* conversations down a telephone line, rather than telephone conversations. Once the bug is installed inside a target telephone, it remains there doing nothing until activated. To get it going you must dial the target telephone in the ordinary way and, as soon as it answers, send a specific frequency down the line (a whistle, or harmonica note). The telephone line is then held open even if physically it appears to be on the hook. The tele-

phone microphone is alive, so that any sound within the room can be heard. Harmonica bugs can be found by physical inspection and by the voltage-test method.

Official methods

All the tapping methods mentioned so far have assumed that they are being carried out by private citizens against private citizens. Official taps, that is taps that have been authorised by a government minister, are carried out at telephone exchanges.[*] They are not detectable and if you can hear 'voices' or played-back tape recordings of earlier conversations, you are either paranoid or someone is trying to make you feel paranoid.

Legal tapping

There is one form of telephone tapping which appears to be legal, though this book offers no guarantee of that.[†] Many telephone answering machines now offer a remote facility, enabling owners to hear messages without returning to base. The answering machine is usually commanded with the aid of telephone 'touch-tones', or, for phones that still work on the old pulse system, with a separate tone pad. If you can determine the make of the answering machine you are interested in you can get an instruction book (call up the manufacturer and say you have 'lost' yours). Some high-end remote telephone answering machines will respond once you have sent a code, often only two digits. If you don't know the code, you can readily break it by brute force: if you have a computer with a modem you can write a short program which will dial the number, switch the modem into 'tone mode' if it isn't there already, and get it to try every possible number in turn. You'll only have a relatively short period during which the answering machine is receptive to receiving code, so your program will have to allow

* The *Guardian* newspaper has suggested that there are 35,000 taps a year carried out by 70 specialist BT engineers, known as 'secret squirrels'. In 1990 the disclosed number of warrants issued was 539. (*Guardian*, 14 June 1991, 16 July 1991; Granada Television, *World in Action*, 15 July 1991.)

† In the UK, if the courts are persuaded that a telephone answering machine is a 'computer', then you could be committing an offence under the Computer Misuse Act, 1990.

for that and ring off and back on again as appropriate.*

In any event, if you are successful, you can hear the messages intended for your target and leave no trace that you have done so – provided you don't wipe the messages in the process, and don't try it while your target is in the vicinity.

Evasion

The *sine qua non* of telephone tapping is access to the right telephones and telephone lines. If you can control these, you can also restrict opportunities for taps to be affixed. So the first line of defence is to ensure that you know who can get into your office premises and what steps are taken to prove that they are who they say they are. Elsewhere I have written how I, with neither training nor any great enthusiasm for clandestine work and armed only with some telephone testing gear in the bright yellow livery of British Telecom, was able to enter the corporate HQ of a company then in the grip of a spectacular take-over, and was taken straight to a room holding the telephone line frame and the computer network controllers.[8]

If you are really concerned, one effective and low-cost technique is to place tamper-evident labels on all phone equipment and keep a log-book of authorised service and modification visits. But of course the labels will remain intact if the interception takes place along a line rather than from within equipment.

In practice, tapping telephone lines in offices, particularly those involving PABXs, is a job for experienced telephone engineers. The only exceptions are: compromising telephone instruments on the desks of targeted individuals or, seeing if any

* Another approach is to buy one of the credit card-sised pocket auto-diallers which not only store your favourite phone numbers but also generate the appropriate tones to save you the labour of keying them each time on the phone. You can program up one of these to spit out every two-digit combination in turn – there are less combinations than you first think: you can nearly always omit 11, 22, 33, etc. and often also those beginning with 0 . . . A still simpler route, if you can get legitimate entry to your target's answerphone ('Oh, what a nice machine . . . . I am thinking of getting one myself . . . . Can I have a look?') is to peer inside the lid holding the cassette mechanism – that is the usual place where the actual code is inscribed. You can then use the code from your own phone from then on.

key executives have direct lines which by-pass the PABX and to which access can be obtained. For this reason, keen tappers are often likely to go for the *homes* of important people. Domestic tapping, particularly out in the country where lines are strung out along poles, is far easier to execute: moreover, the type of people who are thus targeted are precisely the sort who are likely to have important and unrestrained after-hours telephone conversations. If you think you are such a person, it might be instructive to explore the route your telephone line takes as it leaves your house – and see if you can spot the easiest point at which access might be obtained. Then you'll know where to look if ever you start getting really suspicious.

You could start using a cellular phone if you think your land lines may be compromised. The possibilities of eavesdropping on these are explored in Chapter 9.

The main technological aid to evading tapping is the **speech scrambler**. These come at varying levels of sophistication, convenience, and expense. Firstly, it should be obvious, but you have to have a scrambler at both ends of the conversation. Moreover, assuming the scrambler can be set for various combinations of scrambling, the settings have to be the same. In other words, scrambled telephone conversations need pre-planning. The lowest-cost scramblers use a technique called analogue frequency-inversion; it is good enough to defeat the casual listener, but for those ready for it, trivial to counteract. Most scramblers these days use digital techniques – the speech is first digitised (most telephone traffic is digitised routinely once it gets into the exchange) and then encryption applied to the digitised stream. What varies is the extent of the sophistication of the encryption: the more complex forms of encryption can't take place in 'real-time' which means that participants in the conversation will experience curious delays in response. If the telephone path is noisy, recovery of the scrambled speech may be incomplete. Again, the more complex equipment is also less portable.

Telex tapping

It is not only voice conversations that can be tapped. In many ways it is more productive to tap digital data – the information has a greater chance of being important, will be more concisely expressed than an informal chat, there is the possibility that you acquire copies of authentic documents and you'll have no transcription costs. The oldest form of digital data transmission is the telex. To tap a telex line you must first, as with all forms of tapping, get physical access to the line. You must then be able to decode what is being sent along it. These days telex facilities are available on cards which can be inserted inside PCs. Adaptions of such cards are available to assist telex tapping.[*]

Fax

It is also possible to tap fax machines; during a fax transmission the two machines are locked into a call-and-response cycle (to prevent errors, to monitor line quality, and to signify end-of-page) so that tapping fax is more than simply placing a pirate fax machine across a telephone line. Your pirate must suppress the reception of certain signals while faithfully recording the remainder. I have seen adapted regular fax machines performing faultlessly.[†] More sophisticated fax machines, ones with internal memories so that messages can be transmitted to multiple destinations and/or at delayed times, or where a remote user can request

a message to be sent to him, can be hacked quite extensively. The hacker needs a fax modem of the sort sold to go with portable computers and a knowledge of the special diagnostic codes used by the target fax machine. That way, the contents of its messages can be retrieved in the same way as computers can be hacked.[‡]

Computer tapping

The tapping of computer data is in many circumstances technically much simpler than trying to read telexes and faxes; at the lowest level, almost no specialised equipment, apart from the telephone tap itself, is required. But computers have a chapter all to themselves.

(1) *Observer*, 2 November 1986; *Sunday Telegraph*, 16 March 1986; BBC News, late November 1986.
(2) *Sunday Telegraph, Sunday Times*, 16 March 1986.
(3) *Financial Times*, 5 April 1990.
(4) *Financial Times*, 21 February 1990.
(5) *Sunday Times*, 28 January, 4 February 1990; *Independent on Sunday*, 28 January 1990; *Guardian*, 31 January, 1 and 2 February 1990; *Observer*, 4 February 1990.
(6) Among TV coverage of the subject: BBC2 Horizon: 'Spies in the Wires', 1984; Thames TV Reporting London, 1987; Thames TV City Programme, February 1988; YTV First Tuesday, 4 April 1989; BBC2 10×10, 27 July 1989.
(7) Senate Sub-Committee on Administrative Procedures and Practices, 1965.
(8) *DataTheft*, Heinemann, 1987, 1990.

* One of the other 'advantages' of telex cards is that it is very easy to change their notional address – telex number and answerback; in other words you can fool someone into thinking he is sending a message to a particular location when in fact he is sending it to you. You can also originate messages purporting to come from someone else. But this is more likely to be useful in a fraud.
† The use of fax machines to aid frauds is now established. In March 1990, faxes purporting to come from a London firm of solicitors were sent to the British branch of a Middle Eastern bank authorising the transfer of up to £300m. In fact the faxes originated from a machine in a north London newsagent, the notepaper used was adapted from the authentic stationery of the solicitors, and the money was alleged to be required to fund very low interest mortgages (*Independent*, 23 March 1990).

‡ Fax machines, in fact, present considerable security problems to their owners. Confidential faxes which are misdirected are common: I have received material originating in Britain's 'silicon gulch' intended for a military purchaser in Spain which, because of one mis-keyed digit, arrived on my (unlisted) fax phone. A Glasgow employment agency received Ministry of Defence material (*Independent*, 29 September 1089).

8 Covert Sources: Computer Hacking

It seems obvious: most corporate information these days is held on computers – if 15-year-olds can hack into them, then this has to be the single most effective technique available to the industrial spy. Why not hire the 15-year-olds to do their stuff, or why not learn how to do it yourself?

One reason for not doing so is that it is against the law; the UK Computer Misuse Act, 1990, for example, has three main planks – unauthorised alteration of data, unauthorised access to a computer for the purpose of committing a serious criminal offence, and simple unauthorised access to a computer without any other attendant ambition. Many other countries have similar legislation.[1] However, the datathief might feel that the benefits are considerable when compared with the chances of actually being caught. This chapter, like others throughout this book, having explained the legal and other penalties of various courses of action, describes what is technically possible.[*]

We have to begin with some misconceptions about computer 'hacking'[†] Much of what has been printed about the subject has concentrated on a very small number of spectacular multi-national network penetrations. People, including me, have written about them because they are interesting, whereas most computer crime has very few intriguing or sophisticated features.[‡] Unfortunately,

large numbers of the public have persuaded themselves that it is the 'network adventurers' who represent the most substantive threat to computer systems. As I have shown elsewhere,[2] for the most part the network adventurers are interested either in computers for their own sake or in the technological challenge of breaking security systems. Such people, by and large, do not have contact with organised crime or industrial spies. Nor would they necessarily recognise valuable information if they came across it, know to whom it might be significant or have any idea how to market it successfully.

Another part of the public have become fascinated by the use of exotic eavesdropping technologies involving the detection of radiation from VDUs, but, as we will see, for the industrial spy concerned with cost-effectiveness, most of these techniques make sense only when all other measures have been exhausted.

In this chapter I will be concentrating on methods of datatheft in terms of their ease of execution and likelihood of quality of harvest.

Computer-held material has the following attractions for the industrial spy: it can often be acquired in such a way as to leave no trace that it has been stolen; it can be copied or downloaded at considerable speed; it can be held in a highly compact and therefore easily concealed and removable form – the whole of this book, probably in excess of 300 pages of close-typed A4, occupies one high-density 3½-inch diskette; in some circumstances it can be acquired without having to enter hostile premises, sometimes without even leaving one's own office; once in the hands of the industrial spy or his customer, computers can be used to analyse the harvest of information thus acquired.

However, the most useful technique of acquisition isn't hacking in from outside. The definitive method is simple disk file copying.

---

[*] Readers are prompted to have a look at the idealised Management Consultant's Strategic Overview of Information Acquisition Costing Methodology in Chapter 2.
[†] The earliest use of the expression 'hacker' meant unorthodox programmer or computer enthusiast and carried no criminal connotation; it is still used that way by many in the computer industry. I am using the word in a slightly later sense to cover unauthorised access to a computer.
[‡] That doesn't mean to say that computer crime is not important, or that large amounts of money are not involved; merely that the methods used are nearly always in essence extremely simple, typically impersonation of authorised users, or fraudulent input.

Targeting

The danger is to confuse technique with targeting. Whereas for the classic hacker the object of the exercise is to prove one's skills by overcoming a security system, for the industrial spy the aim is directly to acquire whatever confidential files are relevant to the espionage exercise as a whole.

Rather than sitting at a keyboard trying to 'hack in', therefore, the industrial spy needs to form an understanding of how the target company uses its computer systems and which parts of it are thus most likely to have information useful to the intelligence-gathering project. Different parts of a computer system may be protected by different qualities of security – on the whole the more expensive the hardware the more rigorous will be the protective measures.* But there is often no correlation between the value of information held on a computer and the cost of the hardware.

Indeed, most larger companies have more than one computer or more than one computer system. There may be a mainframe or a large mini-computer with many terminals attached which is used for heavy-duty number-crunching or database work. Typical uses are to process information about sales, stocks, manufacturing, trading positions, and to send out bulk mailings. There may be other mini-computers directly in control of manufacturing processes. There may be yet others for 'office automation' (centralised word-processing and internal electronic mail) or to run payroll or personnel. There can be specialised workstations used for design or for desk-top publishing. And there will be large numbers of personal computers. Some of these will be doing no more than acting as terminals to larger systems; many will be running departmental applications – local word-processing, spreadsheets, mailing lists. Increasingly, personal computers within the same office or building are linked together on local area networks so that users can share files and such resources as

laser printers.

It is often possible to discover details of a company's computer systems by straightforward research. There are reference books and indeed databases which purport to cover most of the major computer installations in the countries in which they are published.[3] In practice they are often out-of-date and incomplete, but they provide a starting-point. More promising is the professional computer press which frequently carries news items of contracts awarded and features on interesting installations. Often these features are prompted by the PR departments of the computer systems companies that have done the installing. The industrial spy, posing as a freelance technical journalist, may be able to get further 'product information' from the computer company concerned.

The other element in this area of research is to understand the internal organisation of the target company, as the computer system will often, in one way or another, reflect the organisational structure. As we have seen elsewhere, organisation charts, phonebooks, relevant press clippings and the like are essential to any analysis of a company.†

Fortunately from the point-of-view of the datathief, these days in nearly all corporations the critical planning work, the key memoranda and minutes, the preparation of materials for internal meetings, are all carried out, not on big mainframes, but on personal computers located in a handful of offices associated with the Financial Director or Chief Executive.

Datatheft methods

It is physical proximity to a computer, its screen and keyboard rather than access via a telephone line that should be the initial aim of the datathief. Indeed many of the key personal computers in a target organisation may not be linked in a useful way to the telephone system at all. Even if the PC has a modem (this is the device that enables a computer to 'talk' down a telephone line), it will normally only be active if the PC has a communications program loaded and running. Most PC-users only load their comms programs when they have a

---

* A frequent mistake made by journalists covering 'hacker' stories is to assume that, because a hacker has demonstrated that one part of a computer system appears vulnerable, that the hacker therefore had complete control over all the computers the victim owns. Hacker stories are too often full of 'could haves' – assertions by both hackers and journalists about what could have been done, but in fact wasn't.

† See especially Chapters 2 and 10.

specific need for one – say for online access or for external electronic mail.

Physical proximity to a computer is gained by all the usual methods of getting into offices where you would normally not be welcome. If you are on the staff of the target company and are being disloyal you must, as for any other dirty work in an office, establish times when the computer VDU is being neglected by its owner.* If you are an outsider you need a cover story – the telephone or maintenance engineer ploy, the 'lost' visitor ploy, and so on. Your success will depend almost entirely on the quality of the physical security of the company you are targeting – visitor sign-in procedures, visitor and staff badge systems, keycard access control facilities for various specific offices – will all be problems you must overcome.

Once the datathief gets to a target PC though, there will often be no further technical security facilities. Unlike larger computers, PCs are de-signed as 'single user/single task' machines and there are no in-built security facilities, though pru-dent owners may have tried, with varying degrees of success, to add some afterwards.

Assuming there are no PC security facilities, the datathief needs very few technical skills. One route might be to copy everything on the PC's hard disk on to a series of floppies. However given the size and capacity of many hard disks this may be unnecessarily time- and effort-consuming. What is needed is a selection. The datathief ought to examine the directory of the computer's hard disk to see how it is arranged. Usually the directory will be hierarchical – that is to say, groups of associated files will be arranged together in a series of sub-directories. Since a handful of software packages tend to dominate each of the main categories of PC applications – there are perhaps only four or five significant PC word-processing programs, only one important file format for spreadsheets, per-haps two important file formats for databases – it is not necessary to copy the programs themselves – the datathief simply takes the datafiles and views them later on his own machine. It is quite easy to recognise which file is which – those for the spread-sheet Lotus 1–2–3 have extensions (the three-letter code after the .) .WKS, .WK1 and the like; word-

processor files may have such extensions as .DOC and .TXT. Datafile copying can be carried out either by simple DOS commands, the sort every PC-user learns, or by using utility programs such as PC–Tools or X–Tree which allow the user to point-and-shoot at the desired files. Often PCs have such utilities already on them but there's no reason why a datathief shouldn't prepare himself by having a collection of such utilities about his person.

Where a PC is connected to mainframe or mini, or to a local area network, mere access to the PC may automatically grant access to the larger com-puting facilities. More usually though, these will require passwords. However, if the PC is approached during the middle of the day it is pos-sible that the user has earlier opened up a 'session' with the external computing resources and not closed it off afterwards, thus leaving access to any datathief. Alternatively, most arrangements for connecting PCs to mainframe, minis and local area networks also allow for the downloading of mat-erial from them to the PC's hard disk, in which case it will be available for simple copying-across to floppies.

Hacking techniques

Although PC security protection is often less tough than that employed on larger systems, many of the security packages are quite adequate against the casual datathief. Most datathieves have to operate at speed in order to avoid detection and the more sophisticated cracking techniques will in practice not therefore be available.

These are the well known simple, low-level hacking tricks which, after all the publicity about them shouldn't work but often do. Many of them apply equally to mainframes, minis and local area networks:

- Look around the immediate surroundings of the PC or terminal to see if the password has been recorded in a book or sticky label
- If you are a regular visitor to the office where the PC or terminal is used, see if you can overlook the legitimate owner as s/he types in the password
- Try and guess legitimate passwords – variants on the legitimate owner's name,

* See Chapter 6.

title, department, jokes that the owner might find amusing . . . passwords like *sysman* which may have been provided originally with the access control package and never removed

- In the case of PC access control packages, the simplest of them can be by-passed by using a fresh copy of DOS in the floppy drive and then rebooting
- An alternate route to by-passing PC access control involves the datathief in taking with him a portable PC of his own and then using one of the breed of special file transfer kits used to move data at high speed between portables and desk-top PCs. Their advantage is that they do not require the target machine, in the first instance, to hold appropriate communications software. When first connected, the 'host' machine sends a simple comms program over to the target via the RS232 port. The simple comms program is then used to receive a much more sophisticated comms program which is then used thereafter. This process often by-passes any security package that the target PC has had installed. There is another advantage – data transfer using this method is extremely fast, particularly if the datathief's portable itself has a hard disk.

The other traditional hacker tricks – fake sign-on screens which capture the passwords of legitimate users, password try-out programs which automatically offer guesses at a valid password from a large dictionary of common variants, password file decrypter programs, the exploitation of loopholes in operating systems – are really for the recreational hacker rather than the industrial spy. But even the recreational hackers say that often their best results come not from the development of new technical skills but because legitimate owners do not install or use computer security products properly.[4]

The problem for computer owners is this: many computer security products have to trade convenience of ordinary use of the computer against the security facilities provided. Many security packages are simply too complicated for their owners to operate – with the result that while users kid themselves that because they have spent a suitably large amount of money on something plastered over with approval certificates from government bodies they must be secure, no security product ever made installs itself automatically.

Once a collection of computer files is in the hands of the industrial spy, he can use his own computer resources to analyse his harvest.[*] Text files – memoranda, minutes, reports, etc. – can be 'string searched' for relevant names and other important keywords – all word-processors do this and so do many of the utility programs like Norton and PC–Tools. Database and spreadsheet files can be examined using the datathief's own copies of the relevant applications programs.[†] You can use the stolen database material in new databases of your own design and the spreadsheet data in new spreadsheet formats – you steal not only the data but also save yourself the trouble of retyping the keystrokes.

How many industrial spies actually take advantage of these hacker techniques? As with the other technical measures described in this book it is impossible to know; the most successful practitioners are never caught, or even suspected. The case material we have is about failure.

One stream of cases is very similar to the conventional 'stolen documents' incidents already covered. For example, in 1987 an engineer who hop-scotched between jobs in high-tech companies in the Los Angeles area was caught and charged with stealing trade secrets from two high-technology companies and attempting to extort money from another. The 37-year-old man was alleged to have stolen more than 100 computer disks from a company called ESC Inc., and an engineering manual from another called Electro Adaptors Inc. At the same time he had attempted to extort money from a third company, Matrix Science Corp. in Torrance after he obtained a prototype of an electrical connector – all the companies made specialist electrical connectors – and threatened to sell it to a competitor.[5]

A more entertaining line concerns journalists hacking into the electronic newsrooms of their competitors. This is made easy by the fact that a

---

[*] This applies equally to computer files captured in transmission and obtained by tapping telephone lines.
[†] See above, p. 63.

very small number of suppliers provide facilities to nearly all the newspapers and TV newsrooms. In the UK, for example, the dominant newspaper system is called Atex and the TV equivalent is called Basys Newsfury. Journalists thus have no difficulty in 'learning' a new system; add to this the general job mobility in the industry and it is not surprising that journalists are involved in hacks twice over. I have lost count of the number of times journalists have asked me to hack into systems belonging to their competitors – no, I have never agreed to do so. At Florida television station WTSP Terry Cole, news director and assistant news director Michael Shapiro were fired after raiding the confidential news files of Tampa television station WTVT. Both were later charged with 14 counts of computer-related crime.[6] In Los Angeles a freelance journalist specialising in the more bizarre sort of story was accused of hacking into computers owned by Rupert Murdoch's Fox Television, for whom he had previously worked, to get Hollywood media gossip for onward sale to such papers as the *National Enquirer* and the *Globe*. Fox set up a sting operation; when caught the journalist said he was writing a book which would expose working practices in this section of journalism.[7] In the UK in 1990 there was considerable unhappiness in the current affairs department at BBC Television where long-term BBC staffers were resenting the ascendancy of a group of people who had been brought in from the commercial station, LWT. They managed to hack the computer identity of the deputy editor of news and current affairs to read a memorandum setting out future plans.[8]

Rather more serious was the claim that early in 1990 Sprint Communications Co., the US's third-largest long-distance phone company, allegedly obtained confidential information – possibly through a secret tap of a government computer – that helped it win a federal phone contract called FTS–2000 worth potentially $25 billion to contractors over a ten-year period. At the same time there were reports that two former Sprint employees had filed a lawsuit making similar allegations of industrial espionage against the company. Sprint denied the charge.[9]

The habit has even moved, apparently, into politics. In September 1990 the executive director

of the Republican General Assembly in New Jersey resigned after admitting knowledge of a break-in to computer files owned by the Democratic Party. In New Jersey some 600 people, opposing politicians and New Jersey Legislature officials, all share the same computer system and the Republican official was able to take advantage of security weaknesses.[10]

Database compromise

There is another form of hacking which, under certain conditions, is both useful and seems to avoid most types of unauthorised access legislation. It is called database compromise and consists of using legitimate access to a database to obtain information which the database owner almost certainly intended to deny you. A simple example was provided by British Telecom in 1990 when it launched a trial of a service called Phonebase – I was one of the triallists. Until then Britain had not had an electronic form of the telephone directory – enquirers had had to use printed directories or ring an operator. Phonebase makes a version of the computer system used by its directory enquiry operators available to the public. The British telephone directory permits subscribers to go ex-directory – the names do not appear in the printed versions but are available to BT staff. When Phonebase was first trialled to the public, BT removed the phone numbers, but not the names or addresses to which they referred. As a result the names and addresses of well-known and not-so-well-known individuals became locatable simply by typing the name into the computer system.[11]

A more sophisticated variant consists in developing an understanding of how a database was originally designed, including where it gets its inputs from and then refining the questions put to it so that it is possible to infer more than was intended.[12] Health statistical databases, and those derived from census information are, unless carefully designed, vulnerable to this sort of attack: in both cases information is first collected and then partially withheld in order to meet some legal obligation.

VDU radiation (tempest)

Like the cocktail olive bug, the fact that VDUs radiate enough energy for their contents to be recovered at some distance on the screens of lightly modified televisions is constantly being rediscovered by journalists.[*] On UK television alone one can find endless revelatory features over the last six years.[13] Like the cocktail olive bug too, there is less in the VDU radiation story than first appears.

All VDUs based on the cathode ray tube behave like a very crude television transmitter. Unlike proper TV transmitters though, the signal is spread over a fairly wide frequency band and is not confined to just one channel. The signal that emerges is very unclean and in particular lacks the strong synchronising – 'sync' – pulses that give a broadcast TV picture its stability (so that each line is laid neatly and precisely over the previous one and the picture doesn't swim). At a basic level, VDU radiation detection consists of a domestic TV set which is tuneable below the broadcast UHF band (the VDU radiation is strongest in the frequency band 200–300MHz), with some electronics to allow the operator to re-create the missing sync pulses. On this basis, over a range of a few metres and in an otherwise quiet electronic environment, images will be seen.

Images of what? Images of the contents at that moment of the VDU, typically 80 characters by 25 lines, just part of a letter or memo, what the computer user can see at that precise moment. At this level of technology you are not able to record what you see – for that you require at the very least an adapted VCR, that is a VCR with its tuner section modified in the same way as the cheap domestic TV set. You may need this replay facility, because the image won't be stable and even when it is the individual characters will be indistinct. Domestic TVs have a lower resolution than even the cheapest computer VDUs – if you have had a home computer which you have tried to use with a TV, you'll know that whilst a simple 40 characters-across

screen looks acceptable,[†] 80 characters are an eye-strain, and that is when they are being fed into the back of the TV from a well screened cable. If you are using a modified VCR for recording – VCRs have an even lower resolution than domestic TVs.

This technology, moreover, doesn't even give you a print-out – for that you'll need, typically, an image capture board linked to a personal computer. With some specialist image-processing software you may be able to enhance any indistinctions and with still further software, you may be able to use Optical Character Recognition (OCR) to translate the image into characters which your computer can understand. At this point your budget has moved somewhat beyond the 'black and white TV plus $50's worth of components' type of specification.

You've clarified the image, but you still have two other problems – you need to extend the range over which you can receive and you need to cope with situations where there is more than one VDU in the vicinity. Now, there is a simple, low-cost technology which will increase the sensitivity of any receiver and also help null out unwanted signals – it's called an antenna and we all use it to receive broadcast TV programmes. But, for the most part, since you will want to conceal your eavesdropping from your target, you won't be able to use the ideal arrangement, which is a directional log-periodic (fishbone) antenna on a rotator mounted on some van parked on the perimeter of the target's premises. What you have to do is beef up the receiver side of the equipment. However, by now you are leaving the area where there are bits and pieces of equipment originally designed for ordinary commercial activities which can easily be adapted to your needs – from now on you are dependent on custom-built electronics and the prices these cost to design, test and assemble. With enough money spent you will also be able to cope with the higher resolutions of most VDUs currently in use in offices (though resolutions are going up all the time) – now you have a receiver that is extremely sensitive and with lots of extra controls for tuning, filtering, adding in variable

---

[*] The technology is sometimes referred to as 'Tempest', though in fact this is a set of US standards to reduce emission. It is also sometimes called 'van Eck freaking' after Willem van Eck, a Dutch scientist who produced one of the first open accounts of the phenomenon.

[†] That is one reason why teletext services like Ceefax and Oracle in the UK are only 40 characters wide.

sync pulses, coping with different target screen resolutions, and so on.

This means skilled operators. Consider how the costs have mounted up – from the simple adapted TV set we are into extremely expensive equipment mounted in a specially adapted van and with one or more skilled technicians charging high rates per hour. And they still mightn't find anything of interest.

In other words, capturing VDU radiation has to be a technique of last resort, when you have exhausted all the other methods described in this book and are still certain that there is valuable information out there that you simply must have.

(1) For a partial list, see *Law Commission Working Paper No. 110: Computer Misuse*, HMSO, London, 1988.
(2) *DataTheft* (Heinemann, London, 1987, 1990) and the *Hacker's Handbook*s (Century-Hutchinson, London, 1985-90).
(3) *Computer User's Yearbook* is the one for the United Kingdom (VNU Publications, London).
(4) See, for example, 'How Secure are Computers in the USA?'. Dr Cliff Stoll, *Computers and Security*, Oxford, July 1988 and also his *The Cuckoo's Egg* (Doubleday, New York, 1989. My own *Hacker's Handbook*s are no longer available.
(5) *Los Angeles Times*, 7 August 1987.
(6) UPI, 15 March 1989.
(7) *Sunday Telegraph*, 16 September 1990.
(8) *Guardian*, 23 March, 25 June 1990.
(9) *Washington Post*, 21 February 1990.
(10) *Computer Weekly*, 27 September 1990.
(11) See *inter alia, Sunday Times*, 29 October 1990.
(12) See *Security of Computer Based Information Systems*, V. P. Lane (Macmillan, London, 1985).
(13) For example: BBC1 Microlive, November 1986, BBC2 Money Programme, 23 October 1988; ITN, 13 March 1989.

9 Covert Sources: Radio Eavesdropping

It is much easier to eavesdrop if the target has been helpful enough to make his conversations and data available over the radio. A surprising number of business transactions take place via radio-based systems – cellular phones, cordless phones, delivery vehicle dispatch, buildings security, paging, inter-building and central office-to-vehicle data transmission. It is always worth discovering if companies or individuals of interest use radio-based services to any extent. The only practical way for anyone to get communications on the move is via radio – and if you buy the right sort of radio receiver, you can listen in. For most purposes that "right sort of radio receiver" is the scanner. It can achieve a great deal, but not quite as much or quite as easily as many articles about it have suggested.

Scanning radios first appeared at popular prices in the late 1970s. Unlike conventional radios which rely on large tuning knobs or the more specialist monitoring radios which in those days required a separate crystal for each channel that the owner wished to listen to, scanning radios are controlled from a keypad rather like that on a calculator. They combine digital control with a radio circuit called a frequency synthesiser as a result of which a large number of channels can be tuned into with considerable accuracy. The digital control means that frequencies can be memorised, placed in memory banks which can be sampled later on, and frequency bands – that is, areas of the radio spectrum – can be searched between upper and lower limits, the radio pausing when it finds activity and then resuming. At a leap, facilities which had previously only be available within sigint organisations became an item of consumer electronics. A popular early model was called the Bearcat and this term is sometimes used for all scanners, though the Bearcat company has long since been taken over.

Scanners were, and still are, marketed principally at amateur radio buffs and others such as aircraft spotters. For most of these people, the main use is to 'hear the action' – the radio equivalent of ambulance chasing. Every large-scale accident or public event is inevitably monitored by such enthusiasts. The hobby is illicit, in that it involves breach, in the UK, of the Wireless Telegraphy Act, 1949[*] and in the USA, the Electronic Communications Privacy Act, 1986. For some considerable time, the equipment has also been used by criminals, drug runners and terrorists,[†] who have wanted to observe police activity.[1]

The models available now at the beginning of the 1990s vary as to the range of frequencies covered, the sophistication of the memory and other facilities, the performance of the radio section,[‡] and the packaging. Although one well known international chain store specialising in electronics sells a number of models, better value can be obtained from amateur radio outlets. One full-range scanner available covers from 150KHz (the low end of the LF or long-wave broadcasting band) right through to 1300MHz, which is in the

[*] You can manufacture, sell and own the equipment, but you can only use it on a limited number of frequencies (broadcast stations and amateurs). Prosecution depends on being caught in the act or doing something which shows that you have acquired information which could only have been obtained as a result of unauthorised listening. In practice the authorities are not interested in those enthusiasts who listen to the civil aircraft and marine bands, but take a much dimmer view of those who eavesdrop on police and army activity. In some European countries, for example Germany and Finland, *possession* of scanners is a criminal offence. In the UK a backbench MP called James Cran made an unsuccessful attempt at introducing a Control of Electronic Surveillance Devices Bill in May 1989.

[†] For example, scanners were found in the possession of IRA arms cache-builders Liam McCotter and Patrick McLaughlin, arrested in Manchester in 1987 and New York drug-ring ruler Lorenzo 'Fat Cat' Nichols in 1985.

[‡] That is, its sensitivity, selectivity (ability to distinguish between two adjacent signals), proneness to overloading, and the absence of 'false' signals artificially generated by the circuitry. More expensive receivers can also cope with single side band and even video reception.

low microwave region and way beyond most mobile communications. It is the size, less its antenna, of a bar of soap. Unfortunately in that particular case, the size has been at the sacrifice both of the radio performance and of ease of use. Other hand-held scanners, around the £250 price-level in the UK, are only slightly larger, have almost the same frequency coverage, boast 1,000 programmable channels and ten separately operable search bands. Low-cost models may not have full coverage of all bands. In-car and desk-top models are also available, some of the latter being capable of control from an external computer, thus enhancing the facilities even more.

No one who first sees a scanner demonstrated can fail to be impressed, both with its flexibility and with the vast number of different occupied radio channels that can be heard within just a few minutes.[2] It is all too easy to suppose that scanners can eavesdrop on anything and that, as a consequence, all radio traffic can be easily violated. The rest of this chapter shows why this is not necessarily the case.

The radio frequency spectrum

As you operate the scanner, you'll soon discover that certain parts of the radio spectrum are very crowded indeed – each single megahertz (1MHz) of spectrum may hold up to 80 separate radio channels, each with a distinct use. Your first problem is to find out who is using each or, at least, the spot channel(s) used by the person in whom you are interested.

The use of the radio frequency spectrum is determined initially by international agreement (the International Telecommunications Union and various World Administrative Radio Conferences), then by national practice. The granting of individual frequencies may be carried out by a government department or delegated, in part, to others. In most countries you can buy an official publication setting out the main blocks of allocation, though the level of detail varies. In most countries too, there are unofficial publications, more-or-less openly available, which provide more detail. Finally, there are true underground publications, circulated among 'recreational eavesdroppers' or 'monitors', which purport to give considerable detail on who uses which frequency. But these are often inaccurate and tend to focus on what the compilers find interesting – emergency services, broadcast auxiliary (news reporters and outside broadcast talkback) rather than on commercial traffic.

Finding your desired spot frequency, therefore, may not be especially easy. Depending on what you are looking for, your best bet may be a source within the target company itself or, if you can get close enough to use it, a frequency measuring device.

Fixed frequency services

Most of the older and more traditional sorts of mobile radio applications tend to operate on fixed frequencies. That is to say, once you have found the right channel, the traffic you want will always be there. The emergency services tend to work on fixed channels, as do delivery and dispatch services, taxis, and the like. Indeed, the British police have become sufficiently alarmed at the loss of privacy on their radio channels to have contemplated spending considerable sums on scrambling systems.[3] Fixed channel services are the easiest things to listen to, but in general, from the point of view of the industrial spy, also the least productive.*

One possible exception may be radio microphones, as used by media-aware companies for internal presentations – you know the sort of thing: animated electronic slides and videos of the new product and the new strategy and, because the speaker wants to move around a bit, a radio mike hung around the neck or clipped to a lapel like a TV presenter. CB radio is another example of a fixed frequency service – you have 40 channels to choose from, but once a conversation has estab-

* Not always. A man taped radio conversations that allegedly provided evidence of dangerous working conditions at the Seabrook nuclear power plant in New Hampshire, and turned over 300 hours of scanner-acquired tapes in January 1990 to federal regulators. He had chanced upon control room conversations. US 'monitors' claim to have overheard George Bush berating Vice-President Dan Quayle for making insensitive remarks at a visit to the scene of the 1988 San Francisco earthquake (*Monitoring Times*, 1990 *passim*; *Sunday Times*, 14 October 1990).

lished itself on one channel, it will stay there. CB, by definition, has no privacy, and it is unlikely that anything of commercial value will be heard on it, quite apart from the fact that its image is too down-market for most business folk.

Cordless phones

For reasons we'll see later on, the radio technology that offers far and away the best combination of ease of use and potential quality of harvest is the cordless telephone. It carries, of course, precisely the same traffic as other phones, there are very few channels used and there are two ways of eaves-dropping on them.

The original cordless phones use two sets of radio frequencies, one at 49MHz and one at about 1900kHz – just about the AM broadcast band. (You need a pair of channels so that both speakers can talk simultaneously and not have to hand 'over' each time as you do on traditional radio systems.) The 1900kHz transmissions use the mains power lead as the antenna. The radios have a range of about 100–200 metres. When cordless phones were legalised in the UK, the 49MHz band was substituted by a handful of channels at 47MHz. The newer US standard – which is used illegally elsewhere, abandons the 1900kHz band altogether and has as its pair 49MHz and 46MHz, radio design having improved to the point where you can have transmit and receive frequencies that are close together without interference.

Looking for cordless phone traffic, therefore, means little more than placing your receiver within 200 metres of your target and scanning between 46 and 49 MHz until you hear what you are looking for. Thereafter, having found the spot frequency of your target's phone, you can simply leave the scanner tuned and connected to a tape recorder. If your target is using a cordless phone with a 1900kHz 'base transmit', you can monitor on a communications receiver, and perhaps enjoy a slightly better range.[*]

Interestingly enough, the US Supreme Court

---

* The 'security' devices fitted to some cordless phones are intended, not to stop eavesdropping, but to prevent the use of a handset to hijack someone else's line – the line is only opened if the right digital code is sent from the handset to the base.

decided in January 1990 that cordless phones did not fall within the protection of privacy laws. 'Because there was no justifiable expectation of privacy,' the judge had said in the original case, 'the interceptions did not violate the Fourth Amendment.' The original lawsuit filed revolved around the case of Scott Tyler of Dixon, Iowa. Neighbours using a cordless phone stumbled upon the Tyler family's cordless-phone conversations and concluded that they were hearing illegal drug dealing taking place. The neighbours reported that to the county sheriff, who provided equipment for them to record future conversations. As it happened, no drugs were dealt, but Tyler was convicted in late 1984 of bilking two food companies out of $35,000, even though the court refused to allow the taped conversations as evidence. Tyler and his family later sued the neighbours and county officials for invading his privacy.[4]

The UK is currently pioneering a newer cordless phone technology called CT2 and it may be adopted elsewhere. CT2 phones can be used not only in the home and office in association with a base station connected to a regular phone line but also out in the street, at stations and in shopping malls. In these latter cases, there are public base stations with a range of about 100 metres and when the CT2 phone is taken 'off-hook' within range, it sends an identification code which can be used for billing purposes. CT2 phones can be used in this way for outgoing calls only, though when a CT2 is used at home, in-coming calls can also be received. CT2 technology has yet to take off (and, at this writing, may never do so because the commercial proposition it offers may not be attractive enough for the potential customers) but it has the advantage that CT2 phones can't be eavesdropped by scanners. The speech is digitised prior to transmission.

Cellular phones

While cordless phones are easy to overhear, cellular phones are not. That statement needs qualifying: set the scanner to search the right part of the radio band[†] and you'll hear masses of cellular

---

† For example, 915–960MHz, in the UK, 820–840MHz in the USA, and 450MHz in some European countries

telephone dialogue.* Sit on a hill overlooking central London at around the 6 p.m. rush-hour and you could hear, in turn, fragments of up to 1,000 conversations. The trouble is, they'll all be anonymous and the chances of your finding the conversation of choice these days is almost non-existent.†

Cellular radio is able to support the large number of customers it has because the frequencies allocated to it are constantly being reused. The geographic area over which a particular service operates is divided into cells each of which has a handful of frequencies associated with it. When it is not in use, the cellular phone is always listening out for the nearest of a number of control channels which, when there is an in-coming call or the cellphone owner decides to make an out-going call, tell the cellphone which pair of actual frequencies to use (a pair are used, as in cordless phones, so that both parties can speak and listen simultaneously). The cellphone owner is usually constantly on the move. When the signal strength of the channel in use drops below a certain level, the cellphone immediately scans around looking for another control channel with a stronger signal. If it finds one, it will be in a neighbouring cell and any conversation taking place will need to be changed to a new pair of frequencies. This process, usually accompanied by a brief digital buzz, is called the 'hands off'.

The cellphone owner notices more-or-less nothing, but the scanner owner does – the conversation has vanished. Handing off takes place much more frequently in places of high population because the cell density is much greater. Listening to cellphone conversations in cities is always very fragmentary, and becoming more so, as the cellular service suppliers increase the number of cells to support their new customers.

So, with a simple scanner, you can only hear

* Listening to cellular telephones is governed by the same laws as those forbidding eavesdropping on other parts of the radio spectrum, though the judge in the Dixon's 'biscuit-tin' case (see p. 92) caused some temporary confusion when it was reported that he had said that it appeared not to be illegal (*The Times*, 13 February 1988)

† This has not prevented a whole series of scare-mongering articles appearing in the press, e.g. Gary Murray in *Mobile Communications*, October 1989; *Sunday Telegraph*, 13 August, 29 October 1989.

cellphone conversations at random and you'll not hear any one colloquy for very long. What can be done about it?

First, you could try limiting your eavesdropping to the country, where cells are larger. Second, if you can get in close enough you can try and listen to the signals coming from the cellphone itself. Normally when you use a scanner to sample cellular traffic, what you are listening to are the base stations, dotted around on buildings and towers. The signals from the cellphone can be heard on the other half of the pair. In the UK, for example, this will always be 45MHz *below* that of the base station signal. They will be much weaker, of course, but, provided you are within range, there is an advantage – the scanner will only hear signals in the immediate vicinity and you have a greater chance of finding the signal you want. If you now follow your cellphone owner's car, when the hands off takes place as the car moves into the next cell, you again have some chance that your scanner will locate the selected channel again.

The other alternative, apart from going to the cellphone service with an official warrant, is to use much more sophisticated receiving equipment. This listens on the control channels, interprets the information it hears, and then uses either a couple of scanners linked to a computer or, more usually, an adapted cellphone, to move channel in sympathy with the target cellphone. I have read articles about such equipment but have never seen any.[5]

Nevertheless, where cell sizes are large and traffic (that is telephone traffic) is light, interesting conversations can sometimes be overheard on simple scanner equipment. In early November 1990, Richard Needham, a junior minister in the Northern Ireland office was driving in South Armagh and talking to his wife about Mrs Thatcher, then (though no one knew at the time) in her last few weeks as Prime Minister. Needham, from the liberal wing of the Conservative Party said: 'I wish that cow would resign.' Monitoring him were IRA personnel and they – apparently – released a tape to a Belfast newsagency. Needham later had his apology accepted by Mrs Thatcher.[6]

Before leaving the subject, it is worth reporting on one other feature: billing is often itemised. Get hold of such a bill and you can work out who has been talking to whom.[*]

Packet radio

Increasingly organisations that generate a great deal of radio traffic that relies on detail are going over to systems which send a data message – in the form of instructions which appear on a small screen or via a miniature printer – rather than relying on voice traffic. The UK's Automobile Association – AA – sends information to its mobile patrol staff in this way – the staff can receive detailed information about the AA member, the vehicle and the fault without having to stop the patrol vehicle and take dictation over a radio link. Taxi and dispatch companies use similar systems.

Often the technique used is packet radio, which was originally devised by some experimentally-inclined radio amateurs and uses an adaption of the X.25 packet-switched protocol used for international land line-based high-speed data traffic.

Packet radio equipment – in effect a sophisticated radio modem – is available at lowish cost from amateur radio dealers. To eavesdrop on to commercial traffic you simply connect it to a scanner – find the right frequency and experiment with the speed settings till the read-out begins to make sense. The traffic will be in a slightly compressed format but is usually not difficult to decode.

If you listen over an extended period you could, among other things, calculate how well the company was using its distribution/dispatch services, identify patterns of activity and identify key customers.

Wireless LANs

The computer systems of many companies now consist, not of large central computers but numbers of personal computers linked together on a network, often referred to as a Local Area Network or LAN. LANs are usually based on lengths of cable or wire but since 1990 there has been in-

creasing interest in reducing the costs of networking by the use of radio as opposed to cable. (The cable itself is not expensive on a per metre basis, but installing it is.)

This has resulted in the growth of wireless LANs. US-originated versions operate in the frequency band 902–925MHz but the UK-licensed versions are in the microwave region – 2.412–2.438 GHz. Whereas eavesdropping on to a cable-based LAN requires entering the target building, hijacking a legitimate 'port' on to the cable, making an illicit break in the cable or using sophisticated versions of the cable-tapping techniques described on p. 157, eavesdropping a wireless LAN can be done with the right sort of radio monitor from outside the building where the computers belonging to the network exist.

In practice, none of this is particularly easy, even though the US-selected standard frequencies are within the coverage range of all but the lowest-cost scanners. The main difficulty is that wireless LANs use what are called spread spectrum techniques. In this, all the 'channels' use the whole of the frequency band available and band usage is constantly being changed to make optimum benefit of the resources available. Regular scanners are useless. (Spread spectrum is also used for high-security voice traffic.) Eavesdropping on to wireless LANs, therefore, means purchasing equipment similar to that used by the 'legitimate' members of the network in question and using that as the basis of monitoring kit.

For the moment, the costs of such an exercise are likely to outweigh any benefits an industrial spy might hope to gain.

Microwave, satellite links

In the United States in the mid-1980s it was estimated that just under 70 per cent of all long-distance telephone trunks went via ground-based microwave links. In the UK there is a well known and very obvious network of 'BT' towers centred on the one near Warren Street in London. Increasingly commercial companies with large volumes of data traffic are linking sites (or linking to main network) not by land line but via a microwave link.

It is possible, but not easy, to intercept this traf-

---

* During the run-up to the take-over bid for Gateway Foodstores in April 1989, three directors were identified in this way having held long cellular telephone conversations with the bidding group, Isosceles, and Gateway obtained court orders forbidding any further contact (*Observer*, 18 June 1990).

fic. In the first instance you must interpose your own antenna (almost certainly a dish similar to those used legitimately for transmitting and receiving). An article circulating among advanced hackers since 1987 describes the principle methods used by telecommunications companies to send multiple data traffic from one point to another and discusses how one can adapt domestic TVRO equipment (that is equipment designed for the reception of television satellites), scanners and HF communications receivers to effect decoding of at least some of the telephone and data traffic being carried on microwave links.[7] Similar techniques can be used on those satellites that carry 'business' traffic as opposed to entertainment material.

The article is plausible in its detail though at this stage it is doubtful whether the effort required to assemble the equipment would be commercially viable. What is beyond doubt, though, is the more advanced of the scanner enthusiasts have, for the last several years, found it worth their while to remove the TV sets from their satellite receivers and replace it with good scanners. They are able to find large quantities of unexpected material, not only alternative, foreign-language sound tracks for TV services which they already know about, but news-agency sound services, studio talkback channels used by reporters, often across continents and 'feeders' for international short-wave broadcasters.

Satellite data

But satellites are used for more than broadcasting television programmes and transmitting voice and data traffic. They also watch the world and transmit highly detailed images of the world below – super-accurate almost real-time cartography. Every 26 days every square centimetre of the world is scanned by Spot–2, the largely French-owned commercial satellite. It can produce images down to a resolution of ten metres in black-and-white or 20 metres in full colour. Spot–1 was launched in February 1986, Spot–2 in 1990 and

Spots –3 and –4 should be in place by 1995. Its images, captured and analysed at a centre in Toulouse, are sold commercially to almost anyone who is prepared to pay. Approximately 30 per cent of income is derived from map-making (civilian and military), 20 per cent comes from agribusiness and 18 per cent from mining, oil and similar forms of exploration. The United States has a similar commercial satellite data service which operates at slightly lower resolutions called Landsat. The Russians have made it clear that its space station Mir is available to rent and have made marketing arrangements in the West – they claim their pictures will have resolve down to five metres.[8]

Most customers for such material are prepared to pay for it, but the transmissions from all these satellites can be received over a wide area; already equipment exists enabling enthusiasts to receive data direct from weather satellites – it may not take too long before pirates start siphoning raw data from the cartography satellites.

This however must be, for the moment, one of the extreme edges of eavesdropping technology; the ones you have to worry about are the simple, low-cost ones.

In this next section of the handbook, we turn to matters much closer to the heart of industrial espionage – the specific ways in which you can find out what is really happening inside a company. . . .

(1) *Observer*, 16 April 1990; *Police Review*, 24 March 1989; *Sunday Telegraph*, 18 March 1990; *Financial Times*, 19 March 1990; *UPI*, 9 January 1988.
(2) For example, Tom McNichol, *Guardian*, 14 August 1989; *Los Angeles Times*, 23 February 1986; *Sunday Times*, 14 October 1990.
(3) *Police Review*, 24 March 1989; *Financial Times*, 19 March 1990; *Sunday Telegraph*, 18 March 1990; *Observer*, 16 April 1989.
(4) *Los Angeles Times*, 10 January 1990.
(5) *Telecommunications*, February 1989.
(6) *Sunday Times, Sunday Telegraph* and most other papers, 11 November 1990.
(7) My copy was downloaded from Arpanet; the approximate date – Spring 1988.
(8) *Financial Times*, 11 January 1991; *Guardian*, 8 December 1989.

10 How to Find Out about Companies

The most common target of industrial espionage is businesses. Even if you think you only want to know one or two specific things about a company, there is a bedrock of basic factual material that is essential if you are to understand what makes the company tick. Most of this information is incredibly easy and cheap to obtain. Every rationally run company makes its decisions within the framework of a business plan. All companies have finite resources in terms of skills, assets, cash and capital, and a finite capacity for developing new things or moving in new directions. Every company's ability to raise finance for new ventures depends on what it and its directors have achieved in the past.

You may assume that all you want are recent sales figures from your most obvious competitor, or details of some new product launch. You may believe that corporate analysis is only for merchant bankers and securities analysts. What you will soon discover is that everything your competitor does is likely to be governed by a small number of elemental dynamics and that you need to understand them.

Many of the textbook ways of analysing companies, based as they are on financial disciplines and the well known key accounting ratios, tell only part of the story. People go into business, start companies, change and remodel the companies they are in, for more reasons than to optimise profit. Profit indeed is only one measure of success. Predicting a company's intentions therefore, requires an understanding of its history and culture. The industrial spy needs to be acquainted with some of the more useful recent outpourings from the business schools.

However, corporate research will always mean establishing the simple known facts and building up from there. How far you go depends on what prompted the intelligence requirement in the first place.[*] If all you wish to know is whether you can safely commence a low-level trading relationship, your enquiries will finish quite quickly with a simple credit check. If you are one of two companies competing fiercely in a limited market, or if you are a potential take-over victim – or predator – you'll want to build up a rather more comprehensive file. Like many investigations, competitor analysis, industrial espionage, whatever, begins after a while to exhibit a series of positive feedback loops – you secure the basic material, overcome your inhibitions about opening a formal file on your target, analyse what you have, derive from that a list of what you still need, collect more expensive or difficult material, analyse that . . . and so on, until you feel you are achieving the intelligence goal you set yourself.

Does a company actually exist?

A letter with a company name and address on it, or an advertisement, does not mean that a company exists or that it exists in the form in which the letter or advertisement implies. Fraud squad officers and private investigators continue to marvel at the numbers of people who fail to carry out even the simplest checks.

Most companies are in the Yellow Pages (business phonebooks). The electronic form, in the UK and many other countries, is available for the price of a phone call – in the UK there is no usage charge. EYB covers the 1.8 million UK businesses normally found in the 66 various regional editions of the printed version and is updated regularly. Overseas Yellow Pages equivalents are available from a number of the online hosts. In the US, Dun and Bradstreet have a low-cost Electronic Business Directory covering 8.4 million businesses and a Market Identifiers service with more detail for 2.4 million of these. There are additional D&B

---

[*] See Chapter 1 for how intelligence requirements are formulated.

Basic business information
The chart shows the progression you should follow in a 'typical' corporate intelligence exercise – it covers the basics and goes from the basic but essential (and low cost) through to more expensive and more 'difficult' methods . . . the order given here is not absolute. . . .

Procedure	*Commentary*
Does a company exist?	*Check Yellow Pages etc.*
Published accounts	
Annual report	*The annual report is free.*
Companies House return	*CH return on microfiche is more detailed than online*
Balance sheet	*version – it will give original documents and some*
Profit & loss account	*private addresses of key individuals, for instance*
Source & application of funds	
Directors' report	
Registered office	
Register of members	
Directors, company secretary	
Directors' interests in shares	
Mortgages & charges	
Register of debenture holders	
Catalogues, lists of products and services, specification sheets, promotional literature, advertisements	*These are free and essential*
Trade directory entries	*May be out of date, incomplete and misleading, but costs very little to acquire*
Press comment (easy)	*Easy-to-obtain press comment is available from online services like Profile, Dialog and Nexis. Initial cost*
– on company	*would be in the low hundreds of £s*
– on industry	
– on leading personalities	
Basic credit reference	*Find out what Dun & Bradstreet, Infolink, Jordans, etc. think – at the least they'll have checked the local county (civil) courts*
Market research (published)	*It may not be worth spending a great deal of money*
Stockbroker commentary	*initially, but some of it will be free, or low-cost*
Cross-ownership, holding companies, subsidiary companies	*This means creative use of various databases*
Major shareholdings	*You can get this direct from the annual return, but it may be out-of-date. You can also demand it from the company's registered office. But there are also databases covering the larger companies*
Press comment (more difficult)	*You may need an online database specialist for this, or to get a researcher to visit libraries for more unusual sources*
– on company	
– on industry	
– on leading personalities	

Procedure	*Commentary*

Directors (and other key executives)
    Basic biogs
    Share-holdings
      in company
      in other companies
    Other interests, e.g. other directorships
	You can do online searches in news databases for basic material and look at the CH returns for interests in the target company. Some online financial databases will also reveal holdings in other companies – see also Chapter 11

Professional advisors, e.g.
    auditors
    merchant bank
    lawyers
    PR consultants
    other
	Most of this will appear in the annual report. Check the press for clues as to the identity of non-statutory advisors

Gossip	*Never underestimate the value of informal gossip, from wherever you can get it. Two things – start to write it down, together with the circumstances in which it was heard; you may wish to conceal the fact that you are asking around about someone or something*

Analysis
    financial
        assets
            land
            proprietary rights
        cash resource
        cash flow
        potential for raising further cash
    products/services
        position in industry
    company culture etc.
	You should now have enough to begin a basic analysis – and to decide what more you need

Loop-backs	*At this point you may need to go back up the list to get more detail because you have now discovered its relevance*

Dirty work
    lifestyle checks on directors
    follow-arounds on directors and advisors
    garbology
    infiltration
	Only now do you start with the basic dirty work – most of it based on paying for observation at a distance

services for Europe (1.5 million businesses in 29 countries), Canada and 'International'. In the UK more detailed basic information is available from Kompass.

Published accounts

Companies have two motives in sending in returns to Companies House, the Securities and Exchange Commission, their local chamber of commerce, or whichever regulatory authority has been designated to receive them. The first is to comply with the local law. Usually smaller companies are not required to provide as much detail as larger companies. The second, if they are publicly quoted or hope to raise finance from the public, is to present the sort of description of themselves that is attractive to investors. Additionally, the quoted company will have to obey the listing regulations of the relevant stock exchange, which are likely to require quite high levels of disclosure – as well as timeliness and even-handedness in the publication of information which is likely to affect the share price.* Neither of these ambitions may tie in precisely with the interests of the industrial spy. Would-be investors, for example, are more concerned with dividend income and the possibilities of growth in the value of the quoted share. As a competitor, predator or predatee, you need to know what the company's strengths and weaknesses are. In the published accounts you will find clues rather than answers.

The basic contents of an annual return are as follows:

> Balance sheet
> Profit & loss account
> Source and application of funds
> Directors' report
> Registered office
>> Register of members
>> Directors, company secretary
>> Directors' interests in shares
>> Mortgages & charges
>> Register of debenture holders

You can obtain the full records as opposed to the summaries, either in hard-copy or microfiche form, from (in the case of the UK) Companies House or, at greater expense but more convenience, from commercial intermediaries. You can also place your order online, electronically. The Companies House version will include the Memorandum and Articles of Association. 'Mems and Arts' are frequently assembled from boiler-plate paragraphs with a word-processor, but they may also contain important clues about company powers and aims. The Companies House records will also give in far greater detail information about shareholders, past as well as present, and of any restructuring. Older material may not be on microfiche and you may have to inspect the documents direct at the Companies Registration Office search room. The full version may provide you with other detail that is useful in other aspects of your research – addresses of directors, for example. The Extel Card Service combines material from the Annual Report, six monthly statement, and any company announcements of a 'price sensitive' nature; but the service only covers quoted companies.

The adjacent table provides the definitions of the terms commonly found in annual returns.

Accounting definitions

Fixed assets
> Property, plant, fixtures, fittings, office equipment and motor vehicles all at written-down value; includes leased and capitalised assets.

Intangible assets
> Goodwill, trademarks, patents, copyrights, shown at their amortised book value. These are assets with no physical existence but which are deemed to confer benefits to the company in the future.

Intermediate assets
> Investments in subsidiary and associated companies, trade and other unquoted investments. Amounts due from other group, associated and affiliated companies that appear to be receivable over one year and with no stated repayment terms. Other similar amounts due from third parties, such as directors and employees.

Stock
> Trading stocks, work in progress net of progress payments.

Debtors
> Trade debtors and trade bills receivable within one year.

Other current assets
> Sundry debtors and pre-payments and accrued income due within one year. Other assets held for realisation in the next twelve months; amounts due from other group, associated and affiliated companies that appear to be receivable within one year. Cash and 'near-cash' assets, e.g. marketable investments.

Total current assets
> The sum of stocks, debtors and other current assets – the portion of a company's assets which is realisable within one year.

* This is 'price-sensitive information' – those who have privileged information and buy or sell shares on the basis of it are of course guilty of 'insider dealing'.

Creditors
Trade creditors and bills payable within one year.

Short-term loans
Short-term portion of the company's total debt includes: bank overdrafts and current portion of bank and other institutional loans, hire purchase and leasing obligations that appear to be payable within one year. Current portion of amounts due to other group, associated and affiliated companies that appear to fall due within one year.

Other current liabilities
Sundry creditors, accrued expenses and pre-paid income, including dividends, corporation tax, value added tax, social security and other sundry amounts payable within twelve months.

Total current liabilities
The sum of trade creditors, short-term and other current liabilities.

Net assets employed
The net assets employed by a company are obtained by subtracting the current liabilities from the total assets.

Shareholders' funds
Issued ordinary and preference share capital, capital and revenue reserves, profit and loss account balance; government grants.

Long-term loans
The long-term portion of the company's total debt includes: bank and other institutional loans of over one year repayments, including mortgages. Portion of hire purchase and leasing obligations payable over one year. Amounts due to other group associated and affiliated companies, that appear to be payable over one year, or have no fixed terms of repayment; long term portions of trade and sundry creditors.

Other long-term liabilities
Minority interests, pension funds and similar liabilities; deferred and future taxation, due beyond twelve months.

Capital employed
The sum of shareholders' funds, long-term loans and other long-term liabilities. It is the counterpart of the 'net assets employed'.

Sales (turnover)
All income derived from the principal activities of the company, net of value added tax. May be broken down into domestic and export sales.

Profits before tax
Net profits after deduction of all expenses including directors' remuneration, depreciation, interest paid, but before deduction of tax, dividends, subvention and other expropriations. May include exceptional and extraordinary items.

Interest paid
Gross interest paid by the company. This may be an aggregation of short-term, long-term and credit agreement interest. It may also include arrangements with group, associated and affiliated companies.

Directors' remuneration
Including fees, salaries, health care, pension fund arrangements.

Employees remuneration, number of employees
All but the smallest companies have to disclose this; often there is a further requirement to disclose bands of remuneration and from this it is sometimes possible to calculate the income of specific individuals.

Depreciation
Includes amounts written off tangible fixed assets (including leased assets). Does not include an allowance for inflation drain.

Non-trading income
Non-trading income is usually shown after deduction of non-trading expenses and will include such items as financial and investment income.

Net worth
Shareholders' funds less intangibles.

Total debt
The sum of short-term and long-term loans.

There are of course important limitations to the value of statutory returns. At a Cambridge conference in 1990 the litigation manager of a firm of City solicitors warned delegates: 'Always remember that the last published accounts but one of any fraudster usually have an audit certificate on them stating that in the auditors' opinion the accounts presented a true and fair view of the fraudulent company's affairs.'[1] There need not be a fraudulent intent in producing accounts which, shortly thereafter, turn out to have been misleading. Many more companies fail through over-optimism or sloppiness on the part of their managers than because someone has been deliberately dishonest.

The problem goes further than that, though. Many of the figures in Companies House returns and annual reports which seem so definite and precise (and signed off by prestigious accountants) contain large elements of subjective judgement. The value of stock, for example, can be set either at hoped-for revenue levels over the coming twelve months, defined by the cost of raw materials plus direct production costs, written down to nearly zero almost immediately after production, or set at anything in between. At a stroke the profit figure moves up or down accordingly. It all depends on what you want to show – do you need high profits to impress the City, or do you wish to keep your tax bill low, or throw predators off the scent? You have similar scope for making judgements about fixed assets: how do you value property, for example – at the original purchase price, at the level of the heady days of the late 1980s, or in the rather more depressed conditions of the early 1990s? How on earth do you value 'goodwill', or put a figure on how much you might realise from some patent, or as happened in some of the late 1980s take-overs, the worth of brand-names? When you look at debtors – what provision should you make for bad debt? Even something as apparently tangible as 'cash' can require subjective judgements: what if some of the cash is in overseas bank accounts, or is 'near cash' – marketable investments which have to be sold and the value of which can vary, or what if the cash includes precious metals and commodities held for investment where again you must forecast what you might realise. How do you handle fluctuating exchange rates? In these and other matters, the only thing a company's directors have to do is persuade the auditors that the picture presented is a 'true and fair' one – and that only has to be the case at the time the snapshot for the balance sheet is taken. Auditors are sometimes criticised, particularly if companies fall into spectacular liquidation, but they are not expected to have hindsight.[*]

Alter any of these figures, and the 'key accounting ratios' so beloved of financial analysts start shifting all over the place.[†]

Of course, when you start looking at larger companies, ones which acquire and dispose of smaller ones, things become much more complicated.[2] One trick large secretive conglomerates go in for is frequent internal restructuring. Each operating division has its own registered company, each of which of course files accounts. The master company may produce consolidated accounts or may treat itself as essentially an investment operation, lending money in various forms and receiving back income in a variety of shapes from its subsidiaries. The individual subsidiaries are not absolutely required to follow the same series of subjective judgements about valuations as their parent, though it raises eyebrows if the variation becomes very obvious. In any event, scrutiny from outsiders becomes more difficult.

Other tricks include: reserve accounting (costs charged against the balance sheet rather than profits), off-balance-sheet finance and 'acquisition accounting'.

UK Companies House returns also include details of mortgages and charges on the assets. In the US you can inspect the Uniform Commercial Codes not only for commercial mortgages but also for other finance agreements and this is a particularly useful source of enquiry for the industrial spy – among other things, it tells what equipment a company may recently have purchased.

Product information

Nearly all companies publish an extensive range of sales literature, from advertisements through generalised brochures to detailed catalogues, price lists and product specifications. The information is free, can usually be obtained direct or with only the smallest amount of subterfuge, and is essential. Not only are you acquiring knowledge which you need for product analysis[‡] but you can begin to deconstruct the published revenue figures – and establish which of the company's products or services are likely to be making the best contributions to turnover and profit.

Marketing literature and advertisements tell you how a company is pitching itself at its intended

---

[*] The firm of Stoy Hayward was in the news briefly during the early months of 1991 when a number of its London-quoted clients all collapsed within a fairly short period.

[†] See below, p. 83.
[‡] See Chapter 12.

customers; in part they will also tell you how a company sees itself, which may be almost as useful. Once you have seen the literature and advertisements you may be able to make a guess as to how much the company is spending on marketing.

Credit ratings

If all you intend is to open a modest trading arrangement, then a brief examination of its credit report should be quite sufficient. A number of companies offer simple credit-check data: in the UK, CCN gives ratings via a series of codes: GL, for example, means a credit rating better than £100,000; GX, that 'trading conditions' are adverse; and G*, that information is held which makes it impossible to state a formal credit rating. CCN also holds information about mortgages and charges, county court judgements, and administration/winding-up orders. Infocheck, another service, has more comprehensive reports but on fewer companies, only 325,000. Neither service provides credit references on every single UK company – for many smaller and recently established companies you'll find that details are only obtained after you have specifically asked for them – you may have to wait three days or more.*

Total cost for some peace of mind: perhaps £10. Larger corporations, those likely to want to issue bonds and other debt instruments, and banking institutions are regularly rated by a number of independent assessors whose judgements are accepted by the financial community: they include Standard & Poor Corp., Moody's and, for banks, Thomson BankWatch and IBC Banking Analysis.†

You can also ask for banker's references. The degree of detail will be much more extensive if the subject of the reference has given consent – the bank's first duty is maintaining client confidentiality. The references are normally 'trade' not 'investment', that is to say: banks can comment, usually very opaquely, on the quality of the maintenance of the client's account(s) but not on their long-term business prospects. Typical answers are: 'good for their normal business engagements', 'unable to speak for your figures', 'we do not think that they will enter into any commitment which they could not see their way to fulfil', respectively: 'Go ahead at the figures you have mentioned to us', 'Keep away', and 'Proceed cautiously'. If you ask for a banker's reference without the immediate knowledge of the subject, you must expect that they will get to know quite quickly thereafter.

Press comment

Almost every trade, profession and industry has its own specialist press. Every company of any size can expect, at some point in its existence, to make the pages of the press within its immediate locality; every quoted company will have its activities covered by the financial and national press.

Press coverage provides news of successes and failures, appointments and dismissals. Even if some of this is partially inaccurate you are collecting valuable gossip which can be checked out. It will provide the news, anecdote and detail the annual report leaves out. In my own business I never visit a potential new client without first having accumulated some press comment. At the very least it shows them I care enough to want to work for them; more often it tells me how to 'play' the situation.

The cheapest way of collecting press comment is to purchase the relevant press and spend a few minutes each week clipping out everything of relevance. However, this is better suited to a long-term, non-emergency surveillance than to a crisis situation, or to a newly realised interest.

My own preference is to collect as much material as I can electronically – it is quicker, in the first instance more exhaustive, easier to store and much easier to search through afterwards.‡ Some of the online searches only produce bibliographic results – which means deciding whether it is worth trying to obtain the full text in hard copy, either from a library or from a specialist fulfilment agency.

* Once you have taken the small step of mastering the technology, using computer access is faster and cheaper than relying on print information and telephone calls to human beings. See Chapters 3 and 4. However, more detailed credit information may require joining a subscription service as opposed to something available to all comers; some information will only be imparted in telephone calls and correspondence.
† See also Chapter 12 for credit information about individuals.
‡ See Chapter 3.

You can set up some online services so that, once you have downloaded your historical information about your target, the database carries out regular automatic scans of its new material to see if there is anything of interest to you.

Press comment can also alert you to industry-wide developments that might alter the situation of your target company – rising costs for raw materials or overheads, for example, new technological advances, new laws and regulations, and so on.

As we have seen, not all desirable information is available electronically and, in any case, one disadvantage of online services is that they rarely carry the advertisements that accompany a print publication. Recruitment ads and new product announcements may be of particular value.

Market research, stockbroker commentary

Market research, as we have seen,[*] is sold at price tags that vary considerably. The more expensive it is, the more you will need to find out how far the precise objectives of the research tie in with your needs. Any figure below, say, £100 can usually be justified on the grounds that it will contain a useful compendium of background information on an industry or profession, which would be more expensive to accumulate in any other way.

Stockbroker analysis varies considerably in quality. The main aim, however, will always be to assess a company's potential as an investment for the financial community; you may have other interests. Stockbrokers are primarily interested in forecasting dividend levels and comparing one form of investment with another. Depending on the analyst, a stockbroker's report may look in some detail at the 'fundamentals', that is the factors that will make a company grow, which could be a combination of innovation, management and acquisition.

Directors, major shareholders, key executives

The annual report will list the directors and may also include the key executives. It is they who will

[*] Chapters 3 and 4.

be making the decisions which most interest you. You need to build up personal files on each one – a subject examined in depth in the next chapter.

The ownership of a company, as opposed to who manages it day-to-day, can be very significant. In a private company with significant holdings by family members of the founders who are not themselves employed in the business, for example, those shareholders may have a number of non-obvious concerns – death duties and capital gains, for instance. There may also be deep-seated family feuds. A newly formed private company with institutional shareholders will almost certainly be committed to a high-growth business plan and have its major assets subject to some form of charge or preference. Key employees will be locked into long-term employment contracts and perhaps personal guarantees. Any of these elements could have a substantial influence on the way in which the company makes its decisions.

In a private company some detail on major shareholdings will appear in the Companies House filings. You can also obtain such information from the company's registered office. For publicly quoted companies this information will often be very out-of-date. There are electronic services which provide details of major share purchases and disposals – and also ones which monitor specifically the share activities of a company's directors – often extremely important indicators that something may be afoot. Some of the most interesting shareholdings may be in a series of nominee names. It is only a company that can, in certain circumstances, demand that the identities behind nominees be revealed.

In a mooted take-over of a public company, perhaps fewer than 20 people, acting on behalf of the institutional shareholders, will decide what happens. Any predator must make sure he knows which people he must persuade, and what arguments will most influence them. Even if no take-over is in prospect, companies can be influenced by the fear that one might arise.

Land

A further 'basic' in the collection of information about a company is to look at its ownership of land and to see if it has any plans to change its usage.

The first clues will come from the annual report which often, but not always, indicates addresses or locations of operating premises. There should also be some mention in the fixed assets entry, if the properties are owned as opposed to rented.

In most countries there is a register of property which is open to public inspection.[*] Recent mortgages and charges may be quite significant as a form of financing.

Detailed examination of the design of a building may give clues as to the number of people employed therein (in the case of offices) or of industrial processes taking place within (in the case of factories). At a banal level, the number of car-park spaces may tell you something about the number of people employed. With a few carefully taken photographs you can do on a small scale what the photographic reconnaissance people have been doing for years for the big national intelligence agencies.[3] Ideally you should include in each picture some device that enables you to fix a scale on the detail you require – a vehicle or other known object is usually enough, because the exact size of the object can be obtained from manufacturers' literature. Shadows too, properly interpreted, can be helpful. You can measure buildings, count the number of windows and doors, guess at the size of internal spaces, examine air-conditioning and other ducts, look at fuel stores, supplies of external power, and check any special arrangements for coping with waste. There is a computer program designed for the use of special forces I once saw demonstrated. Its purpose was to help plan rescues of hostages held in buildings. From photographs of the outside of the building the operator could simulate a three-dimensional model on the VDU. He could guess how the corridors would run, how rooms were divided up internally, which way doors would be likely to open, and so on. The special forces commander could then feed in intelligence data about the location of hostages and guards. Then he could 'walk in' to the model, planning his raid meticulously – how many of his men here, how many there, how the timings would need to be worked out, what distractions needed to be created. And so on. Most commercial reconnaissance is trivial by comparison. There are large numbers of aerial photographs already available via specialist agencies – or you can commission them yourself.[†] You can also buy satellite photographs.[4]

Finally, local press coverage about requests for new planning consents, and enquiries with local estate agents and construction companies may produce further results.

Financial analysis

All that you have done so far is to collect some raw information – you must now analyse it. Traditional financial analysis consists of calculating a series of 'key accounting ratios', the more common of which are shown in the accompanying table.

Although they can be very useful, particularly when comparative figures are available for similar companies, they are at the mercy of the accuracy of the information provided in the Annual Report which, as we have seen, may contain large elements of subjective judgement. There is no such thing as a universally "good" figure for any given ratio; in each case they have to be appreciated in terms of how a particular industry operates. A greengrocer buys his goods in the wholesale market in the morning and if he hasn't sold them more or less by the end of the day, he has mis-bought; his liquidity ratio will look very different from a manufacturer who may either have to produce for stock in case a customer comes along, or build to order whilst financing the costs of raw materials and labour. An advertising agency, unlike a manufacturer, normally has few fixed assets or raw materials but may need to offer extremely long credit lines and have large marketing costs. So you compare key ratios across only an industry. Several companies specialise in publishing such figures; in the UK, the most comprehensive range comes from the ICC Information Group Ltd. One of the advantages of comparison is that variations between similar companies may help to identify particularly eccentric "subjective" judgments. The ratios should never be viewed in isolation from other ways of analysing a company. In particular the eye can sometimes be drawn away from a close

* See Chapter 4, p. 28 for more detail.

† See p. 98.

examination of a company's cash position and cash-flow – the relevant ratios are Quick and Liquidity, but it may not be the ratio but the actual sum which is crucial. In difficult times it is cash rather than the prospects of profit which provides immediate survival.

Non-financial analysis

There are other forms of analysis which may be much more useful. These almost abandon the financial approach on the grounds that there are too many opportunities for a company to issue

---

Key ratios

Return on capital
Profit before tax, expressed as a percentage of capital employed.

Profitability
Profit before tax, expressed as a percentage of total assets.

Profit margin
Profit before tax, expressed as a percentage of sales.

Asset utilisation
Sales expressed as a percentage of total assets.

Sales to fixed assets
Sales expressed as a percentage of fixed assets.

Stock turnover
Sales divided by stocks – the number of times stocks are turned over during a year.

Credit period
Debtors divided by sales and multiplied by 365 – the average number of days taken before accounts are paid.

Working capital to sales
Working capital (stocks plus debtors minus creditors), expressed as a percentage of sales.

Export ratio
Exports expressed as a percentage of sales.

Liquidity
Current assets including investments expressed as a ratio of current liabilities.

Quick ratio
The sum of debtors and other current assets divided by total current liabilities.

Creditors to debtors
Creditors expressed as a ratio of debtors.

Gearing ratios
1 Total debt expressed as a ratio of net worth

2 Shareholders funds expressed as a ratio of total liabilities
3 Long-term debt expressed as a ratio of net worth
4 Gross interest paid, as a percentage of pre-interest, pre-tax profit.

Average employee remuneration
Total employee remuneration divided by the number of employees.

Profit per employee
Profit before tax, divided by the number of employees.

Sales per employee
Sales divided by the number of employees.

Capital employed per employee
Capital employed divided by the number of employees.

Fixed assets per employee
Fixed assets divided by the number of employees.

Total assets per employee
Total assets divided by the number of employees.

Wages to sales
Wages expressed as a ratio of sales.

Return on shareholders' funds
Profit before tax expressed as a percentage of shareholders' funds. Also: return on investment

Total debt to working capital
Total debt expressed as a ratio of working capital.

Current liabilities to stocks
Total current liabilities expressed as a ratio of stocks.

Debtors to total assets
Debtors expressed as a ratio of total assets.

deceptive figures. They favour approaches based, among other things, on the building of company chronologies, on assessments of company culture, on examinations of how companies compete and on what happens when technological innovations are exploited commercially. The various forms of non-financial analysis given below are neither non-exclusive nor complementary; rather they are approaches which might suit particular intelligence objectives:

Company chronologies
The aim of a company history is to try to identify the patterns that have determined its growth. To assemble a company chronology in detail you have to acquire all of its Annual Returns and Company Reports and pick the information out. You plot major movements in share ownership, capital reconstructions, changes of directors, career patterns of senior executives, sizes of workforce over the years, occupation of office and factory buildings, patterns of profit, loss and dividend payment – and, of course, product development. For longer-established companies you may find that the company itself has produced some form of history – if only a brochure – and there may be articles in the specialist press. You may also discover suitable materials in a local reference library or at a local polytechnic school of business. Indeed, the company history is an old standby of the business schools. What were the circumstances in which the company was set up? What were the ambitions of the founders? Was it to make money, or to produce particular goods or services? What were the cultural values at the beginning, and how have they changed? What have been the significant achievements in its growth? Which were the key products or services? Who have been the important managers who have shaped its destiny – or have been unmitigated disasters? What forms of corporate restructuring has it been through? The chronology also provides a factual framework for other sorts of analysis.

Company profile
The profile, by contrast, concentrates on the here-and-now. It gathers together the accumulated research and recasts it in a form directly relevant to the intelligence mission. Typical headings might

include:

> Mission and objectives
> Corporate structure
> Significant shareholdings
> Management structure
> Divisional arrangements
> Products/services
> Market position
> Key personnel
> Financial strengths and weaknesses

The profile can also examine more subjective elements: is the company essentially aggressive, predatory, benevolent, establishment-oriented? Does it favour organic growth or growth by acquisition? What are the elements that appear to drive the board decisions: the creation of new products, the need to keep an existing production facility/staff gainfully employed, success in marketing and sales, financial bottom-line, the needs of stock exchange investors, prestige/self-esteem? What is the period of time over which it makes decisions? Are the decisions mainly for the short- or for the long-term? Are decisions kept to or subject to frequent drastic revision? What is the state of employee morale?

Here, much of the material comes from the trade press and anecdote from those who know the company well.

Cultural assessments
Every company has its own internal culture[5] – a system of informal rules that spells out how people within the company behave most of the time. The cultural values may be quite simple to articulate: 'Service (or Quality) Before Profit'; 'We Believe in Long-Term Relationships with our Customers'; 'Never Knowingly Undersold'; 'Optimising Sales'; 'Ruthlessness in the Marketplace'. On the other hand it may take some time reliably to identify what the cultural values are. In any event, supporters of this sort of analysis claim that companies always make their plans within the framework of their cultural beliefs.

One typical tool of the analyst of corporate culture is to look at the career paths of key employees. If people stay in the same job for a long time and if there is a considerable amount of promotion from within, the company is probably extremely stable, has a fairly high employee morale but may also be resistant to change. If many of the senior managers have been recruited from outside the company and if few of them have been in their jobs for more than three years, you have an operation which may be very dynamic and aggressive, but which is also likely to have pockets of discontent and be prone to instability.

A related tool is to examine the style of the chief executive – is he also chairman of the board or is there some body other than the notional shareholders' meeting to whom he has to account for his actions? Are there non-executive directors around, and if so, are they likely to be sufficiently knowledgeable and experienced to be effective? In the case of large companies – is there also an audit board? Is the CEO also the founder of the company, or a family descendant of the founder? What shares does he own?

Another indicator of corporate culture is to examine environmental trivia – the type of premises used as headquarters,[*] the type of receptionist, the quality of the office furnishings and plants, the perks the senior management take to themselves, the extent to which the CEO becomes involved in public affairs that are not immediately relevant to the company's areas of activity, the degree to which the annual report departs from the sober presentation of the facts, and so on. It can also be useful to examine how employees as well as managers are cared for.

Shadow business plan

In the shadow business plan, the analyst places himself on the board of his target company and tries to identify its prospects as the board members would perceive them. He constructs shadow management accounts complete with cash flows. He seeks to visualise what the sales and marketing reports are like, he reviews reconstructed production reports, he looks at industry opportunities – the possibilities of technological innovation, targets for acquisition – *as the target company would look at them.* He also looks to see which parts of the operation may need restructuring, downsizing or selling off – and works out what costs may be incurred and benefits obtained.

Product analysis

Product analysis, as the name implies, consists of examining the company's range of products and services and setting them in the contexts of their competitors, direct and indirect, and of the market(s) for them. The subject of how to find out about 'things' – technological innovations, new production methods – is more fully examined in Chapter 12.

Analysis is not an end in itself; each one of these analyses may suggest other forms of enquiry. . . .

(1) Mourad Fleming, CIDOEC 1990, Volume 4, p. 662.
(2) *Interpreting Company Reports and Accounts*, Geoffrey Holmes and Alan Sugden (Woodhead-Faulkner, Cambridge, 1991).
(3) See *Deep Black* by William E. Burrows, essentially about spy satellites but with interesting coverage of the US National Photographic Interpretation Center (NPIC) and the National Reconnaissance Office (NRO).
(4) *Guardian*, 8 December 1989; *Sunday Times*, 7 January 1990.
(5) See *Corporate Cultures: the rites and rituals of corporate life*, Terrence Deal and Allen Kennedy (Addison-Wesley, New York, 1982)

---

[*] In the 1958 classic *Parkinson's Law*, the author suggests that really vibrant organisations run themselves from conditions of chaotic and creative squalor; companies that have immaculate corporate HQs are already on the downward slide.

11 How to Find Out about Individuals

There is an argument which suggests that the idea of privacy is essentially an invention of the late nineteenth century and that it has had little meaning since about 1985. The person who is born into a small community which he never leaves can have few secrets from his neighbours – they knew his parents, his relatives and siblings, they knew him as a child, they watched his sexual adventures, they witnessed his marriage, they can see how much wealth he has and what his earning capacity is. The possibility of privacy comes from geographic and employment mobility – the more a society lets you start afresh in new surroundings, the greater the extent to which individuals expect constantly to be meeting new people with whom to make friends and do business – the greater the opportunities for privacy. Privacy is a function of good-quality transport and of large cities. Even today, people who are born into ruling élites enjoy rather less privacy than the rest of us – a small network of schools, universities, regiments, clubs defines the village in which they live. The computer is ending this brief period in human history – so much of our lives is recorded in computer files, formal and informal, official and unofficial. 1985, give or take, was the date when a combination of the quality, quantity and availability of electronic information achieved critical mass. Computer databases replace the knowledge and gossip of the small community.[*]

The world is full of con artists. For every person who sets out to don the complete mantle of someone else, there are 50 who gild the lily of their own resumés, endowing themselves subtly with slightly better social and academic qualifications than they actually have (or, occasionally, pretending to come from more modest circumstances than is the case), or who take sole responsibility for achievements they ought really to share with others, whilst suppressing those parts of their autobiography which show a less-than-inevitable line of successes.

If you are considering employing someone, say at a normal executive salary, you can demand a CV which you can then verify; you can also expect the right to call on referees. Increasingly, potential employees are not surprised to be asked to undergo a day's psychological profiling as part of the assessment process. But if you are entering into a multi-million dollar contract or a joint venture where the status and probity of the leading figures are crucial, you can do no such thing. If you are about to sink your future into starting up a company, perhaps mortgaging your home to provide start-up finance, you may know surprisingly little about your co-directors – and also find considerable social constraints on how much you can ask them.[†]

But information about individuals is important outside the specific territories of employee or business partner recruitment. It can be critical to evaluating a company's overall strategy. Companies, even the largest ones, are run by individuals, or small groups of individuals. The company culture – its way of doing business, its values and so on – tend to come from these people.[‡] So, in many ways, the key to understanding the company is to identify and understand this group.

[*] In passing on this view I am making no judgement as to whether I think this state of affairs is a Good or Bad Thing.

[†] Tim Healey's book *Networks* has an anecdote worth repeating about how these things are sometimes still done. Oliver Lyttleton, Lord Chandos, was one of those figures who were frequently asked for their opinion about 'chaps' who were being considered for directorships, bishoprics, and the like. Chandos always had the same answer, 'Yes', but he had a hundred inflexions ranging from: 'Yes, what a simply marvellous idea, an ideal fit' to 'Yes, you are considering X and there is a whole murky undergrowth of rumour and fact which you had better sift through before you go any further.' However, the networks of which Healey wrote so engagingly in 1983 can't always be accessed by those who might need the information, and they are not always particularly reliable.

[‡] See Chapter 10.

Vast amounts of information about individuals, particularly if they have ever been company directors, or have ever had any prominence in their industry, can be obtained quite legitimately. Much more can be obtained by simple enquiry from targets' friends and acquaintances. Private detectives can be employed to follow them around simply to see what they do and where they go. At the darker end of the spectrum are zoom lenses, tape recorders, garbological expeditions, bugs, phone-taps, pretext calls and breaking-and-entering homes and offices in the search for information.

As with so much of the material in this book, judgements about ethics are being withheld in favour of describing what is possible. However (and you will have seen this is a recurring theme throughout this book), the best methods are often the ones which do not involve breaking the law or even areas which seem to mount a direct challenge to ordinary business ethics. For example, one of the first things you discover is the relative uselessness of that traditional holy grail in personal intrusion: personal banking information. A balance on one bank account (which can only be obtained by subterfuge), for example, tells you almost nothing about the financial health of an individual. Most people with a bank current account will also have at least one entirely separate savings account, a savings scheme and various pension and insurance arrangements. Most of the people of interest to industrial spies will have much more complicated personal financial arrangements than that.

The target biography

When, for whatever reason, you have decided that someone is of interest, the first and most important discipline you must impose on any enquiries is the compilation of an accurate life history in strict chronological order. This is the direct equivalent of the company history mentioned in the previous chapter.

The chronology – up to a point the more detailed the better – will reveal home, educational and career information in a way that no amount of unstructured anecdote ever can. If there are gaps in public knowledge about someone, if there have been unacknowledged periods of career setback, the chronology will soon make it evident.

How do you set about preparing a biography? Nearly all people of any prominence publish some information about themselves or have it published on their behalf – in corporate literature, during public appearances at conferences and seminars, in interviews with journalists, in responses to directories such as *Who's Who* and the many trade-specific equivalents. In fact most business people publish several biographies of themselves – you can check them for consistency – and some tycoons seek every opportunity for self-publicity. If the target has ever sought employment with someone with whom you are friendly, you may be able to obtain a more formal, self-written CV.

Once there is a framework, you have the basis for checking out and filling in the details. Home addresses may not be immediately available from publicity material in all cases (though they are sometimes given in company prospectuses and Companies House filings), but the telephone book and the various telephone number enquiry services will fill the gap, and if they don't the electoral and community charge (local tax) registers will. Did the subject really attend the schools, universities, regiments and so on claimed? These institutions themselves will hold records which can be verified.* To go back further, are the published details about birthdate and parentage correct? If necessary a visit to the registrar of births and deaths, or to a local church where a christening might be assumed to have taken place may provide much-needed confirmation. Similar processes should reveal details of marriages and children.

Once into a career, can you list out all the employment situations, start and stop dates, positions held, responsibilities taken, results or otherwise achieved? Much career information can be obtained from back issues of relevant trade magazines, local newspapers and, if the subject is im-

---

* This was the technique used to identify anomalies in the 'official' biography of one of the UK's best-known entrepreneurs, James Gulliver, while he was head of the Argyll supermarket group and involved in a take-over of the Distillers Company. Gulliver had claimed in his *Who's Who* entry that he had been educated at Harvard; in fact he had attended a three-week course there. This bit of 'dirt' was uncovered by a private detective and later released to the press by a PR man retained by Distillers. (*Sunday Telegraph* and *Sunday Times*, 16 March 1986).

portant enough, from national newspapers. None of this requires much effort – trade and local papers are usually published weekly so that even if they are not available online, as we saw in Chapter 4, there are only 50 issues for each year of interest to scour. National newspapers can be scanned electronically at low cost. If the subject has ever been a company director then the various online services of corporate information are invaluable: some of them permit a search on director's name – that way you can identify all the current companies (and some recently dissolved ones) of which an individual is a director. These same database services will contain details of the size of shareholdings while other databases can tell you of significant holdings in other public companies (provided, that is, the holdings are not too heavily disguised in nominee names).

All careers have some form of inner logic which defines their progression. Wealth is either earned or inherited. Wealth can only grow according to a limited number of patterns. No one is plucked from total obscurity into jobs of great responsibility – whoever made the appointment must have known something about a previous track record which justified the risk, if that is what it was. Your chronology should show it.

Personal details

All this information has come from public records which can be inspected without the subject having even the slightest idea that they are beginning to be the subject of a 'file'. A great deal of useful analysis

---

Lifestyle checks

Estimate income
  Salary (from annual reports, from comparisons with other rates in the same industry)
  Inherited wealth translated into income
  Shareholdings – as declared
  Estimates of other investment income
  Other income, e.g. licenses, fees, copyrights (you may be able to get sales figures for the goods in question and also details of the contracts which specify levels of royalty etc.)

Estimate capital
  Shares (for many entrepreneurs, the fact that they hold large numbers of shares at given market value does not mean that they are in a position to dispose of them, or that if they did they would realise everything at a 'stock exchange' price)
  Land-holdings, including houses (from credit databases, land registry, estate agents etc.)
  Other, e.g. works of art

Family details
  Estimate any income or capital from spouse or children
  Previous marriages
  Dependent relatives, including parents
  Other dependents, e.g. non-married relationships

Estimate regular outgoings
  Mortgages

Family support/household
Children's education
Office costs etc. personally borne
Hobbies etc.
Spending habits of dependents
Special costs e.g. gambling, drink and drug dependence

Ambitions
  Personal finances
  Social
  Business targets

Secrets
  (areas which the subject would prefer not to be in the public domain)
  Family background
  Business failure
  Socially 'unacceptable' relationships
  Drug/drink dependency

Identify pressure points
  (pressure points are those areas likely to influence behaviour; they need not completely reflect the 'real' world, merely the subject's perception of what the world is like)
  Cash flow (e.g., difficulty in maintaining a desired standard of living, despite having a high income)
  Social ambitions
  Political ambitions
  Business ambitions

is possible from just this, but there are further techniques.

As we have seen earlier, there are a number of companies who specialise in what they call 'due diligence' enquiries. One of the main services they offer is called the lifestyle check.

All, or nearly all, the information listed in the table can be obtained quite legally and usually without the subject being aware of the enquiries.

In contrast to the chronology, the lifestyle check concentrates on the present situation.

To find someone's income, you don't need access to private bank accounts. The salary and remuneration package may be a matter of public record – the annual reports of public companies are required to indicate the numbers of employees receiving remuneration within certain given bands. Alternatively, the press may have made some mention. Failing this, reference to recruitment advertisements, or informal chats with corporate headhunting firms,[1] for comparable positions, should give a fairly accurate guide.[*]

Information on creditworthiness, as opposed to a bank balance, can be obtained with relatively little subterfuge. Public registers of mortgages and credit agreements of land and personal property are available in many countries. In the USA, credit agreements are registered at State level as a Uniform Commercial Code (UCC) and similar

arrangements apply in many European countries. In the UK there are no direct equivalents and resort must be made to credit reference agencies, who make their databases available online. Officially, such services on 'consumers' (that is, private individuals) as opposed to companies are only available to those who can demonstrate a need to use them, in other words, those who give credit. The credit reference agencies are supposed to require subscribers to produce a letter from a local Office of Fair Trading supporting the requirement for access to personal credit data. In practice the agencies want to sell their data as widely as possible and are unlikely to make extensive enquiries of potential new subscribers. Private detectives use three techniques to get around the restrictions: they befriend a local trader with a legitimate requirement for personal credit data and simply pay them a fee for each enquiry; or they ask initially to join the credit agency's *company* credit database service (on which there are no restrictions) and then at a later stage quietly request an extension to permit access to the personal data; or they make a series of masquerade calls, a technique with very wide application – they pretend to the credit agency, bank, tax office, whatever, that they are someone with a legitimate right to financial information.

The personal credit databases are based on the electoral register – everyone of voting age is on them. Since most of the databases are designed to be very flexible it is possible to locate someone's address on quite 'fuzzy' information. You can also search for the names of all who live at a particular address – unmarried and gay couples living together may be identified that way. The other information all the databases have are unpaid county court judgements – public information, but usefully collected together.[†] But most of these services also carry more specific credit *ratings*.

[*] There are several ways of trying to 'get a balance' on a credit-card account. You need a garbological expedition; if you are fortunate you may find a discarded statement; more reasonably you can expect to find discarded counterfoils which will give you the credit-card number. The credit-card companies usually respond to telephone requests for information by asking one or more questions which they believe only the legitimate cardholder will know. If you are proposing making a masquerade call of this kind you need to have a file of information about the maiden name of any wife, relevant dates of birth, business phone numbers, and so on. Alternatively you can masquerade as a credit-card 'merchant' – a retail outlet seeking authority for a particular transaction. You'll need to be the sort of merchant that regularly handles high-value transactions. You can get the special phone number to call and the validating merchant identity number by calling in on the relevant retail premises and watching and listening carefully as a genuine credit enquiry is handled. The credit-card company doesn't tell you the actual balance, just whether it is prepared to authorise a transaction of a particular size – it will then issue an authorisation number.

[†] In the UK, CCN Systems, one of four credit data agencies, holds 30 million items of financial information and 2.5 million 'personal profiles'. It is based on the electoral roll, census information which gives 300 socioeconomic variables, the Post Office's postal address file, the National Shopper's Survey (compiled from people who have filled in detailed questionnaires on appliance guarantee forms and the like), and county court judgements. Its annual turnover is £50m (*Guardian*, 2 November 1989).

These are made by collecting from participating credit companies details of all agreements – and any defaults – made by each individual. The rating an individual gets depends on, among other things, where they live (each postal or zip code carries its own weighting derived from overall census data), the number of credit agreements successfully fulfilled – and the amounts involved.[*] More controversially, some of these services also carry any history of default associated with the individual's current address – so called 'third party' data.[2] In the UK the Data Protection Registrar is seeking controls over this. If someone has been declared a bankrupt that information is held, in the case of the UK, at the Royal Courts of Justice in the Strand.

Other types of information may be obtained from some of the databases that are used to support direct mailing activities. These now operate down to the postal (zip) code level.

The next component in the exercise is to try and estimate the true net worth of the subject. In the USA, *Forbes* magazine has tried to calculate the fairest and most useful way of measuring an individual's wealth in order to identify the world's richest 400 men and women,[3] and a similar exercise is carried out each year by the *Sunday Times* magazine for UK-based people. This is an approximation of the rules the *Sunday Times* sets itself:[4]

- 'wealth' means identifiable wealth in the form of land, property, racehorses, art treasures, or significant holdings in public companies – it does not include cash at a bank or portfolios of small equities holdings

- the *Sunday Times* recognised that many landholders were unable to sell their lands for legal reasons, but included values for them as they were able to enjoy the benefit of them

- similarly, many company directors with large shareholdings in their own companies would be unable to sell them, either at all, or at anything like the market price. Nevertheless

these too were included in the *Sunday Times* valuation, though that might be inappropriate for the present purpose. Fortunes based on the paper value of shares can fluctuate wildly

- whilst shares in publicly quoted companies can be valued at the 'stock exchange' price, those in private companies cannot. A rule of thumb is to value these either by reference to a comparable publicly quoted company or to estimate the total shares in issue as being worth 12.5 times the most recent post-tax profit figure. But this calculation only applies to larger companies – directors of small loss-making companies have been able, at least in times of high business confidence, to sell their shares for considerable amounts of money – provided they can find some larger company who wants their business badly enough

- family-held shareholdings and family trusts can sometimes create a nightmare for the researcher trying to guess the value of them to individual participants

- land can be valued according to publicly available tables. (The *Sunday Times* doesn't mention it, but the value of houses etc. can be obtained by reference to advertisements for comparable properties)

- artworks can be valued according to auction records

- since the *Sunday Times* was principally interested in UK-based rich people, their research team was particularly interested in typical aristocratic sources of wealth – sporting rights, and farmland

Outgoings can also be calculated from simple observation – a few days of looking at a subject's house, guessing the cost of its upkeep, working out a monthly mortgage figure from its original cost and whatever capital gain accrued from the sale of a previous house, following a spouse and children around to see their spending habits, their hobbies, checking where the children are being educated, looking for second homes, working out who owns

---

[*] One of the consequences of this is that a person who doesn't borrow very much may have a much poorer credit rating than someone of an otherwise broadly similar profile who does.

and pays for the cars[*] – soon provides close-enough figures.

Once income, capital and outgoings are known, a fair idea of idea of an individual's real freedom from financial worries can be readily calculated.[†] It is clearly important to distinguish wealth based on large shareholdings held in a publicly quoted company (which may be subject to formal restrictions as to selling or in any event which could not be sold without having an adverse effect on the company – and not at the regular quoted price) and true 'discretionary' wealth. Discretionary wealth is what you can spend *without* having to refer to anyone else. Self-made businessmen usually only acquire large quantities of discretionary wealth by keeping their companies private, by persuading shareholders that the sale of a small proportion of the total shareholding can be sold without damage to the company's prospects, or by getting a large company to buy theirs out for cash. Rather smaller chunks of discretionary wealth are obtained if an employee's services are dispensed with and a good pay-off is negotiated.

The next stages require more intrusion and involve more subjective types of information: friends and business associates can be chatted up, though some skill may be required to conceal the purpose of the enquiries.[‡] A close visual inspec-tion of the home (from the outside) may produce clues as to the level of spending – how recent is the decoration, is there any evidence of recent large capital expenditure – swimming pools, conservatories and the like? Or does the house look neglected, the curtains faded, and so on? That could indicate that there are substantial cash-flow worries.

A further technique is the pretext call: a private detective calls, usually on a stay-at-home wife, pretending to be a market researcher, antique dealer, charity worker, anything that will cause them to be accepted to the point where they will be invited in. At the very least the detective will be able to see much more of the home circumstances than from outside. Books, photographs and clutter will all give clues to family interests and social aspirations. With luck the wife can be persuaded to talk about herself and her family; in a prosperous house, a housekeeper or au pair may be almost as useful. An astute detective can, without breaking any law and without giving anything away – women appear to be particularly good at this sort of activity – build up a highly detailed social and psychological profile of family circumstances in an 'interview' lasting less than 30 minutes. Alternatively, it can be neighbours' homes which are visited for local gossip.

The local gossip may also provide you with information that cannot normally be obtained except through subterfuge of a quite dangerous kind – medical and criminal records. Not the records themselves, of course, but gossip about what they might contain. The gossip can be cross-checked against other sources. So far as criminal records are concerned, however, there are other methods of gaining some information without resort to bribing a police officer. It is a staple of local newspapers that they cover details of any court appearance within their district or any individuals who live in their area. Any more serious offence may be covered in the national press which can be searched electronically.[§] Looking at old news-

---

[*] In the UK, information about the ownership of cars is not publicly available. As a member of the public you have to show 'reasonable cause' (for example, an accident where the driver has not stopped) before the Driver and Vehicle Licensing Centre will provide the information. Private detectives often obtain such information by bribing a policeman to interrogate the Police National Computer which carries DVLC data. However, in many US states, ownership of cars, and any associated credit arrangement, is a matter of public record.

[†] Fraud investigators have a four-stage formula which they use to establish a net worth and thus uncover funds from unknown or illegal sources:

1 Assets – liabilities = net worth
2 Net worth – previous years' net worth = annual net worth growth
3 Annual net worth growth + living expenses = income
4 Income – legal or known sources = illegal or unknown sources

(C. Griffiths, in *International Criminal Police Review*, No. 377).

[‡] This is a classic situation for the recruitment of unaware agents – see Chapter 5.

[§] Newspaper files are not subject to the Data Protection Act, 1984, which is concerned with data files where the primary aim is to collect information of a personal nature – the primary aim of newspaper files is news (letter from Assistant Data Protection Registrar to *Computer Weekly*, 27 June 1991).

paper material and databases constructed from them makes it possible to circumvent the effects of legislation like the Rehabilitation of Offenders Act, 1974. The Act provides that, by law, an individual may conceal and indeed lie about any past criminal conviction that is regarded as 'spent' – there is a table of offences and punishments and periods after which the offence is regarded as expired, provided there has been no further trouble with the law. The same legislation can, in certain circumstances, prevent someone publishing information about spent convictions. However there is nothing to prevent the researcher from seeking out *old* publications that have the necessary information.

Once you are using private detectives, of course, you can also commission them to follow your subject around to see where s/he goes. A week's thorough surveillance is usually considered enough to reveal clues as to any anomalies in an individual's lifestyle – irregular sexual liaisons, illnesses concealed, gambling and alcohol and drug dependency. Once you have such information, of course, you have to decide how relevant it is.

Evidence of how extensive the use of 'lifestyle' checks are come from one of the more spectacular recent British cases of industrial espionage gone wrong, the Dixons/Comet case of 1986. It is often chiefly remembered as the first successful prosecution for the use of telephone taps by private detectives – the biscuit-tin bug case[*] – but tapping and bugging was only a small element in an extensive operation.

In April 1986, Dixons, a successful national chain of electrical appliance retailers which had already recently expanded by buying a rival called Currys, launched a bid for the UK end of the Woolworth group which included, among other things, the electrical appliance warehouse operation, Comet. The bid was worth £18.2bn. Dixons' security advisor hired a company called Cornhill Consultants to carry out many of the activities described in this chapter, focusing in particular on two Woolworth directors, Geoff Mulcahy and Nigel Whittaker, who had been credited with much of the success of Woolworth UK since it had split away from its US parent. After everything

had become public, the *Independent* newspaper reported:

> The surveillance included reports on their families and wives. The investigation covered everything from their financial situation to the value of their house. A resulting report even noted that one of the Woolworth directors made occasional visits to his local pub. Nothing to the detriment of either . . . Mulcahy or . . . Whittaker was found. . . . The dossiers – each page is headed re: opposition – were sent to Dixons' head of security on April 26 . . . [the dossier] describes the Woolworth chief executive's life as characterised by 'early morning departures to work in his Daimler/Jaguar and an equally late return each day. We were unable to discover anything to the family's detriment in this area.' Dixons learned further that the Mulcahys lived in a substantial detached dwelling of five or six bedrooms. . . . 'The family moved to this house some two or three years ago and little is known about the family apart from the precise job Mulchay holds. Local residents maintain a very high security profile with each house subscribing to the Crime Watch organisation for self-help. As such, making discreet enquiries in the area was a very precarious affair.' . . . Similar investigation was carried out on Mr Whittaker's wife and family. . . . Woolworth got wind of the investigation after neighbours reported approaches from unknown men seeking personal information on the Mulcahy and Whittaker families.

The surveillance also included enquiries into a private (and legitimate) venture of a director of another Woolworth subsidiary specialising in home improvements, B&Q.

The bid failed in July 1986 having cost Dixons £12.8m. The following month, Peter Hopper, appliance purchaser at Dixons and five others left Dixons for Comet. Dixons suspected them of, at the very least, unethical activities and breach of contract. By the following the month they believed there was a leak of very confidential information – business secrets such as the buying prices of new products and their availability were, they thought, being leaked. Broad-based surveillance of Woolworth and its various subsidiaries was restarted, in-

* See Chapter 7.

cluding the watching of retail outlets in order to assess sales.

Cornhill Consultants decided that mere exterior surveillance was not going to be enough and they, in a move typical of the security industry, sub-contracted two men to bug, or rather tap, Peter Hopper's home.* The following month the biscuit-tin bug was found, the two technicians caught, and they in turn pointed the way to Cornhill Consultants and its boss, Michael Anderson.† Woolworth themselves started to employ a corporate security company specifically to identify the extent of the surveillance operation.

When the tapping case came to court in February 1988, Judge Rodwell QC attracted a great deal of press attention when he went out of his way to say that companies are entitled to engage in industrial espionage such as undercover surveillance work.[6]

It is the combination of this information, the chronology, the estimates of wealth and expenditure and the personal details which makes it possible to identify what makes an individual tick. Few people are interested in money for its own sake – they may want high rewards because that tells them how clever they are, they may have unrealised social ambitions which stem from their upbringing, they may have an unusually well developed moral conscience, they may, in the midst of apparent prosperity, be struggling with personal difficulties. You may be able to hear about some of these things as simple gossip, but if you collect data and analyse it properly your knowledge will be much surer.

Individuals as businessmen

But it is all too easy to become fixated by the minutiae of people's private lives – that can be a consequence of relying too much on private detec-

* One man was called Terry Rowe and the other Terrence Rowe. They were not related.
† In another move typical of these types of incident, Woolworth's merchant bank N. M. Rothschild asked for and obtained a categorical denial of involvement from Dixons' financial advisors, Warburg's. There seems little doubt that Warburg's passed on their assurances in good faith and it is still not clear whether Dixons' entire management team knew of the full extent of the surveillance operation.

tives; too many of their clients seem to relish the pornographic thrill of spying on their rivals rather than understanding how an analysis of their rival's business weaknesses might improve their own companies.

A careful examination of an individual's career details and the way they express themselves in public may provide a wealth of clues as to how they might move in the future. A 1987 article in the academic management journal *Long Range Planning* shows the sort of conclusions that can be reached:

What can be inferred from the executive's experience and from the objective record of his career? Is his age significant? A young executive may be dynamic, but may lack experience and knowledge. Where do his strengths lie? His career progress can tell us, for example, whether the subject is a risk-taker or a more steady company administrator. We should be alert to clues that suggest, for example, that his experience with only one company may have restricted the executive's knowledge of how other companies are run. Or perhaps having specialised in one function he may ignore considerations foreign to his background. For example, as an economist he may focus on statistically significant trends, dismissing small technical advantages by competitors until their cumulative advantage is established. . . . It can also be informative to research the executive's social or non-professional life. Is he interested in events outside his sphere of business? Clearly, a well-informed manager is better able to anticipate new opportunities and organise a timely response to environmental changes. What are his social contacts? What is his social milieu?[7]

There can be other clues too, from the personal style of individual chief executives. Although subjective judgements can degenerate into clubland snobbery – 'Did you see his suit – and those shoes – all that male jewellery – and that car? Far too flash and obviously putting up "front" on someone else's money' – or amateur psychology – 'Clearly an anal retentive and desperate to become "accepted"' – such indicators should not be dismissed out of hand. Companies which are named after their founders and which have buildings with the chief executive's name on them are often run by people whose sense of self-esteem can push them into making bad judgements. Some securities analysts are supposed to have begun to worry about the Coloroll conglomerate when they noticed that its chief executive John Ashcroft started to hand out coffee mugs with his photograph on them – the Group collapsed in early 1990. Lavish expenditure by directors on offices, personal transport and other creature comforts may also be a sign of weakness and, in times of crisis, vulnerability lest the company-funded lifestyle is taken away suddenly.

(1) *Observer*, 12 August 1990.

(2) *Financial Times*, 30 August 1990; *Guardian*, 1 September 1990. The four leading UK personal credit reference agencies are: CCN Systems, Infolink, Wescot Data and Credit, Credit and Data Marketing Services. The US field leader is TRW Systems. See also: *Independent*, 23 July 1990.

(3) The *Forbes* listings usually appear each October. See also *Financial Times*, 6 October 1990; *Washington Post*, 5 December 1988, 2 January 1990; *Los Angeles Times*, 10 October 1989, 8 and 9 October, 1990.

(4) *Sunday Times* Magazine, 2 April 1989, 8 April 1990, 14 April 1991; *Sunday Times*, 16 September 1990.

(5) *Independent*, 22 November 1987.

(6) *The Times*, 13 February 1988.

(7) 'Assessing Your Competitor's People and Organisation', Richard Ball, *Long Range Planning*, 1987, Volume 20, No. 2.

How to Find Out about Products, Research and Development

At around 4.40 a.m. on the morning of 25 March 1987, thieves scaled the 6-metre walls of a Milan palazzo and, inside 12 minutes, had removed just over 1,700 samples of fur coats, suedes and sheepskins, knitwear, gold lamé dresses and other prototypes from the showroom of the designer Krizia. The value was not in the garments themselves but in the opportunities for sweatshops in Hong Kong, Taiwan, Korea and the back streets of London to produce accurate copies.[1] One of the more desperate ways to research how products are made is to steal the genuine article. Other products stolen in order that they might be copied have included micro-chips[2]* and pharmaceuticals.[3]

But there are many less risky and criminal methods to obtain information about products, designs, processes, research and development. The thing to remember is that nearly all new products tend to evolve out of old ones and, while they are being created they leave all sorts of clues along the way. The objectives of technically oriented industrial espionage need not be obviously high-tech or state-of-the-art. For every company that seeks to invent completely new products, many more make money by finding more efficient ways of manufacturing well established items, or by making that subtle design difference which hits the marketing button.

Whereas the intelligence analyst of companies needs to have some form of education and experience in financial and corporate matters, the analyst of products and processes requires credentials in technology and science. This is necessary not only because of the material that has to be evaluated but because many of the agents that may be used will only respond to someone who is himself technically literate. However, commercial companies only embark on research which they hope eventually to be able to sell – the analyst who forgets this does so at his peril.

As with the other industrial espionage 'targets' we have been considering, technically oriented investigations work most effectively when there has been a great degree of preparatory work in the accumulation of openly available background material. This helps define more specific intelligence requirements.

Literature scans

The more technology- and science-oriented the product you are concerned with, the greater the level of assistance you will get from the world's electronic databases. As we saw in Chapter 3, the genesis of the online business was in scientific papers. There are three separate skills the researcher needs to develop: fluency in the various online search languages; a knowledge of the huge variety of overlapping electronic publications available; the ability to use the sources creatively – testing where information may have been withheld or, equally surprisingly, revealed.

The feature about many large technologically based innovatory companies that most aids outside researchers is that the companies tend to be quite large and that often the salesmen and technologists within them despise each other. As a result, it is not unusual to find one group busily revealing what the other has been making strenuous efforts to conceal: technologists eager to boast of their achievements to their peers while the salesmen

---

* The main customers of chips-for-copying have been the Russians. The Japanese appear to have been more interested in reverse engineering. There is a quite separate trade in *stolen* chips – large well-organised gangs, some of them Vietnamese, steal chips from California's Silicon Valley and Orange County, mostly for eventual inclusion in low-cost clone printed circuit-boards assembled in electronic sweatshops in Taiwan, Singapore and Korea. See *Los Angeles Times*, 9 April 1989, 16 October 1989 and 13 March 1990.

Product-oriented industrial espionage:

Product/specification sheets	*What the target says about itself; can be obtained by direct request, via friendly intermediaries; at trade shows*

Literature search
  trade
  academic
  conference papers
  collateral trade
  FOI requests
  patent searches
	Can be both online and print-based; academic material will talk about new theoretical developments, trade press likely to be better on contracts signed etc. 'Collateral trade press' means the trade press of essential suppliers to your target company

Trade shows	*Great for gossip and the recruitment of agents*

External scrutiny of premises
  photography
  offices
  factories
  research labs
  crate-ology
  garbology
	Much is possible simply by external observation

Examine target's R&D staff
  personnel lists
  organisation charts
  qualifications
  achievements
  new unusual appointments
	Seeing who is working on a project may tell you about its likely outcome

Garbology
  discarded documentation
  invoices for materials, manufacturing and test equipment, etc.
  effluent, swarf, etc.
	The items worth hoping to find

Agent recruitment
  unaware
  aware, corrupted
  aware, volunteer
  aware, professional
	See also Chapter 5

Reverse engineering
  legitimate purchase
  theft
	Most reverse engineering is not illegal, though it can shade over into product piracy

Forbidden material
  samples
  finished documentation
  test results
	Material you can only obtain through illegal or obviously unethical methods

hope for surprise in the market-place or, conversely, salesmen attempting some pre-emptive strike against their competitors with a 'product' with which the technologists are not entirely happy. This clash of cultures – in the computer industry it is referred to as 'sandals' and 'suits' – can sometimes be detected by comparing the coverage of a topic in a journal (as read by the technocrats) and in a newsletter or trade magazine (as read by marketing men).

In certain industries there are specialist market research operations which attempt to forecast the demand for products which do not yet exist.

Online databases are also essential for carrying out the futurologist/normative exercises to be described shortly.

Patent rights

One of the more important areas of technological investigation is seeing what patents have been filed. Much of the information is available through specialist online services, though for more thorough work, a patent agent may be needed. The advantage of patent ownership is that, once obtained, it is a monopoly which can be enforced through the courts. The proprietor has the sole right to manufacture, use, import or sell the protected product and to deny others the right to compete. The disadvantages are: the process of the definition of a patented invention is complex and time-consuming; the process itself creates publicity which might be unwelcome; the owner, not the Patent Office (or its overseas equivalents) has to do the enforcing and find the resources to do so; patent protection has to be sought individually in every country in which the product may be exploitable.[*]

Within the UK, the procedure is laid down under the Patents Act, 1977.[4] Patents last for up to 20 years, provided that all the fees are paid in due time. An invention must be new, involve an inventive step, be capable of industrial application (in other words, be a real product and not just an idea), and not be 'excluded' on the grounds that it

is merely a scientific discovery, mathematical method, an aesthetic creation (you use the copyright laws for protection here – this book is the author's copyright but I couldn't get a patent for it), or a design (for which there is separate legal protection). The inventor begins by 'filing' the application with the Patent Office, including a full description of the invention. The description must include everything that is wanted in the invention and must be sufficiently clear and complete so as to be understandable by someone who may wish to use the patent. The date of filing is the one used to test for 'newness' – the invention must never have been made public in any way, anywhere in the world. The claim is put through a preliminary check by a Patent Office Examiner to confirm that the invention is genuinely new and *is then published* as a claim. At this point it becomes available for public scrutiny. The Examiner then subjects the application to a full examination for compliance with the 1977 Act and, assuming that he is satisfied, the grant of patent follows. The timetable is: Claim must be filed within 12 months of the Application; Publication occurs approximately 18 months after Filing Date; First Full Examination Report is issued approximately 18 months after Publication of Claim. There is a time limit of 4½ years from the Filing Date for an application to meet all the requirements.

There are almost 60 patent-related online databases available. In the UK, you can hire the Patent Office itself to do some of your research – it has a Search and Advisory Service. One of its free publications says: 'Patents are . . . an ideal vehicle for monitoring the activities of a competitor.'

In the United States, disclosures under the Freedom of Information Act can be exploited.[†]

Trade shows

In many industries regular attendance at trade shows is an essential route to finding new customers and striking new deals. During my own career I have attended, both as exhibitor and visitor, trade shows in such varied industries as book publishing, online databases, over-the-counter investments, computers for the financial services industry, personal computers, large computers, counter-ter-

* Inventors within the EC can apply for protection under the European Patent Convention and it is also possible to get coverage under the Patent Cooperation Treaty to which the UK and nearly 40 other nations are party.

† See also p. 129.

rorism, computer security, and support services for insurers. Everyone who exhibits has to plan carefully if they wish to maximise the benefits. They have to decide their objectives – immediate sales, sales started on the stand but completed sometime afterwards, a widening of the list of prospects for sales or a belief that, if they don't attend, everyone in the industry will think they have gone out of business. They have to decide which visitors they wish to attract and how to repel those who will take up a great deal of time but never buy anything: at publishing trade shows the last person anyone wants to see is a prospective author – it is booksellers and overseas publishers who are wanted; at computer shows all exhibitors will shun anorak-wearing 16-year-olds, that is unless the object is to sell computer games.

The industrial spy proposing to 'work' a trade show needs to understand something of the approach taken by the exhibitor in staffing his stand. At a well run stand, the people to the fore-front are essentially greeters – their task is to be pleasant, establish who each visitor is, dump the ones lacking in any potential in the nicest possible way, and filter the prospects to the experts who will keep well to the back. Depending on the sort of trade show, the greeters may not even be permanent employees, but out-of-work actresses and models. In fact, once the spy has collected all the product literature of interest, the most useful people to home in on are not those officially staffing the stand but employees of the exhibitor who are just visiting, perhaps as part of a perk. It is from this group that the recruitment of the most useful sort of unaware agent can be made. They can be spotted by the fact that, although they hang around the stand a great deal, they obviously have no definite role.[*] You need to establish their particular expertise and then insist that they answer your questions. From there it is a matter of building up your skills of invisible inquisition and flattery.[†]

If you are using a trade show both as an opportunity for intelligence gathering and for promoting your own wares, you must expect to be subjected to hostile surveillance yourself. If you are using your technical staff as agents investigating the technical staff of your competitors, you must expect that they will both be gathering information and giving yours away. . . .

External scrutiny of premises and other indirect and collateral techniques

As we have seen earlier, it is possible to make surprisingly accurate guesses about the activities going on inside a building by intelligent surveillance of the outside.[‡] There are plenty of examples:

In a 1968 case a construction crew building a methanol plant for du Pont in Beaumont, Texas noticed a small plane flying overhead. It had been hired because competitors had hoped that, while the building's roof was still incomplete, aerial photographs of the interior would show details of a new process du Pont were rumoured to be developing. The photographers claimed that they were flying in 'public airspace' and that as a result, everything they saw was in the public domain.[5]

Leonard Fuld, who runs a competitor intelligence agency called Information Data Search Inc. in Cambridge, Massachusetts, believes strongly in the importance of corrugated boxes. He says that 95 per cent of all products manufactured today ultimately wind up being placed in corrugated boxes. If you identify the manufacturer of the boxes (the name is often printed on them) you can find out from him how many boxes have been supplied and from that calculate how many items are being shipped from the factory of interest. Fuld also supplies a complete Checklist for Plant and Site Inspection which covers many of the subjects included in this book.[6]

The corrugated box is of course only one type of 'collateral' source. Others include information from raw materials suppliers, from suppliers of specialist test equipment and from recruitment agencies which supplied specialist staff.

The CIA has a special term for one aspect of in-

---

* You should also try to identify those staffers who are present primarily for their technical expertise rather than their selling skills.

† For more on the recruitment of unaware agents, see Chapter 5.

‡ See, for example, p. 8 and Chapter 10.

telligence-by-visual-inspection – crate-ology. The term seems to have come into use during the Cuban missile crisis of 1962. Victor Marchetti, one of the CIA whistle-blowers, said it was 'a unique method of determining the contents of large crates carried on the decks of the Soviet ships delivering arms. With a high degree of accuracy, the specialists could look at the photographs of these boxes, factor in information about the ship's embarkation point and Soviet military production schedules, and deduce whether the crates contained transport aircraft or jet fighters.[7]

Futurology: the normative technique

A rather more sophisticated type of analysis is that used by the futurologists. In the early 1960s attempts were made to discover methods by which technological forecasting could be made more reliable.[*] Scientists and politicians were realising that the speed of technological change was increasing and that it would be useful to make predictions about which innovations could be expected when, and what sort of social and commercial consequences might occur as a result. Despite its sci-fi name, most of futurology was (and is) concerned with relatively small areas of technological innovation rather than broad sweeps of change. Attempts at predicting, say, the flat-screen colour TV display are much more likely to be usable than generalised forecasts of the future of an Eastern European computer industry over the next 30 years.

Technological forecasting falls into two main categories – **anticipatory** forecasting which starts from the present and seeks to extrapolate to the future, and **normative** forecasting which identifies a desirable goal and then works backwards to see what steps are necessary in order to realise it.

It is an adaption, or perversion, of the normative technique that is of greatest use to the industrial espionage analyst. The analyst identifies a technological innovation which it is believed that the target company has, or may soon, develop. He then

draws up a list of ingredients that are going to be required if the innovation is to become reality. Most of the ingredients will be already available to the innovator – the task is then to concentrate on those that might not be and to home in on evidence that the innovator is taking steps to acquire or master them.

The technique can also be used by specialist journalists. The famous 'Zircon' story resulted in the raiding of BBC premises and the home of the journalist Duncan Campbell in 1987. Campbell had been alerted to the possibility that the United Kingdom was about to launch its own spy satellite by a friend who edited a specialist newsletter. The friend had received a press release from British Aerospace about a contract for a UK armed forces communications satellite. However, the information given about its intended positioning in a geostationary orbit did not fully tie in with the published information about the proposed satellite communications system; it had a footprint (the part of the globe over which communication may be made) that made little sense. On the other hand, it occurred to Campbell, the footprint did make sense if the UK wished to make a contribution to the NSA/GCHQ global spy satellite arrangements in which GCHQ was very much the junior partner. The way to test the story, it seemed to him, was to guess what form a British spy satellite might take and who would be involved in designing and building it, apart from British Aerospace. There was a great deal of information available in the United States about the general capabilities and manufacturers of successive generations of spy satellite. Like Peter Laurie many years before,[†] he also re-read large numbers of UK government statements about defence to see if there had been some oblique reference or budgetary provision which would make sense in the context of his hypothesis. Eventually he felt he had enough collateral information with which to challenge civil servants.[8]

Reverse engineering

The difference between copying and reverse engineering is that the aim of the copyist is usually to manufacture a counterfeit article that can be

---

* Readers may like to get hold of *Technological Forecasting in Perspective*, Erich Jantsch (OECD, Paris, 1967) which is still one of the best overviews on the subject.

† See p. 10.

passed off as genuine but which is cheaper to make because there have been no development costs and because lower-quality raw materials and production techniques are used. The purpose of reverse engineering is identify the key ideas behind a product but then use them to develop something new and distinctive; the aim is to save on development costs but not to pass off the new product as a counterfeit of the original.

That at least is the formal distinction, but it is not always possible to make it in practice. Occasionally , for example, an engineer may have such a poor understanding of the underlying technology that he is studying, and be so anxious that the result will integrate properly into the overall product being manufactured, that he will copy rather than reverse engineer. That is almost certainly what happened when the Soviets copied chips originally manufactured by Intel and at the time not available to them commercially under the CoCom rules.* Intel engineers, shown examples of Russian chips, found that they had even copied non-functional squiggles on the chip mask.[9]

Two other cases which have pre-occupied the personal computer industry illustrate the difficulties. In 1981 IBM came out with the IBM PC. It used an operating system – MS–DOS – that was generally available to computers using the microprocessor upon which the IBM PC was based, the 8088/8086 family. What was proprietary to IBM however, was one particular component, the BIOS chip, which handled the Basic Input and Outputs to the System – in other words it was the chip which made the central processor, the memory banks, the screen, keyboard, disk drives, printer and modem ports, all aware of each other. Initially IBM thought it was protected against pirates because the BIOS chip had legal protection. In the early days of the PC you thus had a number of almost similar but in fact incompatible computers, all based on the MS-DOS operating system. In the UK, for example, the Sirius and Apricot computers of the time were more popular than the IBM PC. After a time, however, it was discovered that it was possible to produce a chip which had all the *functions* of an IBM BIOS, but

did not achieve the results by direct copying of the genuine article. What made it easier for the 'clone' engineers was that the IBM BIOS had one function which no one really wanted – the capacity to handle a cassette drive.† The cloners were able to get rid of the cassette player port and thus produce a 'reverse engineered' chip rather than a copied one. The Japanese manufacturer NEC had more difficulty when they tried to introduce a reverse engineered clone of the 8088/8086 called the V20/30. The court case hung on the extent to which the original internal workings – the microcode – of the 8088/8086 chip had been copied, and how far new features had been added – one new feature was that the NEC chip allowed easier emulation of an earlier PC chip called the Z80.[10] The computer industry is full of long and expensive law suits involving reverse engineering and copying.‡ In Europe there is a considerable concern that a Directive on Software Copyright is so tough in its wording that, in seeking to prevent reverse engineering, it will stifle legitimate competition from clone makers and will also make it difficult for any form of maintenance to take place on systems unless provided by the original installer.

Dirty work

When reverse engineering also involves theft of original samples and of internal documentation, it becomes dirty work.

Other forms of dirty work include the compromise and corruption of employees, specialist journalists, securities analysts and other independent industry-watchers.§

A particular favourite is the false contract offer, of which the Chesebrough Ping-Pong Ball case is one of the best known. A man called Harold Han-

---

* The aim of which was to deny the Soviets technology which might be used in the arms race.

† In the days when floppy disk drives were expensive and hard disks seldom seen on personal computers at all, programs were loaded via adapted audio cassette machines.
‡ For example, the extended disputes between IBM and Fujitsu over copyright on software for a mainframe computer family, and the 'look and feel' disputes involving the on-screen appearance of certain types of PC software in which Apple, Microsoft, Hewlett Packard and Digital Research have participated, and the separate efforts of Lotus to protect the type of 'user interface' adopted in its 1–2–3 spreadsheet program.
§ See Chapter 5 on the recruitment of agents.

sen, an employee of a music and record publisher/distributor invented a device a little like a snorkel with a ping-pong ball, the purpose of which was to help players of woodwind instruments to improve their breathing technique. It was thought that the invention might also be useful for patients with lung problems and an approach was made to a health division during which prototypes and detailed drawings were supplied. In due course Chesebrough-Ponds offered the public two similar products which they claimed they had developed themselves. Hansen's employers eventually won their case.[11]

(1) *The Times, Daily Telegraph*, 27 March 1987.
(2) See *High-Tech Espionage* by Jay Tuck, *The Steal*, by Brian Freemantle and *The New Wizard War* by Robyn Shotwell Metcalfe, *passim*.
(3) *Los Angeles Times*, 22 August 1990.
(4) The Patent Office, an executive agency of the Department of Trade and Industry, is at 25 Southampton Buildings, London WC2 1AY. It publishes a series of free booklets and guides which can be obtained from The Patent Office, Cardiff Road, Newport, Gwent NP9 1RM.
(5) Cited in *Industrial Espionage: Intelligence Techniques and Countermeasures*, Bottom and Gallati and *Corporate Intelligence and Espionage*, Eells and Nehemkis.
(6) *Competitor Intelligence*, Leonard M. Fuld.
(7) Quoted in *Deep Black*, William R. Burrows, pp. 112-113.
(8) BBC2 Secret Society series, 1987–8.
(9) See *The New Wizard War*, Robyn Shotwell Metcalfe, and *High-Tech Espionage*, Jay Tuck, *passim*.
(10) *Los Angeles Times*, 8 May 1988.
(11) See, for example, accounts in Eells and Nehemkis, and Bottom and Gallati, *op. cit.*

13 **Counter-Measures**

So far this book has more or less assumed that your aim in life is to be an industrial spy. As well as being an industrial spy you are very likely to be a potential victim. In this chapter we consider counter-measures.

To be in business at all is a risk. If you want the privileges of limited liability you must, each year, place in the public domain information about the ownership of your company, its assets and an outline of its activities. If you desire the benefits of investment from the general public, you must open nearly all of your activities to the public's scrutiny. Unless you think you can sell your products and services solely on the basis of some mysterious 'word-of-mouth' you must tell your intended market what you have to offer. Even if you avoid all these hazardous opportunities for detail of your activities to fall into the hands of, among others, industrial spies, you still can't stop them from scrutinising you and your place of business from the outside.

What we are talking about, then, is balancing various risks: the risk that competitors and predators get to know more about you than you wish – against the risks that your potential customers don't get to know that you exist, and of trying to grow a business without being able to take advantage of publicly raised finance.

An information security program is thus only partly a question of buying-in the most impressive forms of protective technology and of hiring the right sort of ex-policeman or army officer as your security manager. You have to think quite fundamentally about how you want to do business. Not every business can afford to remain private because organic growth – ploughed-back profits as the sole source of new investment – would simply be too slow. Some businesses have to be large – and become so quickly – if they are to survive. Many high-technology companies can only sell on specification – if they don't disclose what their products do and how they do it, customers won't buy.

But, within these constraints, there are choices to be made . . . .

Just as there are industrial espionage programs which are long-term and those that are brought into being to meet some immediate crisis, so counter-espionage effort can be for the duration or brought suddenly into action to tackle an emergency such as suspected leakage or sudden bout of take-over fever. The emergency package will never be as effective as the long-term plan – too much about you will already be in the public domain and, because you haven't thought about it previously, you probably won't even know which items of information are most in need of protection. Worse still, the very act of taking panic action may draw attention to the fact that something unusual is about to happen.

That was almost certainly the case in a situation I was involved in at the end of the 1980s. I was asked to investigate a series of suspected hacking incidents at one of those large industrial companies that tend to dominate the area of the town in which it is situated. The streets and pubs were named after the company's founding family and many of the workers were third- and fourth-generation employees. The company was having to restructure itself; it had expanded geographically, had bought other companies in the same industry but elsewhere in the UK; now, among other things, in the face of an overall contracting and more competitive market, it was having to 'rationalise' its production capabilities. There were two bits of evidence to sustain the hacking allegation: first, the computers seemed to be breaking down rather frequently. Secondly, whenever the company was planning a further round of 'rationalisation', the people in the town always seemed to know about it, even before the board had completed its deliberations. This was not a ruthless and heartless company, but the board felt they needed to be able to make difficult decisions in private. They wanted me to discover the hole and plug it. The computer evidence was sketchy; the computer system had been breaking down – on the other hand, it was a bit of a lash-up to say the least; on to the basic system had been added all sorts of additional modules which over the years various managers had said the company needed. There was no single software supplier and there had been quite a turn-over of computer staff, as the best ones moved on to make their fortunes elsewhere. The Head of DP complained bitterly of underfunding. There was no obvious evidence of hacking in the form of audit logs or electronic graffiti, either by staff or by out-siders. The computer was probably breaking down because it was poorly set up, overstretched and not properly maintained. 'What do you do about in-formation security in general?' I asked the Finance Director. I had arrived slightly early, been kept waiting quite a long time, and had been able to walk around the head office – in a converted Geor-gian mansion – unchallenged. 'Whenever we have something important going on, we double-up the commissionaires on the front and everybody around here is reminded to lock their offices and not leave them unattended,' he told me, 'but mostly we want employees to feel we are approachable.' What had happened seemed quite clear – the employees had seen the increased security and realised that important decisions were being made. Not being noticeably stupid they real-ised that, at any one time, there were only a small number of such decisions that could be made – and their first guess was usually the right one. The board was all but announcing its intentions.

Risk analysis/management

Too few companies do it properly, or don't com-mission such an exercise at the optimum time, but the most effective technique for limiting your losses via industrial espionage is to carry out a risk management exercise. In talking about the **manag-ing** of risk (the technique can be used for any sort of risk, including fire or fraud or receiving an ex-torsive demand), you acknowledge that while risks can't be eliminated, you can inform yourself soberly about the nature and probability of occur-rence of various risks, identify the possible counter-measures and their costs – and then make some prudent decisions: you are managing the

situation rather than just letting it happen to you. The process goes something like this:

Identify the threats
What are the things that could happen to your business that you most fear? Do you know what your secrets are – have you ever carried out an information or secrets audit? Can you identify individuals and organisations who might want to pry or take hostile action against you? What specifically might they be interested in – tech-nology, business plans, your staff, your custom-ers, your suppliers? How much do you know about these potential industrial spies? How far do you think they might go? What further level of hostility do you think you should protect against in case you are underestimating your enemies?

Identify what you must protect
What sort of artifacts, documents and people are your enemies likely to want to get their hands on? Reread the earlier chapters of this book to get some ideas – and also look at the ac-companying table.

Identify the protective measures available
Protective measures can include: your methods of doing business – deciding not to take your company public, not to issue product literature, not to employ freelance staff; administrative measures such as restricting access to important information, making staff subject to formal con-fidentiality agreements using sign-offs; techno-logical devices, such as physical and computer-related access control, closed circuit television and computer-based surveillance, etc. etc.

Associate probabilities and losses should the identified threats become real
What are the chances of any one occurrence taking place, and what would the size of loss be if it did?

Associate costs of implementing the various security measures
Of the various measures available, what would the above-the-line and below-the-line costs be? The purchase price of most security technology

is the above-the-line cost; administering it properly and the possible reduced efficiency with which you now find you are conducting your normal business affairs are the below-the-line costs.

Calculate what protective measures you should implement

In a perfect world, you try to identify the annualised losses you will suffer from the various threats. You derive an annualised loss by saying that you think that you might suffer a significant information leak say, every five years, and that each such leak might lose the company say, £1m in profits. The annualised loss is thus £1m divided by 5, or £200,000 a year. You thus derive, according to supporters

of this approach, an annual budget for protective measures of just under £200,000. The trouble is, neither the assessment of probabilities of threat nor of the losses you might make are in any way precise. . . . Indeed, the costs of the protective measures mightn't be that precise either. How, for example, do you calculate the benefits and risks of allowing the publication of a technical article in the trade about a new process, an article which both stimulates your customers into giving you orders, and tells your competitors what they must do to undermine your business?

Successful evasion

There are a few individuals and companies who have been remarkably successful at staying out of the public eye while accumulating vast wealth and power and about whom astonishingly little is known. It is only when operations like the *Forbes* 400 and *Sunday Times* Top 200 are attempted that

---

The secrets audit

The key step in managing your secrets is to identify what those secrets might be:

Obviously secret
industrial processes
forward plans
product launch details
product costings
discounts, arrangements with customers
arrangements with suppliers
financial planning
personnel records
(in the case of professional companies): client correspondence etc.
proposals for new business

Information of collateral use to a competitor
organisation charts
phone books
PR coverage
product information/advertising/catalogues
informal industry 'scuttlebutt'

Garbage
wastepaper basket contents etc.
typewriter ribbons etc.
raw materials wrapping

People
those on your staff who, for one reason or another, may be targeted, corrupted, or become disloyal

---

Philosophies of secrecy

There are two broad approaches to handling organisations with secrets to protect: permission granting and information denial. An alternative name for this is Closed and Open Systems. In a Closed System everything is deemed to be secret – the individual is informed of things on the basis of 'need to know'. In an Open System, everyone has access to everything except those items which have been specially identified as 'secret' or 'confidential'. In defence and military situations, the Closed System tends to be favoured, in commercial contexts, the Open. The problem with Closed Systems is that people who might need certain items of information in order to do their jobs properly may needlessly be denied them. The problems of Open Systems are of identifying the secrets and ensuring that they can't be identified by means of 'database compromise' (see page 65). Most organisations operate an uneasy hybrid of the two.

some of them begin to become identified.[*] Overwhelmingly there are two features that have enabled these immensely prosperous families (and in some cases, businesses) to avoid public attention: the companies are invariably private – if they have ever had to raise finance it has been on the basis of mortgages and debt, never equity; secondly, these people never, or hardly ever, give interviews.

I have my own list of favourites among the successful attention evaders who were identified by the *Sunday Times*; it is remarkable how little firm fact about any of them is available in the sorts of sources that have been covered in this book:

Clemens and August Brenninkmeyer own the Dutch-based international retail store C&A. Forbes reckons they are worth £2.7bn.

Gad and Hans Rausing are Swedish tax exiles living in Sussex whose £2,000m fortune comes from the food packaging company, Tetra Pak. Another Swedish tax exile living in the UK is Eva Larson, the daughter of a construction mogul.

Charles Feeny runs the world's largest duty free business, Duty Free Shoppers, which has an annual turnover of $2bn. The *Sunday Times* describes him as a frugal and secretive millionaire. His main vehicle is thought to be a Bermuda company, General Atlantic Holdings. His fortune hovers around the £1,000m mark.

The Barclay twins are in property having started out in estate agency. They once owned the Ellerman shipping line and offered to pay to keep Canova's *Three Graces* in the UK. They are said to be worth about £450m.

David Thompson is unusual among this group in that he was once involved with a publicly quoted company, Hillsdown Holdings, though his stake is long since sold. The *Sunday Times* labels him: 'easily Britain's most reclusive millionaire' and says that no picture of him has ever appeared in a newspaper. His wealth of £400m compares with the £90m or so that the *Sunday Times* ascribes to Britain's current best-known predator-tycoon, Lord Hanson.

The Thomson family are the controllers of D. C. Thomson, the Dundee-based publisher of, among many titles, the *Beano* and the *Dandy*, but also many regional newspapers. The company's premises are unmarked, as are its vehicles. It never makes public statements, and photographs of key members are almost unknown.

Ian McGlinn has a 30 per cent stake in the international cosmetics franchise, Body Shop, being one of its original backers. Value in April 1991: £100m. He plays no part in it.

Forbes and the *Sunday Times* are only concerned with those domiciled, respectively, in the US and the UK – neither lists the Reichmann family of Toronto who are perhaps slightly less well concealed than they used to be: they are the owners of the global property development company Olympia and York which includes London's Canary Wharf but also First Canadian Place in Toronto and the World Financial Center in New York, an oil and gas company, a pulp and paper company and investments in railroads and retail. It has been the slump in the property market in the early 1990s and their need to find occupiers and make deals involving the public sector that has made them slightly less reclusive. However, when I did a literature search I could only find three instances in which Paul, their only spokesman, had talked on the record to the press. Attempts to 'expose' them, noticeably by the *Toronto Star*, have been met by fierce litigation. Even in Britain, where they have been established for only a short period, the myriad of corporate entities, addresses from which they operate, and nominee arrangements is quite awe-inspiring. Why do some recently formed Olympia and York companies use as a registered office a dusty insurance broker's retail shop in a 'forgotten' part of North London whilst more established vehicles operate from the West End?

There appear to be no organised surveys of the discreetly rich of Japan, Scandinavia, Europe and the Arab Gulf.

There seem to be some general lessons to be drawn from these and similar examples:

Individuals
- don't ever take your company public
- make the minimum legal disclosures
- use a complex network of companies to

---

[*] See also Chapter 11. *Forbes* in particular has a fascination with these ultra-rich, super-secretive people.

handle your affairs – not all of them need be active
- live in a country other than that in which you base your core business interests
- use nominee directors as much as you can
- hide your shareholdings in nominee accounts as much as you can
- operate in as many different jurisdictions as you can; locate your master company in a country with minimal disclosure requirements
- don't break any laws of any kind
- don't ever seek publicity, even by anonymous donations of such startling generosity that the finger may point at you – but also don't make an obvious fetish of avoiding publicity
- live modestly:
  - don't buy flash houses
  - don't frequent nightclubs
  - don't attend race meetings
  - don't buy expensive pictures
  - don't have affairs with showbusiness folk
  - hope that your children and relations behave as quietly as you

Businesses
- have as complex a corporate structure as you yourself can understand
- make your master company, if quoted, essentially into an investment operation – let the operating companies stay private and thus have a lower requirement for disclosure
- keep changing the structure, always of course for some sound managerial reason, but also to make it difficult for outsiders to track
- change the year-ends every so often – that will make it more difficult for outsiders to compare like with like
- have as many different classes of shares as possible
- don't talk directly to the press; if absolutely necessary, arrange for spokesmen to brief discreetly on your behalf – and periodically dismiss as speculation rumours you have yourself started

Products
- if patentable, or even if not, keep filing misleading claims
- keep a law team ready to enter prolonged litigation to protect your rights, irrespective of whether there is either a sound legal or sound commercial reason for doing so – the aim is to intimidate and distract
- if possible within the framework of what the product actually is, keep changing its shape and its name, even if actual technological innovation is minimal. Hire an ex-IBM staffer to help you do this.

14 National Intelligence Agencies and Industrial Espionage

This has been a book principally about commercial companies spying on commercial companies. Commercial companies have always been one of the targets for NIAs – national intelligence agencies and the world's largest conglomerates have always had a relationship with NIAs that was both wary and symbiotic. There are distinct signs that the relationship is becoming both closer and more intense.

NIAs have been interested in the commercial world for a whole variety of reasons. Banks in particular have always been watched because it is through them that questionable commercial transactions can be most readily traced – the unauthorised sale of military hardware or of computer components, money laundered by international organised crime, drug money, payments to spies.[1] Companies manufacturing and trading in chemicals expect to be asked about purchases of supplies that can be used to produce weapons or refine narcotics. Electronics and computer companies know that their products and components can end up in weapons systems. Defence industry companies have had to rely on a whole series of formal and informal relationships to tell them with whom they can safely trade.

Any company that does a great deal of international business can provide 'cover' for a spying operation, either for the placement of a full-time NIA employee or for the recruitment of agents.[*] British businessmen asked to work by SIS and whose activities have become public have included Greville Wynne, who was the contact for Oleg Penkovsky, James Rusbridger, Kenneth and Keith Littlejohn, Anthony Divall and Bill Graham.[2] Companies of course provide cover for the opposition as well as for your own people.

It has never been particularly hard for NIAs to arrange 'placements' or 'recruitments'. The largest companies have always known that they needed to have a good relationship with the NIAs in the countries in which they operated. In times of crisis or war, countries in the free world depend on the large companies involved with natural resources, essential commodities, raw materials and food – they hold key buffer stocks and can make the difference between survival and defeat. The protection of the buffer stocks, oil wells, ports, etc. then becomes a matter of national as well as commercial interest. NIAs and these large companies need to have some arrangements for talking to one another. It is partly for this reason that so many of the large companies have recruited as their security managers former NIA employees.[†]

Sigint Surveillance of Private Companies

A good deal of the industrial activity of NIAs has relied on various forms of sigint; in particular the routine reading of telex traffic, a fact which journalists and writers frequently seem to rediscover.[3] It looks as though the practice has never ended although since 1985 it has been technically illegal for the intelligence agencies to tap lines without a warrant. According to a former administrative officer at the Joint Intelligence Committee, GCHQ currently circumvents the legalities by posting British Telecom monitoring staff to its telex tapping point in Palmer Street, London SW1.[4] The tapping of telex messages has always been attractive to the authorities (and others) for two reasons: the messages tend to be compact and relevant; they lend themselves readily to auto-

---

[*] Journalism is, of course, another occupation well suited to providing cover or the furnishing of freelance agents.

[†] Another reason is that the NIAs are frequently believed to provide the best training for commercial security staff.

mated scanning for names and words of interest, operating somewhat like a spellchecker in a word-processing program. (By contrast, reliable programs to do this for voice transmissions are still several years off as there are still many unsolved difficulties in computer-interpreted speech recognition where the computer is asked to understand more than a few simple words and where there can be no arrangements for the computer program to be 'trained' against the linguistic patterns of the target of interest.)

Telex, however, is of diminishing importance in commercial communications which now rely on a series of public and private high-speed computer links, mostly using variants of the X.25 packet-switch protocol. One of the more important private networks is run by SWIFT, the Society for World International Financial Transactions, which carries instructions for most global international bank instructions. Many large International conglomerates have their own networks or use the facilities of a provider like GEISCO. For a NIA, the technical difficulties of tapping these networks are no greater than tapping telex links and indeed many network engineers can pinpoint quite precisely one or more nodes within their knowledge where this takes place. Because in most cases the telephone authorities are nationally-owned, local NIAs are also able to lay down rules to the international conglomerates about the sort of encryption they can use on their networks as they pass through the NIA's home territory – usually enough, it is hoped, to prevent a company from being spied on by its commercial competitors but easy enough so that the NIA can decrypt.

In addition to this a few writers have sought to tabulate evidence of more aggressive forms of NIA-sponsored computer-based espionage – the equivalent of professional hacking. A paper given to a computer security conference in Helsinki in 1990 by Wayne Madsen[5] provided a table rating each of the world's NIAs in terms of their capabilities in this area, those of the following countries being describes as 'excellent': Australia, Canada, Finland, France, Germany, Israel, Japan, Netherlands, New Zealand, South Africa, Sweden, Switzerland, United Kingdom, United States. Strangely, Madsen gave the USSR only an "improving" rating whilst Bulgaria, often though to be

an important surrogate of the KGB's technical espionage activities, was dubbed 'average'.

Easier to tabulate has been the Eastern block use of Western online databases. At the Moscow Institute of Automated Systems there exists a National Centre for Automated Data Exchanges with Foreign Computer Networks and Data Banks and this has provided very many Russian research institutes with access to all the online services described in Chapter 3. The facilities date back at least as far as 1978. The data links have been watched with particular anxiety by the CoCom administrators, anxious to restrict any opportunities for 'leakage' of high military technology knowledge; they in turn have been strongly opposed as many US academics who have felt that academic freedom was more important and that they hoped for a corresponding exchange of research results with their Soviet opposite numbers. In 1988 the FBI attempted to obtain access to the usage logs of the big online hosts in order to scrutinise the reading habits of various of their Eastern block customers under the so-called Library Awareness Program.

Redefining the aims of national intelligence agencies

What is altering the relationship of NIAs to commercial companies is the redefining of the aims of the NIAs themselves.

During the early months of 1990 and carrying on for most of the rest of the year, large numbers of journalists were the recipients of careful clandestine CIA briefings about the future of the agency. To a lesser extent, SIS carried out a similar exercise.[6] The story being put out was this: with the ending of the Cold War and with the prospects of East-West *détente*, there was even greater requirement for secret intelligence. The emphasis though had to change from military to economic and industrial targets. More, even if we in the West didn't change our aims, then other countries' intelligence services undoubtedly were already doing so – which meant that Western counter-intelligence services had to be alert.

Journalists and writers who receive briefings and take part in off-the-record conversations have to be careful – they mustn't allow the glamour of contact with the secret world or the feeling that they are receiving privileged information blind their judgement. Occasionally they may be told outright lies – more frequently they are used as a means of getting a particular item of information, or particular set of opinions out into the public domain in a convenient and deniable form but which, the briefers hope, will influence the politicians who control the budgets of the NIAs.

Employees in NIAs fear redundancy through obsolescence as much as the rest of us. Already the CIA's China specialists had taken a knock in the 1970s when Richard Nixon, looking for an international statesman's role to compensate for the messes of Watergate, had sought to bring Peking back into a more normal trading and political relationship with the West. The Chinese specialists, with their long investment in learning the language, found their services being dispensed with. In early 1990, the prospects for CIA Kremlinologists and authorities on the Warsaw Pact did not look good as *perestroika* and *glasnost* seemed that they would alter for ever Russian internal politics and as, one by one, many of the former satellite nations sucked in by Stalin after World War II sought independence from Moscow. A year later, of course, the instant Westernisation of Eastern Europe looked a great deal less definite.

The CIA, and presumably also SIS, thus had to persuade politicians of the continuing need for their existence. As far as one can detect from the speeches occasionally given during this period by key figures in the US intelligence community and from the well briefed newspaper articles that appeared, the CIA offered the following as the essential agenda for the 1990s: economic intelligence; religious and regional problems;* narcotics; international terrorism; arms control/weapons proliferation; environmental issues, including biohazards and global warming; medical issues, in particular the spread of AIDS which was thought likely to have profound political consequences. The arguments also fluctuated over the humint/

sigint controversy,† in effect a reworking of rivalry and budget-bidding with the National Security Agency.

The more specific targets for economic intelligence were said to be: oil, commodities and agribusiness as determinants of the political behaviour of countries and regions, the threats of Japan and the European Economic Community as predatory economies that could threaten the US, and, as a counter-intelligence activity, the continued attempts of the Soviet bloc to steal strategic and non-strategic US high technology.

William Webster, until May 1991, Director of the CIA, presented the case several times during this period: 'Economic strength is the key to global influence and power. In the years ahead international friction is likely to be increasingly expressed in economic terms . . . The right information will be critical. Providing that information is, of course, the business of intelligence,' he said on one occasion, and on another: 'As the 21st century approaches, it is clear that economic considerations are increasingly tied to national security issues. There is now universal recognition that economic strength is key to global influence and power.'

Other sources were suggesting that the KGB were giving industrial espionage an even higher priority than they had in the days when the Farewell documents were being compiled (see p. 2). One theory on offer was that Gorbachev had made a deal with the KGB: reduce the level of 'internal' spying on alleged dissidents, back Gorbachev's reform programmes and in return, be backed to increase the level of commercial spying which, in any case, Russia will need if it is to catch up quickly with the West.

By May and June of 1990 the arguments in favour of an increased emphasis on economic matters were showing in terms of increased recruitment of economists, with several articles and advertisements appearing specifically to tell university students with the appropriate qualifications that the CIA was interested in talking to them.[7]

But 'economic intelligence' and the espionage effort that goes with it raises two interesting questions: how far should its agenda extend, and,

---

* This was a direct response to the criticism, already mentioned earlier in this book, that the CIA had known almost nothing of the determining movements and individuals in Iran, Iraq and Eastern Europe.

† See Chapter 5.

what methods are going to be used to collect the raw data?

The agenda of economic and industrial intelligence

For countries where all the key industries are state-owned and state-run the harnessing of the resources of the national intelligence agency to collect industrial as well as military and political intelligence presents few problems – all the material goes to strengthen the state. As we have seen, the USSR has, or at least had, a highly formal structure to achieve just this.[*] But in the 'free world', of course, industrial enterprise is substantially in the hands of private businesses. Who then, in the West, is the customer of economic and industrial espionage collected by state-funded agencies?

Unnamed CIA officers have sought to draw a distinction between what they called 'contract intelligence' – information gathered specifically to aid the securing of an identified contract in which the beneficiary would be one particular US company – and very broad trends in economies. The aim of the latter is to assist, among others, US Trade officials involved in international trade negotiations (presumably over such arrangements as the General Agreement on Tariffs and Trade – GATT – and in bilateral arrangements with trade groupings like the EC), and at identifying governments that subsidise their companies and help them set up in the US or enable them to undercut US companies.

As far as contract intelligence is concerned, officials quoted with approval what former CIA director Stansfield Turner wrote in his book *Secrecy and Democracy* about the setting up of a pilot program of industrial espionage in the late 1970s: 'Within a day, a group of six top officials in the CIA came to my office to argue that helping business was not what the CIA had been created to do,' he wrote. 'It did not, in their view, further national security; it was not the kind of worthy cause for which they had signed up.' Turner wrote that he ended the project.

But the problems are more complicated than this approach suggests. First, the CIA appear to be

acknowledging that they will be spying on the activities of their traditional friends as well as their enemies. In March 1990, William Webster said: 'Political and military allies are also our economic competitors.' In the first place, this creates difficulties because the CIA and the NSA rely on the goodwill of these traditional allies to allow them to site local stations and listening posts on their territory, goodwill which would dissipate rapidly if a British government, for example, thought that the eavesdropping activity it was providing facilities for was being directed, not at the Warsaw Pact but at conversations between British ministers or between British ministers and EC officials. Secondly, a number of the 'broad sweep' issues will initially manifest themselves as contracts which may be to the detriment of just one US company.[†] Thirdly, a number of very large international companies operate in so many territories that they are able to negotiate with governments over which countries will benefit from hosting their production facilities. These negotiations can have important benefits for the successful bidder – it is not only the number of people who would be directly involved in the venture, but the range of support services and industries that would benefit from new activity coming to the region. Motor vehicle, consumer electronics and pharmaceutical conglomerates all fall into this category. Full-blown economic intelligence, in these circumstances, implies not only trying to find what the conglomerates are thinking, but also what special deals a number of sovereign states are thinking of offering. Is this 'broad sweep' economic intelligence or 'contract intelligence'?

Collecting economic and industrial intelligence

Even supposing that it is possible to derive a clear and non-controversial agenda for this sort of activity, some of the spying methods are different from those used to collect political and defence-type secrets. Much of it will use precisely the methods described earlier in this book – it will need to be done by a NIA as opposed to an open

---

[*] See p. 2.

[†] There is no reason whatever to suppose the US is the only country likely to carry out this sort of activity; it is, however, the only country where the debate has appeared, however slightly, in the public domain.

ministry simply because governments will not want to acknowledge the files they open on their allies. An increasing amount of the information will have to come from private businesses because, in the West, that is what the economy is made up from. Moreover, one of the more significant sources of information will be businessmen themselves.

Their role, however, will be different from that played by Greville Wynne and similar figures. The stories of these people are to an extent misleading – few of the 'agents' recruited to aid economic intelligence will be asked to do anything covert – no clandestine photography, no using of dead-letter boxes, certainly no microphotography. More typically we are talking of information being exchanged in convivial social circumstances – over a drink or a meal. At such meetings the businessman provides informal assessments of overseas businessmen, politicians and officials. Perhaps the occasional photocopy of an agreement or other document is supplied. Rather more rarely a businessman might be asked to make a more formal presentation to a group of 'civil servants' whose precise role is not always clearly identified.

Why does the businessman thus recruited cooperate? Partly out of patriotism, partly because he is flattered to be asked, but also because the 'civil servants' can help him as well – with information and their own predictions of how governments might move in certain circumstances. The best agent-runners, as we have seen,* are intelligent sociable souls – spying, as far as many of the globe-trotting businessmen are concerned – is largely about friendship with a well-informed and helpful

* See p. 35.

companion. The swapping of information, up to a point, is in everyone's interest.

Are these people 'agents'? This ambiguity about what industrial espionage actually is and when one stops being inquisitive and helpful and becomes a spy has threaded through these pages. It seems as good a point as any to stop.

(1) Although known about for years, the use made by the CIA and SIS of banking information surfaced as the BCCI scandal emerged in July 1991. See, for example, *Financial Times*, 15 July 1991 and *Guardian*, 23 July 1991. The *Financial Times* also alleged a quite separate banking 'oddity' involving the Midland Bank's Midland International Trading Service subsidiary which concentrated on proving finance for arms industry deals and which apparently had strong links with British Intelligence. The Midland Bank denied many of the *FT*'s accusastions. (*Financial Times*, 15 July 1991.)
(2) *Guardian*, 4 April 1991.
(3) See, for example, Ronald W Clark's *The Man Who Broke Purple* (Weidenfeld & Nicholson, London 1977) for events just after World War I; James Bamford's *The Puzzle Palace* (Houghton Mifflin, Boston, 1982), Jeffrey Richelson and Desmond Ball's *The Ties that Bind* (Allen & Unwin, London, 1985) and Patrick Fitzgerald and Mark Leopold's *Stranger on the Line* (Bodley Head, London, 1987) for more recent events.
(4) *World in Action*, 15 July 1991; *Guardian*, 16 and 17 July 1991.
(5) Data Privacy: Legislation and Intelligence Agency Threats, published in *Computer Security and Information Integrity* (North Holland, Amsterdam, 1991).
(6) The reader may like to examine: *Los Angeles Times*, 8 April 1990; *Boston Globe*, 6 September 1990, 10 May 1991; *Washington Post*, 13 November 1990; *Guardian*, 9 April, 16 June, 13 October, 29 December 1990, 4 April, 9 May 1991; *Sunday Times*, 28 April 1991; *Independent*, 20 August, 28 December, 9 May, 15 May 1991; *Sunday Telegraph*, 4 March, 29 July, 10 February, 24 March 1991; *Sunday Express*, 24 June 1990.
(7) *Washington Post*, 13 November 1990.

I Industrial Espionage Terms

Many of these terms are from inter-nation spying, but applied to the industrial version; some come from journalists or librarians; some are unique to industrial spying.

Agent Human source of information, paid or unpaid, not on the permanent staff of the intelligence organisation using them.

Agent of influence Term favoured by Cold War warriors to identify those who are thought to be sympathetic to an enemy regime but who do not actively, or even consciously, work for it. In the industrial sense – may mean little more than someone who gossips too much with outsiders.

Analyst Intelligence organisation employee who sifts, compares and compiles material from various sources and provides conclusions, sometimes called estimates.

Asset A strategically placed human intelligence source, often within the enemy camp.

Asset tracing Activities carried out, usually by private investigators, where there has been a suspected fraud and the original owner wishes to get his hands back on goods which have been stolen from him.

Audit A detailed review by a third party; the object can be accounts, or security procedures, or valuable information assets.

Bagman A security technician specialising in rapid, covert work with a technical skill, e.g. breaking-and-entering, planting bugs, etc. Also **black bag job**.

Bibliographic Database containing references to articles and books on a subject, but not the full text.

Bugging, buggist Use of radio transmitter devices to eavesdrop; the buggist (rather than bugger) is the person who does the job.

Burnt Exposed, as in bug or telephone tap or human surveillance which has been discovered by the target.

Case officer In espionage organisations, the individual who controls an external agent or group of agents and who is responsible for an area of espionage activity.

CD–ROM Compact Disc-Read Only Memory. The same technology used for audio CDs adapted to hold large quantities of text – up to 600 MBytes at a time. Typically CD–ROMs hold large databases which can be searched using a personal computer. It is not possible for an ordinary user to *write* information on to a CD–ROM.

Chinese Walls Imaginary boundaries within City and professional organisations designed to prevent one part of a company taking advantage of information another has acquired in confidence. The trouble with Chinese Walls, it is said, is that they have chinks in them.

Classification The process of designating degrees of sensitivity to information resources and hence who should be allowed access. Traditional classifications include Confidential, Secret, Top Secret, etc., but could include Noforn (no foreigners or outsiders) and Nocontract (not to be seen by outsiders who have not signed a contract or non-disclosure agreement), etc

The Company US Central Intelligence Agency, CIA.

Competitor intelligence One of the polite pseudonyms for legal industrial espionage.

Counter-espionage Activities designed to prevent and detect espionage against oneself.

Counter-intelligence Activities designed to anticipate and forestall the intelligence methods of enemies and competitors.

Cousin UK intelligence slang for CIA staffer. An ex-cousin is someone in private security who once worked for the CIA.

Cover-name Name chosen for individual, company or project to conceal its real identity.

Cover story An explanation designed to conceal the real reasons for a particular set of activities. Also: **legend**.

Covert Hidden, or clandestine. Coverted equipment, such as radio transmitters, is designed to be readily hidden while in use.

Crateology The deduction of the contents of large containers leaving a factory by careful examination of its outside.

Cryptology The science of preparing and transmitting messages which can only be read by those authorised by the sender.

Cut-out Device to prevent an activity being traced backed to its source. This can involve the use of human intermediaries, or dead-letter boxes, or companies whose inner workings, for one reason or another, cannot be fully inspected.

Database Collection of inter-related information stored on a computer in such a way that individual elements can be rapidly searched for and extracted.

Database compromise Interrogating a computer database in such a way that it reveals more than the originator had thought possible.

Defector An individual who foresakes his original employer and joins the opposition.

Deniability The process of commissioning a course of action in such a way that, if discovered, the fact of ordering it can be plausibly denied. The usual technique is to employ some form of cut-out.

Desk man In an intelligence agency – an analyst or bureaucrat.

Desk research Work carried out from existing sources, e.g. by collection, compilation and analysis, as opposed to *field* research, where original data is collected.

Dewey Short for Dewey Decimal System – frequently used by libraries, though some have their own classification or use the one developed by the US Library of Congress.

Disinformation Propaganda or other material published deliberately to mislead the opposition.

Dog Slang for phone, from the Cockney 'dog and bone'; as in 'your dog is sick' meaning that your phone is tapped, or 'dosing the dog' – attaching a phone-tap.

Double agent A human intelligence source who works for both his client and the client's competitor.

Download Collecting information from one computer on to another which you control. Once data is on your own computer you can analyse without building up telecommunications and other costs.

Drop The rapid and usually clandestine passing of a parcel of information.

Due diligence The phrase used in corporate finance by bankers and lawyers to investigate the claims by those wishing to make a contract or raise finance. The expression includes the use of specialists to vet the personnel involved.

Dummy recruitment The making of a job offer for employment which does not really exist; the point is to use the job interview as a means of obtaining information.

Electronic mail, e-mail Computer-based messaging. There are public e-mail services such as Dialcom, I-net, CompuServe, and so on, but large companies may also have their own internal e-mail facilities, either within a single office (on a Local Area Network, for example) or between various offices.

Estimate A summary of intelligence findings; it need not necessarily include figures.

False flag Potential agents and other suppliers of information are often only willing to serve certain customers and would regard it as unacceptable to serve anyone else. In a false flag recruitment, the true ultimate customer is concealed. Thus a technical director might be prepared to pass information on to a journalist, but not to his employer's direct competition.

Field man An intelligence officer who works away from the office of his employers, as opposed to a desk man, who may never leave it.

Five Slang for the UK Security Service, MI5. Also referred to as Box 500.

Freelance Technician or other security professional who is not permanently on the staff of any organisation, but works for a variety of clients.

Friday night drop Phrase used by financial journalists and by financial public relations specialists. One of the best places to get maximum impact for a press story is in the Sunday newspapers. The best time to ensure full coverage is to leak the story on Friday evening, after trading hours, but giving the journalist enough time to check and build the material he has been given.

Friend Slang for a member of the UK Secret Intelligence Service, SIS or MI6.

Full-text database A computer-held database in which the complete text of relevant material, as opposed to summaries or bibliographic information is held. Every word in the database (except commonplace ones like 'the', 'and', etc.) can be searched.

Full-text retrieval, FTR A database program which takes raw text and converts it into a full text database.

Hacker A computer hacker used to mean 'enthusiastic innovative computer programmer'; more commonly it refers to unauthorised access to computers.

Honeypot False, but attractive-looking, information left so that it can be picked up and treated as genuine by an industrial spy. Can be a fake internal document or computer file.

Honey trap The use of sex to compromise and then blackmail someone into revealing information.

Host A large computer upon which several databases are held which provides search facilities and allows several subscribers to use them simultaneously.

Information provider Company which has collected data in electronic form so that it can be converted into a database.

In place An agent in place would typically have a job inside the 'enemy' camp.

Laundering A means of converting dirty assets (e.g. ones obtained by illegal activities or by tax evasion) into respectable funds. Can also refer to information originally obtained by unacceptable means – it is cleaned up to disguise its source or make it appear as though it was obtained openly.

Legend Detailed cover story for an individual, complete with appropriate supporting documentation.

Lifestyle check A package of enquiries, usually carried out by private detectives, into the fabric of someone's life to make sure that it 'adds up'. It includes assessing the value of the target's home(s) and key possessions, likely income and expenditure, friends and sexual habits.

Masquerade/impersonation Beyond the obvious meaning – the use of the identification card or password of a real person in order to extract information.

Menu-driven A computer program where the user is given a series of choices to select what to do next. This is in contrast to *command-driven* programs, where the user has to remember a series of words or expressions in order to get the computer to do anything.

Microfiche Storage medium consisting of much-reduced photographic sheets. Often used for companies data and legal documents. Requires special reader.

Microfilm Similar to microfiche except that reels of film are used instead of sheets. Often used for archiving newspapers etc. Microfilm can also mean photographs (usually taken covertly) with sub-miniature cameras like the Minox.

Microform Collective term for microfiche and microfilm.

Mole Hostile agent or traitor buried deep within an intelligence organisation.

Mr Phelps From the 1960s TV series 'Mission Impossible'; Phelps was the leader who would receive his commissions via a self-destructing tape which always concluded with the warning that if he or his operatives were caught, their actions would be disavowed. 'Mr Phelps' is thus a security professional who may, if necessary, have to take the rap and who guarantees not to reveal his client.

Net worth investigation Investigation and calculation of how much an individual is worth once liabilities have been subtracted from assets – a financially oriented form of the **lifestyle check**.

Numeric database Database with mainly statistical information.

Overt Open, as in open sources, and as opposed to covert.

Passive Short for passive bug. Most bugs are miniature radio transmitters and hence can be detected by use of specialist radio receivers. Passive bugs don't themselves transmit, but, if you flood them with an external radio waves, they will react by modifying the transmission so that an adjacent receiver will be able to hear what is going on in the room where the passive bug is located. Passives are quite difficult to detect.

Pavement artist Security professional specialising in following people on foot.

Perception management A sophisticated form of public relations in which the aim is to change the way in which the public (or a section of it) perceives a company, organisation, product or person.

PNC Check Police National Computer. Access by outsiders, or access by authorised users for an unauthorised purpose is an offence against the Official Secrets Act; however many private investigators claim that it continues to be easy to arrange a PNC background check on individuals despite several prosecutions of police officers.

Pretext call Making an enquiry by telephone and pretending to be someone authorised to obtain confidential information, e.g. banking or social security details.

Rupert SAS slang for officer; used in security consultancies with ex-SAS personnel.

Sanitise Prior to releasing information – removing compromising or confidential details.

Shrieker (or **screamer**) Bug-detection equipment which relies on audio feedback: a whistle is heard as the bug is located back.

SIC Standard Industrial Classification.

Six Slang for UK's Secret Intelligence Service, SIS or MI6.

Spook Intelligence or security operative.

Stringer Freelance operative.

Sweep Use of electronic counter-measures equipment looking for bugs and taps.

Tapping Surveillance on telephone, telex and data lines, as opposed to bugs, which rely on miniature radio transmitters. Some surveillance equipment is both bug and tap, as when a telephone line is eavesdropped, but the results are then transmitted by radio to a listener, as opposed to being captured locally on a tape recorder.

Tempest Actually one code-name for a set of measures to prevent stray electro-magnetic radiation from leaking from such equipment as VDUs and printers and the cables that connect them. Now used informally to cover the radiation leaking itself.

Trade (of information) Exchanging one item of information for another, not necessarily contemporaneously. This frequently happens between journalists, who share non-critical information, hoping for a similar favour to be returned at some future time.

Twenty-two Slang for the UK's Special Air Service, or SAS; the full name of the regular (non-territorial) unit is 22SAS.

Turned An intelligence agent who has been uncovered by those on whom he was originally spying but who has been left in place, in order to pass misleading information to his original client.

Walk-by A preliminary survey of a building or computer that is later to be penetrated: the operative 'walks by' for a good look without drawing attention to himself.

Walk-in In private security this means someone who executes a job simply by walking into a building (as a repairman or cleaner, for example). In orthodox spying, it is someone who defects unannounced by walking in to an embassy or other building where they hope to be welcome.

Watcher Someone specialising in physical surveillance.

II Linking to Online Services

Computer Requirements

To link up to online services, you need a simple low-cost personal computer, preferably though not essentially with a hard-disk, a modem (the device for linking a computer to the public telephone line) which these days typically comes as a card which fits inside a personal computer, and some communications software.

It is only these two last items that can cause any difficulty at all. As of the time this book is being written, modems suitable for online services should operate to the international standards referred to as V.22 bis. This allows information to be received at a maximum speed of 2,400 baud, which is roughly equivalent to 240 characters a minute – this is slightly faster than most people can read.[*] Faster data speeds are possible but not common and there is as yet no universally agreed way in which this is to be done (it involves various forms of compressing data as it is sent and then uncompressing it at the reception end). Nearly all modems now sold conform to what are called Hayes standards (sets of commands the modem accepts to change speed, alter from receive to transmit, decide whether to dial number using pulses or tones, etc.) which means that most popular communications software will work immediately.

Modern communications software provides for automatic dialing in to a host and then capturing the result on screen and, if required, also saving on to disk. The shareware package Procomm and the commercial package Odyssey are particularly recommended but there are others. The Terminal within Windows 3.0 is quite adequate for occasional use. The software may need some initial setting up to match the exact way in which the host at the far end is itself set up. If you don't get a good match you may find your computer screen filling up with corrupted or nonsense characters.

Communications Settings

The usual things you have to set up are:

Speed
Word length (usually 7 or 8)

Parity (usually even, odd or none)
Stop bit (usually 1 or none)

A typical 'formula' would be 1200 7e1 – meaning a speed of 1,200 baud, a word length of 7, even parity and 1 stop bit. You don't need to understand what any of this means so long as you can match the requirements of the host (their literature should tell you what that is) to your software.

MNP

Increasingly, you may also see some reference to 'MNP'. MNP refers to a series of protocols for automated error detection and compression. The aim is to remove some of the errors that occur as a result of line noise and also to speed up the process of getting data from one computer to another by compressing the data just prior to transmission and then decompressing it at the other end. Depending on the type of data being sent, you might be able to get a 75 per cent improvement. MNP comes in various classes – indicating degrees of performance. You can acquire MNP either by buying a modem with MNP facilities or from some communications software. You can connect to a service that says it offers MNP even if you don't have the right sort of equipment – the modem at the far end will detect that you do not and will then switch itself automatically to 'ordinary' mode.

Terminal emulations

You may also see some reference to 'terminal emulations'. To receive most online services you can either ignore this bit, or set the emulation to 'ANSI' or 'VT100'. If you are receiving a videotex (viewdata) service, you may need to use the emulation called 'PRESTEL'.

Directories

Again, most communications software provides you with an automatic telephone directory – you can set up the telephone number for each host service you call together with its specific 'formula'. Once you have done this, logging in then becomes simply a matter of a few keystrokes. Some communications software has a

[*] Hosts tend to charge the same connect-time rate whatever the speed you use for accessing their facilities. At 2,400 baud you are capturing eight times as much information as you are the speed of the very simplest and cheapest modems – 300 baud.

'scripting' facility so that it deals with network and pass-word instructions completely automatically – the soft-ware 'learns' from your keystroke the first time you con-nect to a database/host service and then can be made to 'remember' it for the future.* Some hosts provide soft-ware which is ready-tailored for their needs – but that software may not work well with other hosts.

Most database services are available directly at the end of an ordinary telephone number, no matter where

the hosts are actually located. The Londoner who wants to reach the Palo Alto-based computers of Dialog dials a local London number which is actually answered in Cali-fornia. Elsewhere in the UK, it may be more economical to use a data network service such as PSS or I–Net. These too will be local or semi-local phone numbers, but in this instance you will simply be connected to a net-work and you must then tell it where you want to go. The commands to do so may appear rather obscure, but most host services provide instructions which you can follow quite adequately without understanding what is going on. Again a 'scripting' facility in your communications software will mean that you can automate the network connection process.

* This can of course present a security risk, if your 'script' con-tains details of confidential passwords – the way round this is to use the script for everything except the final entry of the pass-word itself.

III Desk-Top Databases

The task of maintaining a library of information is made much easier by the existence of the desk-top computer as a cataloguing device. It is even possible, given the low cost of large hard disks, to store useful amounts of raw data, but it is important to understand where the substantive costs actually fall. As we saw in Chapter 2, the elements are:

- capital cost of computer hardware
- purchase price of database package
- costs of categorising raw intelligence material
- costs of inputting selected materials
- ease and speed of retrieving desired materials when required
- maintenance and back-up costs
- the costs of any system of internal security you may need to impose (what you have gathered by way of intelligence may be of considerable direct value to your opposition as well as telling them what you know, and by implication, what you might be thinking)

In reverse order of expense: the price of the database software, the price of suitable hardware to run it on, the human beings who must make it all work.

Bibliographic databases

In terms of what computers can deliver, the big divide is between a **bibliographic** approach – where the computer acts as a catalogue of material which is kept in its original print form – and **full-text**, where all or a significant amount is held in electronic form and can be summoned immediately to a computer screen and then printed out if required.

Much of the raw intelligence material most companies acquire is in print form – trade magazines, articles ripped from newspapers, copies of catalogues, price lists, annual reports, market research findings, and so on. This fact appears to favour the bibliographic approach. The raw material is kept in box files, on shelves or in cupboards and given a simple **shelf mark** or **accession number** so that it can be located quickly. Someone has to act as librarian, receiving and evaluating the material, making sure that each item can be found in a variety of ways – by author, title, subject-matter and content. The content is usually described in telegraphic style using a series of **keywords,** which are what subsequent searchers will use when they embark on an information retrieval exercise. The librarian has to try to anticipate all the ways in which later readers may want to find a particular item, so the keywords have to include certain thesaurus-like qualities. However if the thesaurus is too broad, users may find that the computer is finding too many irrelevant entries. On the other hand, if there is no thesaurus and the librarian's anticipation has been poor, the searcher may miss useful information. In some bibliographic database systems it has been judged advisable to use a formal dictionary of approved words to get over the problem – but of course this then adds to the costs of the administrative overhead.

There is a further problem, common to all print libraries – how do you discipline your readers so that they return the borrowed material – and replace it in the correct place?

The choice of a software package for bibliographic catalogues is not completely straightforward. At relatively low cost, around £100-200, it is possible to purchase what are called 'flat-file' database packages. Essentially, these create on-screen versions of the orthodox card-based filing system still used by many traditional libraries. They are simple to set up and use but their main drawback is that the number of ways in which they can be searched is limited: you will be able to search by author, title and subject, and when you do you will have the 'file-card' presented to you on screen. The card will probably have some space for what is called 'free form' text, but the software will probably not search it – if you place keywords there, the software will not 'know' about them. Many of the low-cost flat-file databases are designed principally for name-and-address applications and may not directly suit a more sophisticated cataloguing system. Another aspect to watch for is that low-cost data retrieval software packages often have a strictly limited capacity. There are a couple of specialist 'shareware' packages for the IBM PC which may be worth exploring if your needs are modest – PC-Lit and Business Librarian.[*] However, it is not worth skimping on such software, the capital cost of which will only be a very

* Sources of shareware programs can be found from the advertisements in the more serious type of computing magazine.

small part of your budget. If you make a mistake and buy an underpowered package you may have to re-input all your data into a new one. Estimate your future needs carefully.

Up the market, both in price and facilities, are the so-called 'relational' database packages. One of the field-leaders is the dBase family and there is an important family of sophisticated database packages using principles known as SQL. Prices for these are at the £350 plus level. However, what you acquire when you buy these packages are not instant solutions – essentially they are special-purpose programming languages which enable you (or someone you pay) to design the particular database you want. The result, however, can be highly effective, provided you are clear about what you want the database to do.[*]

Full-text storage

Given all this complexity, the **full-text** approach is less costly than may at first appear. At the heart of it is a rather different sort of software package which takes raw text files (or files converted from word-processors) and then indexes *every* word in the file, with the exception of a small list of everyday words like 'of', 'the', 'and', 'but' and so on. Once started the indexing is completely automatic and all the human supervisor has to do is to select which documents to put in. When a researcher wants to locate information, they type in collections of 'relevant' words, linking them with 'and' or 'or', as appropriate.

The computer searches its resources and then comes back with lists of files which contain the selected words. The searcher can refine or change his or her demands if the computer comes up with too much or too little by way of information.[†] The searcher then selects the files

he or she wishes to view and the software presents the appropriate material on screen – it can usually be printed out as well.[‡]

Prices for software in this category are usually above £500 for full-featured packages – a cut-down version may not be powerful enough for the workload.

However the full-text approach is not without its disadvantages as well. In the first place, the print material has to be converted into electronic files. Some material may be available in electronic form already, in the form of word-processor material or, as we will see in the next chapter, downloaded from online services.[§] But to get most print material into electronic form you have only two choices: hire a copy-typist or use an optical character reader (OCR) scanner. Details about these appear in Appendix IV.

The next problem is that full-text retrieval software tends to create rather extensive supporting files as it indexes. In order to get the necessary speed of searching, it is not the original files which are searched, but indexes containing pointers to the contents of the files.[**] These indexes are created when the files are entered into the database – this process itself can take significant amount of time if the raw text is of any length. The indexes themselves take up space on your computer's hard disk, often at least as much as the original text files themselves. So you need a very large hard disk – 80 Mbytes, at least, even for a modest application. The price of hard disks is falling rapidly, but you need to make the calculations (or have them made for you) carefully.

The great advantages are: the computer produces its material immediately, rather than simply telling you where to go to find it; there are almost no 'librarian'-type costs; there are no unique originals which can get mislaid (the database files should, of course, be backed-up, but this is inexpensive). The disadvantages, apart from capital costs are: you can get false 'hits' by not framing your requests for information clearly and unambigu-

---

[*] If you have a very large budget, you could consider buying an all-in so-called 'optical storage' filing cabinet. These are often used by insurance companies, lawyers and others who need to retain written documents in their original form. The 'filing cabinet' contains a scanner which photographs the original documents which are then stored on a high-capacity optical disc. The filing cabinet also contains bibliographic-type software with which the various electronic photographs can be retrieved. The only thing that is 'searched' are the bibliographic-type entries, not all the words on the photographed sheet, of course.

[†] By way of refinement it is also possible for some full-text retrieval software packages to find articles which contain occurrences of words *within* so many words of each other. Thus, if you were looking for references to computers and crime, you may not want articles in which those two words were widely separated because the article may not be relevant to your needs. On the other hand if you ask the software to search for the phrase 'computer crime', it will search only for that. The solution, if the software will let you is to ask for 'computer' and 'crime', but within, say five words of each other in an article.

[‡] Full-text retrieval software packages available at the time this book went to press and which have the requisite features include ZyIndex, Personal Librarian, and FetchIt. But see if you can try before you buy.

[§] The contracts of supply of some online services seek to prohibit the re-use of material in electronic form. The main purpose of such clauses is to prevent commercial republication of material, but they can also have the effect of denying the re-use in private retrieval systems of the sort described in this chapter.

[**] All word-processors have facilities for what is called 'string searching' – they will work their way through a file looking for occurrences of a particular sequence of letters. This technique is far too slow for full-text retrieval software: string searches can only find one sequence at a time and going through several hundred thousand words from the beginning even if they are all stored on a fast hard disk takes far too long to be practical.

ously (but you can always retry); the efficiency of the operation can depend critically on the size of individual document, you place into the system – if your documents are too long you may discover that the software is finding too many marginally relevant 'hits'.[*]

* You can of course combine the full-text and bibliographic approaches within a full-text package. In fact, this is what I do. Longer, less-wanted articles are not stored in their entirety; instead I prepare a 'bibliographic' entry on my word-processor which provides keywords and lists a physical location (shelfmark) for the actual print material. The bibliographic entry is then entered into the full-text database. During a search, therefore, I may find a combination or materials both immediately on the computer and in 'hard copy'. With some packages you can even combine *images* and text – useful if you wish to store pictures as well as text, or if you are prepared to store some 'dif-

Nevertheless, integrated systems which include OCR scanners and full-text retrieval software do work and, depending on the quality of your originals and the overall expectation you have of the results, can easily justify themselves. I put together such a system for a computer disaster and crime database a few years ago when prices for the components were higher; today a ready-built total package along similar lines (not built by me) has been a modest commercial success and is used, among others, by the Serious Fraud Office and the Metropolitan Police Computer Crime Unit.

ficult' text originals as images. FetchIt, for example has a limited capability to do this. However, images stored on computer take up a great deal of disk space.

IV **OCR Scanners**

OCR scanners are used to convert printed material – typescript, articles from newspapers and magazines – into computer-readable form. They are similar to those used to scan picture images for later inclusion in desk-top publishing, for example. Typically, scanners are either roller-fed (like a typewriter but with a scan-head instead of a print-wheel) or flat-bed (where the page stays still and a moving scan-head passes across it).* For a full-text database to work properly, it is not enough, of course, for the mere image of a chunk of text to be scanned into the computer – the scanned image has itself to be translated into individual characters.

For most computers currently to be found on desk-tops, this procedure is not trivial. It is easy enough to 'read' clean typewritten originals in 10- or 12-pitch, but most text printed in magazines is of a smaller size, there are often several sizes of print on the same page, there is quite a variety of typeface in common use, the characters will be proportionally spaced as opposed to mono-spaced, some characters may be touching each other, and some scanners react badly to certain colours and cer-

tain paper qualities.

If the raw material is 'clean', then a conventional image scanner and some specialist software may give acceptable results, though to work at reasonable speed, they will need a PC with a fairly powerful processor – a '386 or '486 rather than a '286. For most purposes, how-ever, OCR scanners that can cope with all the variants that occur in newsprint need to have their own internal computing power (in the form of a special board inserted inside the PC) rather than using the PC itself.† These can easily cost as much again as a top-line desk-top PC, and even then may require more manual supervision and post-scan editing (correcting the resulting text file for mistakes the OCR software has made) than is entirely convenient. 'Difficult' originals can take quite some time to be read in and may have quite a high error rate. Try the equipment on typical originals you will be using before you make a purchase.

---

† Some manufacturers refer to ICR as opposed to OCR. ICR stands for Intelligent Character Recognition. Such scanners use artificial intelligence or pattern recognition techniques rather than the slower 'exhaustive' methods used by conventional OCR software.

---

* The hand-held scanners used for capturing small images for inclusion in graphics and desk-top publishing software are not really suitable for serious OCR scanning.

V Costs

What are typical costs of industrial espionage? Much of it costs almost nothing. There is negligible expense in gathering together the sales literature and annual report of companies in which you are interested. There are almost no costs involved in the careful filing away of the trade magazines to which you already subscribe, or in cutting out clippings of interest from national newspapers. These raw materials form the basis of almost any industrial espionage exercise you may wish to commission.

Beyond these, the costs of the products and services available bear very little relationship to the benefits you may obtain. Whatever you do, the real cost is in people, not technology. The key is to have a sufficiently clear idea both of what you want to achieve by way of end-result and which low-cost forms of information are available. Hence the chart which has been referred to throughout . . .

Online Searches

Most of the online information you will want you will obtain via various online hosts – see Chapter 3 for more details. Sign up costs vary from zero to about £250 – the higher fees usually include training and documentation whereas the zero sign-up cost services sell these as extras. Thereafter there is little consistency in pricing and so giving "typical" price indications is difficult. Apart from special out-of-business-hours tariffs, expect to pay between £1.40 and £4 a minute. Some services charge you all the time you are logged on to the service, some charge you principally while downloading "useful" information – and they may charge for this on a per-record or per-line basis. You keep costs down by being highly disciplined while connected to the various database services.

Libraries

Public libraries are free, though any realistic costing has to include travel and waiting time for whoever is using the library – and photocopying costs. Private libraries usually charge on a subscription basis but their tariff may also include arrangements for searches to be carried out on your behalf by library staff – and in some cases for the results to be faxed to you.

Professional Information Intermediaries

Professional Information Intermediaries – those that concentrate on business topics anyway – charge from £40-100 per hour plus any online costs. There will also be a start-up fee and you may be required to pay a deposit against fees to be incurred. The reasons for the differences in price are: speed of response, range of online materials instantly available, level of confidentiality offered. You keep the costs down by defining the objectives as carefully as possible and by asking for delivery in stages, sanctioning further expenditure based on the quality of the results so far received and the searcher's

---

Idealised Management Consultant's Strategic Overview of Information Acquisition Costing Methodology:

- Define information required
  - define data
  - calculate value to customers
- Select & cost methodology/methodologies
  - is information available openly?
  - what benefits are expected?
  - cost out – what is cheapest method of acquisition? Which is easiest, or runs least risk?
  - is information time-critical?
  - if information not available openly
    - are you prepared to use covert methods?
    - what are the consequences of discovery
      - in commission?
      - afterwards?
    - what value do you place on the risks?
- Estimate costs of collecting raw data
  - direct fees (e.g. online services, external staff fees)
  - support cost (e.g. telecommunications costs, transport, own staff, staff working expenses)
  - amortised costs of capital equipment (e.g. computers, specialist electronics)
- Transcribe raw data (if material is not instantly usable, e.g. tape recordings, print material needed in electronic form, computer-readable material requiring to be transferred into another format)
- Analyse data and prepare report
- If necessary, redefine information required

estimates of what more could be achieved. If you can guarantee the searcher a given level of work, costs may come down further. The smaller and more discreet intermediaries usually don't advertise. The alternative is to have someone with the appropriate skills and knowledge on your own staff.

Private Detectives

You can hire a basic gumshoe to follow someone around, take photographs, retrieve the odd bit of garbage, for under £100 a day plus expenses. You mightn't get very much class at that price. You can also pay more than £1000/man/day from one of the top-line companies and if you are obviously involved in takeover bid. The difference in price is down to quality of work, quality of contacts, quality of education and the fact that the detective has expensive offices full of fine furnishings and well-brought-up secretaries.

Debugging costs from £300/day, to reflect the price of the equipment used. The best deals are available if you retain someone to carry out regular sweeps – that is if you believe you are a potential victim of electronic eavesdropping.

Bugs, Taps

See chapter 7 for details. Looking first at equipment you can use without breaking the law: miniature tape-recorders cost from £30 up; if you want an ultra-compact one, expect to pay £90 or so. there are versions adapted for the "security" market which offer extra-long playing time by slowing the tape speed right down; these cost approximately 75% more than their unmodified equivalents. Long-distance mikes sold for use with video cameras cost £40 or so; ordinary sub-miniature mikes cost from £10.

Manufacturers of bugs and taps tend to charge what they think the market will bear. These are guide prices for mass market products; you'll pay much more if you commission a one-off special.

Bug modules (that is, for incorporating in housings of your choice) cost from £10 in kit form (£20 for a little more sophistication) and £30 ready-built for simple but effective "airband" work. Complete bugs, disguised as power-plugs, pens, calculators, lighters, and so on cost from £100; again most of these will operate in the "airband". More stable bugs, operating away from the usual frequencies will cost £250 and above. You can buy compact radio mikes for use with video cameras or for stage work for about £45. Radio receivers modified to receive bugs sell for around £150 but you can also use scanners (see below).

Taps, ready built, cost from £70, but simple tape-interface kits cost about £20. If your tap has a radio

transmitter attached, prices start around £120. Harmonica or infinity bugs are priced at £250 and up.

De-bugging equipment

Simple bug-detectors are fairly useless but are priced at £120 and above. Up to a point, you can use a scanner as a bug detector. Professional bug-detection equipment sells for £5000 and up. A reasonable quality spectrum analyser costs about £4000 but you can pay a great deal more.

"Tempest" detection equipment

Equipment you can actually use in the field, as opposed to play around with on a work-bench costs in excess of £10,000. In practice you need quite a bit of skill to operate this sort of kit, so the best thing to do is to hire engineers with the kit. Daily rates start at £500; probably rather more if the technology is being used non-defensively.

Scanners, etc

A scanner can be used to carry out some forms of bug detection and also for eavesdropping on cellular and other radio-based conversations – but see chapter 9. Rather limited scanners, not well suited to UK use, can be bought for under £100. At a practical level you need a scanner capable of receiving from 25 MHz to about 1000 MHz and able to receive both narrow band AM and narrow band FM transmissions. Handheld models cost from about £250 and are best bought from amateur radio outlets rather than High Street electronic goods shops. Versions for in-car use cost £10-20 more. Computer-controllable scanners cost from £450. The most popular semi-professional model costs about £800.

For UK use for the purposes described in this book, the minimum specification is: frequency coverage to include 46-50 MHz (the cordless telephone and other "low power" devices band; 68-88 MHz (VHF low band); 108-136 MHz (strictly speaking the VHF air band but also the most popular bug band - note that you must be able to resolve this in narrow-band frequency modulation and not just in AM); 138-175 MHz (VHF high band, the marine VHF band and also some radio mikes); 410-470 MHz (commercial UHF band); 915-970 MHz (UK cellular bands). Guidance as to who is licensed to transmit where is to be found in the *United Kingdom Table of Radio Frequency Allocations* published by HMSO. You should also ensure that the scanner can step in 12.5 kHz channels – some low costs scanners operate only in 5kHz increments. Most scanners have some gaps in their coverage – it makes their design easier – the most usual being 550-800 MHz or so, which is used for television.

VI Useful Addresses

A truly comprehensive list of addresses relevant to the subject-matter of this book would occupy several times the number of pages of the existing text. The addresses given here are merely a starting point for enquiries. Inclusion does not imply any special recommendation nor are there necessarily sinister reasons for any exclusions. The list is optimised for a UK readership – if you live outside the UK your local reference library is probably the best place where to start finding local equivalents. Such is the speed of change that some information here may be out-of-date by the time you come to try to use it.

The two standard reference guides to UK information sources are Aslib's *Directory of Information Sources in the United Kingdom* (Aslib Publications 20-24 Old Street, London EC1V 9 AP, 071-253 4488) and Croner's *A-Z of Business Information Sources* (Croner House, London Road, Kingston-upon-Thames, Surrey KT2 6SR, 081-547 3333). Local reference libraries should have both.

Online Hosts

These are the organisations through which individual databases are obtained.

Dialog Information Services, 3460 Hillview Avenue, Palo Alto, CA 94304 (415) 858 2700. Dialog Europe, PO Box 188, Oxford OX1 5AX, (0865) 730275

FT Profile, PO Box 12, Sunbury on Thames, Middlesex TW16 7UD 0932 761444

Maxwell Online, Achilles House, Western Avenue, London W3 0UA, 081-992 7335 (includes BRS)

Reuters Textline, 85 Fleet Street, London EC4P 4AJ, 071-250 1122

BT Managed Network Services, Network House, PO Box 402, Hemel Hempstead HP3 9XT, 0800 200 700

Nexis, International House, St Katherines Way, London E1, 071-488 9187

Istel I-Net, PO Box 1488, Redditch, Worcestershire B98 8PD, 0527 28515

CompuServe, PO Box 676, Bristol BS99 1NZ, Freephone CompuServe

Credit Databases

Infolink, Coombe Cross, 2-4 South End, Croydon CR0 1DL, 081-686 7777

Infocheck, Scrutton Street, London EC2R 4RQ, 071-377 8872

CCN Systems Ltd, Talbot House, Talbot Street, Nottingham NG1 5HF, 0602 410888

Dun & Bradstreet International, Holmers Farm Way, High Wycombe, Bucks HP12 4UL, 0494 422154

Libraries

British Library Business Information Service, 25 Southampton Buildings, London WC2A 1AW, 071-323 7454, 071-323 7979

City Business Library, 106 Fenchurch Street, London EC3, 071-638 8215

Information Intermediary Services

The two biggest are:

London Business School Business Information Service, Sussex Place, Regents Park, London NW1, 071-724 2320

Financial Times Business Research Centre, London SE1 9HL, 071-873 3000

Financial Information

Companies House, Crown Way, Maindy, Cardiff CF4 3UZ, 0222 388588; 55-71 City Road, London EC1Y 1BB, 071-253 9393

Interpretative material, or for non-UK companies, is available via various online services – see Chapter 3.

Key Ratios

The company with the widest range of reports for UK companies is: ICC Information Group Ltd, 16 Banner Street, London EC1Y 1AU, 071-253 9736

Telephone Numbers

Phone Base, British Telecom, Tinsley Park Computer Centre, Units 1, 2 & 3, Tinsley Park Close, Sheffield S9 5DE, 0800 91999

Patents

Patent Office, Cardiff Road, Newport, Gwent NP9 1RH, 0033 814000

Search and Advisory Service, Hazlitt House, 45 Southampton Buildings, Chancery Lane, London WC2A 1AR, 071-438 4747

Law Courts

Major civil matters are dealt with at The Royal Courts of Justice, Strand, London WC2, 071-936 6000

The Writ Office has details of writs served. The Royal Courts hold details of judgements and orders made as a result of their judgements; however, if the two parties settle, even after a hearing has commenced (and this is what happens most of the time) no judgement is made and so nothing will be recorded. The details are held for ten years at the Royal Courts and all judgements made since 1947 are available on the Lexis database. The Lexis database also holds reports of cases in which some new point of law is involved.

Minor civil matters are handled by the various local County Courts, details in the telephone book. All judgements where £10 or more is outstanding one month after the date of judgement are registered with Registry Trust Ltd, 173-175 Cleveland Street, London W1P 5PE, 071-380 0133. County Court judgements are also held by the various online databases.

Land Registry

Land Registry, 32 Lincoln's Inn Fields, London WC2A 3PH, 071-405 3488

Details of charges on land, planning consents, etc are held by the relevant local authority.

Motor Vehicles

DVLC, Swansea SA99 1AA, 0792 782576

Births Deaths Marriages

General Register Office, St Catherine's House, 10 Kingsway, London WC2B 6JP, 071-242 0262

Public Records

Public Records Office, Chancery Lane, London WC2, 071-876 3444 *and* Ruskin Avenue, Kew, Richmond, Surrey TW9 4DU

Somerset House, Strand, London WC2R 1LP, 071-405 7641

Bibliography

Much of the material has come from articles and electronic services rather than books, but the following were consulted. The publisher given is the original one; most US books have a separate UK publisher, and vice versa. A number of these titles have also appeared in paperback editions.

Allen, Thomas B. & Polmar, Norman, *Merchants of Treason*, Delacorte Press, New York, 1988

Andrew, Christopher, *Secret Service*, William Heinemann, London, 1985

Bamford, James, *The Puzzle Palace*, Houghton Mifflin, Boston, Mass, 1982

Barlay, Stephen, *Double Cross* (called *The Secrets Business* in the United States) Heinemann, 1973

Bergier, J., *Secret Armies: The Growth of Corporate and Industrial Espionage*, Bobbs-Merrill, Indianapolis, 1975

Bosworth-Davies, Rowan, *Too Good to be True*, Bodley Head, London, 1987

Bottom, Norman R. and Gallati, Robert J., *Industrial espionage: intelligence techniques and countermeasures*, Butterworths, Boston, Mass, 1984

Burn, Gordon, *Somebody's Husband, Somebody's Son*, William Heinemann, London, 1984

Burrows, William E., *Deep Black*, Random House, New York, 1986

Campbell, Duncan & Connor, Steve, *On the Record*, Michael Joseph, London, 1986

Cornwall, Hugo, *The Hacker's Handbook*, Century-Hutchinson, London, 1985, 1986, 1988, 1989

Cornwall, Hugo, *DataTheft*, Heinemann, London, 1987, and Mandarin, London, 1990

Corson, William R., *The Armies of Ignorance*, Dial Press, New York, 1977

Corson, William R., Trento, Susan B., Trento, Joseph J., *Widows: the explosive truth behind 25 years of Western intelligence disasters*, Crown, New York, 1989

Deal, Terrence and Kennedy, Allen, *Corporate Cultures*, Addison-Wesley, New York, 1982

Dobson, Christopher and Payne, Ronald, *The Dictionary of Espionage*, Harrap, London, 1984

Drucker, Peter, *Technology, Management and Society*, Heinemann, London,

Eells, Richard and Nehemkis, Peter, *Corporate Intelligence and Espionage*, Macmillan, New York, 1984

Ernst & Whinney, *Attitudes of Companies in Britain to Fraud (Consensus Research)*, London, 1985 & 1987

Ernst & Whinney, *Computer Fraud* (report presented to National Commission on Fraudulent Financial Reporting), New York, 1987

Fraud Trials Committee Report (Lord Roskill), HMSO, London, 1986

Freemantle, Brian, *The Steal: Counterfeiting and Industrial Espionage*, Michael Joseph, London, 1986

Fuld, Leonard M., *Competitive Intelligence*, John Wiley & Sons, New York, 1985

Garson, Barabara, *The Electronic Sweatshop*, Simon & Schuster, New York, 1988

Gibbons, Don G., *Society, Crime and Criminal Careers*, Prentice-Hall, Englewood Cliffs, NJ, 1968

Gordon, Ian, *Beat the Competition!*, Basil Blackwell, Oxford, 1989

Gordon-Lee, J. N., 'Industrial Espionage and Business Intelligence: their role in business', unpublished thesis, University of Bath School of Management, 1985

Hamilton, Peter, *Espionage and Subversion in an Industrial Society*, Hutchinson, London, 1967; 2nd edition, Peter Heims, 1979

Hamilton, Peter, *Computer Security*, Cassell/Associated Business Programmes, London, 1972

Hamilton, Peter (ed.) *Handbook of Security* (loose-leaf), Croner, London, frequently updated

Hayes, Dennis, *Behind the Silicon Curtain*, South End Press, San Francisco, CA, 1989

Heald, Tim, *Networks*, Hodder & Stoughton, London, 1983

Heims, Peter, *Countering Industrial Espionage*, 20th Century Security Education, Leatherhead, Surrey, 1982

Henry, Stuart, *The Hidden Economy*, Martin Robertson, London, 1978

Hodkinson, R. and Wasik, M., *Industrial Espionage: Protection and Remedies*, Longman Intelligence Report, London, 1986

Hood, Roger and Sparks, Richard, *Key Issues in Criminology*, World University Library, London, 1970

Hooper, David, *Official Secrets: the use and abuse of the Act*, Secker & Warburg, London, 1978; Coronet, London, 1979

Hougan, Jim, *Spooks*, William Morrow, New York, 1978

Jones, R. V., *Reflections on Intelligence*, Heinemann, London, 1989

Kahn, David, *The Codebreakers*, Macmillan, New York, 1967, 1973

Lane, V. P., *Security of Computer Based Information Systems*, MacMillan, London, 1985

Law Commission, *Breach of Confidence*, (Law Com. No. 110), HMSO, London, 1981

Lawton, Patricia, 'Industrial Espionage: a state of the art review', unpublished thesis, City University, London, 1987

Lee, Stan, *Dunn's Conundrum* (novel), Michael Joseph, London, 1985

Legal Industrial Espionage, 2nd edition, Eurofi, Newbury, Berks, 1988

Leigh, L. H., *The Control of Commercial Fraud*, Heinemann Educational Books, London, 1982

Levi, Michael, *The Incidence, Reporting and Prevention of Commercial Fraud*, privately published by the Home Office and Arthur Young, London, 1986

Levi, Michael, *Regulating Fraud*, Tavistock, London, 1987

Macrae, Norman, *The 2024 Report*, Sidgwick & Jackson, London, 1984

Metcalfe, Robyn Shotwell, *The New Wizard War*, Tempus/Microsoft Press, Redmond, WA, 1988

Naisbitt, John, *Megatrends*, Warner Books, New York, 1982

Naisbitt, John and Aburdene, Patricia, *Re-inventing the Corporation*, Warner Books, New York, 1985

Naisbitt, John and Aburdene, Patricia, *Megatrends 2000*, (UK edition) Sidgwick & Jackson, London, 1990

Northmore, David, *Freedom of Information Handbook*, Bloomsbury, London, 1990

Norton-Taylor, Richard, *In Defence of the Realm?* Civil Liberties Trust, London, 1990

Nown, Graham, *Watching the Detectives*, Grafton, London, 1991

Office of Technology Assessment (US Congress), *Electronic Surveillance and Civil Liberties*, Washington, 1985

Office of Technology Assessment (US Congress) *Management, Security and Congressional Oversight*, Washington, 1986

Parkinson, C. Northcote, *Parkinson's Law*, John Murray, London, 1958

Paulos, John Allen, *Innumeracy*, Hill & Wang, New York, 1988

Porter, Michael E., *Competitive Strategy*, Free Press, New York, 1980

Poundstone, William, *Big Secrets*, (UK edition) Corgi, 1983, 1985

Richelson, Jeffrey T., *Sword and Shield: Soviet Intelligence and Security Apparatus*, Ballinger, Cambridge, Mass, 1986

Richelson, Jeffrey T., *American Espionage and the Soviet Target*, William Morrow, New York, 1987

Richelson, Jeffrey T., *The US Intelligence Community*, 2nd edition, Ballinger, Boston, Mass, 1989

Richelson, Jeffrey T. and Ball, Desmond, *The Ties that Bind*, Allen & Unwin, Boston, Mass and London, 1985

Sammon, W. L., Kurland, M. A. and Spitalnic, R. *Business Competitor Intelligence: Methods of Collecting, Organising and Using Information*, John Wiley, New York, 1984

Schweitzer, James A., *Computer Crime and Business Information*, Elsevier, New York, 1986

Slee-Smith, P. I., *Industrial Intelligence and Espionage*, Business Books, London, 1970

Sutherland, Edwin H., *White Collar Crime*, Dryden Press, New York, 1949

Tapper, Colin, *Computer Law*, 4th edition, Longman, London, 1989

Toffler, Alvin, *Future Shock*, Random House, New York, 1970

Toffler, Alvin, *Power Shift*, Bantam Books, New York, 1990

Tuck, Jay, *High-Tech Espionage*, Sidwick & Jackson, London, 1986

US Department of Justice, *Computer Security Techniques*, Washington, 1980

West, Nigel, *GCHQ: The Secret Wireless War 1900–1986*, Weidenfeld & Nicolson, London, 1986

Wingfield, John, *Bugging*, Robert Hale, London, 1984

Woodward, Bob, *Veil: the secret wars of the CIA, 1981–1987*, Simon & Schuster, New York, 1987

Unkovic, Dennis, *The Trade Secrets Handbook: Strategies & Techniques for Safeguarding Corporate Information*, Prentice-Hall, Englewood Cliffs, NJ, 1985

Van Eck, Willem, *Electronic radiation from video display units*, PTT dr Neher Laboratories, Netherlands, 1985

The following books appear in some bibliographies, but were not traced in researching this book.

Moreau, L., *So You Want to be an Industrial Spy?* (Gozo Press, 1977)

Saunders, M. *Protecting Your Business Secrets* (Craven, 1985)

Walsh, T. J. and Healy, R. J., *Protecting Your Business Against Espionage* (Amacom, NY, 1973)

Index

This Index covers the main text only, and excludes the appendices and bibliography